JOHN SCHROEDER is in many ways the quiet man of British pop music, a production genius who has largely been content to remain in the background, building up an enviable track record while others grab the limelight.

The simple truth is that few British record producers can claim such a wide-ranging success as that which this soft-spoken, slightly built man has carved out for himself.

Virtually every field of popular music has been touched by his talents, from the orchestral jazz-based stylings of SOUNDS ORCHESTRAL, through the pop-soul of GENO WASHINGTON, the progressive sounds of STATUS QUO, the straight pop of HELEN SHAPIRO to the exciting black rock of CYMANDE, an outfit which was the first British-based black group to break the American R&B charts wide open.

John has experienced the worst of what the music industry is about: the excitement and joy of big hits, the frustrations of bad deals and the machinations of music's own bureaucracy. It is this which has led him after many requests to put pen to paper and write his story in his own words. He has many adventures and tales to tell, all of which have contributed to a career filled with more ups and downs than a ride on a roller coaster.

Often tongue in cheek, John Schroeder succeeds in imparting some amazing stories, factual information and events surrounding the music industry of the 60's and 70's enhanced with picturesque collages and photographs.

ROGER ST. PIERRE

Also by John Schroeder

BUCKINGHAM

A delightful story, beautifully illustrated, that explores
the extraordinary therapeutic powers of the cat.

ALL FOR THE LOVE OF MUSIC

John Schroeder

To James (as promised) A & E
Thanks for all the help
Best Wishes
Hope You Enjoy It!
John Schroeder

November 19th 2016

Copyright © 2016 John Schroeder

The moral right of the author has been asserted.

Apart from any fair dealing for the purposes of research or private study, or criticism or review, as permitted under the Copyright, Designs and Patents Act 1988, this publication may only be reproduced, stored or transmitted, in any form or by any means, with the prior permission in writing of the publishers, or in the case of reprographic reproduction in accordance with the terms of licences issued by the Copyright Licensing Agency. Enquiries concerning reproduction outside those terms should be sent to the publishers.

This book is a work of non fiction based on the life, experiences and recollections of the author. In some limited cases the names of people, places, dates, sequences or the detail of events have been changed to protect the privacy of others. The author has stated to the publishers that except in such minor respects not affecting the substantial accuracy of the work, the contents of the book are true.

The author has made all reasonable efforts to contact copyright holders for permissions and apologises for any omissions and errors in the form of credits given. Corrections may be made to future printings.

All other images are from the author's personal collection.

Matador
9 Priory Business Park,
Wistow Road, Kibworth Beauchamp,
Leicestershire. LE8 0RX
Tel: 0116 279 2299
Email: books@troubador.co.uk
Web: www.troubador.co.uk/matador
Twitter: @matadorbooks

ISBN 978 1785891 656

British Library Cataloguing in Publication Data.
A catalogue record for this book is available from the British Library.

Printed and bound in the UK by TJ International, Padstow, Cornwall
Typeset by Troubador Publishing Ltd, Leicester, UK

Matador is an imprint of Troubador Publishing Ltd

*To my darling wife
without whose love and support
this book may have never come into fruition*

ACKNOWLEDGEMENTS

When the time came to write this very important page I found it more difficult than some of the parts of the book itself. Those who have come in and out of my life over the years helping to make so many of my achievements become reality deserve the biggest acknowledgement of all with a huge thank you from the bottom of my heart.

Although my years in the Music Industry have seen happiness and tragedy, success and failure I have had the honour of meeting and working with some of the most dedicated and genuinely talented people of all time. Musicians, Arrangers, Artists, Music publishers, Record Company Management and Staff are just a few that come to mind and also include those in America and the rest of the World.

Without a doubt the biggest thanks of all goes to my own Memory as without it I could never have written a word. Thank God I have been able to remember names and re-live situations as if they had happened yesterday. I really do not believe there is one Artist or recording session that I cannot audibly and visually hear and see in my mind.

In all honesty I did not want to write this book. What, another bloody autobiography?! But I prefer to call it a story, my story and in relation to what I have achieved I justifiably believe my efforts over the years have contributed something towards The History of British Pop Music.

Those around me exerted the right amount of pressure making me finally put pen to paper. I hope that by telling this story myself you might enjoy and appreciate some of the highs and lows of the always unpredictable Music Industry. I hope you will have a semblance of what it is really like to produce a Hit Record and likewise how it really feels to produce something that fails dismally.

Apart from my memory this book could also never have come to fruition without the amazing computer wizardry of Ron Docis.

I have to thank Tony Barrow, the Beatles ex publicist for his invaluable advice and I also have to thank Adam White at Universal whose love for Motown and his connections with it managed to furnish me with my photographic needs of that time.

I hope what we have achieved and the story I have told has been worth the effort but only you dear Reader can be the judge of that!

PROLOGUE

One reason above all else made me realise that music had to be my chosen career. I knew it would be hard, maybe impossible, especially as I had no idea where to begin or what qualifications were necessary.

That one reason was my younger brother being academically brilliant in almost every subject except music. Fortunately he had no interest in it or desire for it!

On hearing what I had in mind, my father virtually disowned me, especially as I had miserably failed to consummate any of his wishes such as Accountancy. John Schroeder CA. I don't think so!

If I got lucky I would not only be working doing something I truly loved but it would also provide me with the opportunity of making something of myself by myself, that my parents would hopefully be proud of! It was the combination of dedicated perseverance, implicit patience and of course surprising luck that fuelled the belief that I would one day make it into the music industry.

In 1957 I was proud to join the staff of E.M.I Records. There was no lower position than a junior in the Sales office so the only way to go was up!

At last I had my foot in that door and I was going to make bloody sure the rest of me was going to quickly follow!

The discovery of the Beatles created a massive musical explosion that was to turn the world upside down and inside out! It was not only the music industry but other affiliated industries such as Fashion and the likes of Mary Quant and Twiggy that were to find themselves happily seriously affected! They were about to attain universal recognition and in the process earn a fortune!

For anyone working in or directly connected with the music Industry at the time, the 60's and 70's indescribable charisma, coupled with so many exciting 'out of the blue' opportunities, could not have given them anything but a massive dose of adrenalin. I can only describe it as a giant creative 'kick up the arse' which incredibly for me came just at the right time!

Competition became nothing less than aggressive, which actually made for better and better product. The Charts were the Industry's Bible, but without that magic Hit, life could be very frustrating both creatively and financially, for all those concerned.

The Swinging' Sixties or Sex Drugs and Rock 'n' Roll as the media preferred to call it, was such an excitingly unpredictable era that I implicitly believe it could not and never will be repeated! It produced some amazing songs and some amazing artists that were to become deservedly universally acclaimed, respected and loved for all time.

I am deeply grateful to those who have afforded me the opportunity of producing and creating such a vast and varied catalogue of music over the past fifty years of my life. Although it has been a highly emotional roller coaster ride I have been lucky to have done it and done it *all for the love of music!*

CHAPTER ONE

One morning there it was – that long awaited letter from E.M.I!

I couldn't believe that it had actually come! I stared at the envelope for a good five minutes, too scared to open it! Momentarily I felt quite ill. Both my stomach and my heart were struggling to cope with this sudden avalanche of stress. Finally, *"casting my fate to the wind"*, I opened it!

30th April 1957

Dear Mr. Schroeder

We are pleased to offer you a position in our Sales Office as from Monday May 6th 1957. Your starting salary will be £7.00 per week.
    Please confirm that this is acceptable.

Yours sincerely,

L.G. Wood
Managing director
Electric and Musical Industries Limited.

I had to read the contents of that letter at least six times before it registered as to what it actually said!

I felt I was on cloud three hundred and nine, let alone cloud nine! My intuition had done me proud.

What will my parents think now? The thought of that made me feel good!

When they finally got the news my mother, practically overcome with emotion said

"Oh, darling congratulations. I am so pleased and relieved for you. I know you'll do very well, mark my word."

The only acknowledgement I got from my father was a big grunt, a big sigh and directed at my mother he said

"Well it could be worse. Now he's got what he wanted I might eventually get some money back"

What did my wife think? Sadly Christine did not feel too inclined to share in the pleasure of my achievement!

With almost uncontrolled excitement I immediately sent back the requested letter of confirmation. I really couldn't believe that I was actually going to start work in the Music Industry the following Monday.

I thought I was going to die of shock when on the Friday before, I received another letter from E.M.I. Had they had now changed their mind and didn't want me?! With considerable courage and biting my lip, I opened the letter. Once again the contents were hard to believe but the biggest surprise of all was who it was from. Why would the Chairman of the entire Company write to me, a mere minion about to start work in the Sales office? The answer to that burning question did not emerge till many years later.

TELEPHONE NUMBER SOUTHALL 2468.
CABLES: "EMITRON, LONDON"
INLAND TELEGRAMS: "EMITRON, TELEX, LONDON"

ELECTRIC & MUSICAL INDUSTRIES, LIMITED.
BLYTH ROAD,
HAYES, MIDDLESEX.

OFFICE OF
THE CHAIRMAN.

2nd May, 1957

J. F. Schroeder, Esq.,
"Dendles",
The Santway,
Clamp Hill,
STANMORE, Middlesex.

Dear Mr. Schroeder,

    Thank you for your letter. I am very pleased to hear that you have been offered and accepted a position in the Record Sales Office. I hope it will turn out to be a job that will lead to something better and provide you with a successful career, and, equally important, of benefit to E.M.I.

Yours sincerely,

(J. F. LOCKWOOD)

The big day, the most important day, my first day in the Music Business had unbelievably arrived at long last.

It was Monday morning and I felt scared and excited as I walked along East Castle Street for the first time towards E.M.I's offices. I still couldn't get over the fact that the Chairman of the entire Company had written to me. Someday I'd find the answer to that.

Surprisingly my mental state changed the moment I was introduced to George Dawson, the Manager of the Sales Office and my immediate boss. He greeted me like a long lost friend and made me feel so welcome that it seemed I had been working there for months!

George was a man in his fifties with grey hair, a genuinely affectionate smile and such a gentle and reassuring way that he reminded me of a doctor with a wonderful bedside manner. He immediately introduced me to the other guys in the sales office who all seemed to treat the job with a take it or leave it attitude! I decided to keep myself to myself and just get on with things, showing genuine willingness, enthusiasm and initiative, and concentrate on gleaning as much knowledge as possible on the internal mechanics of a record company, after all this was what I had been waiting for!

George had sensed my sincerity about this being a career move because he went out of his way to spend time with me going through all the different departments, explaining their role in bringing the finished product to fruition. He mentioned E.M.I Studios, a place I was in great awe of, and the factory at Hayes where the records were physically pressed and finally packaged and distributed.

I felt that the Sales Office could well have been re-named Customer Services due to the amount of calls and enquiries we took, both from the trade and a very inquisitive public. It was therefore imperative that I became very conversant with the company's three labels, namely Columbia, Parlophone and HMV and the Artists that those labels represented. I knew the names of the Label Managers but due to them having this rather inaccessible image, George had not come up with a good enough reason to introduce me to them.

From what I had learnt so far it occurred to me that the current record catalogue could be made a lot simpler and easier to understand and to provide more interesting and valuable information. Basically I had all the necessary ingredients available to me, so in what spare time I had I began to carefully compile and lay out my envisaged format as a sample for a revised catalogue.

The opportunity had arisen for someone to go down to the factory at Hayes and work there for a couple of months or so. George was emphatic that I should go as I would learn and understand a lot more. I was more than grateful to George for this and I was really looking forward to it.

Hayes opened my eyes to many things. I had the enviable experience of 'hands on' training on an actual record pressing machine, seeing and learning the co-ordination necessary with the handling of the art work for the labels, the packaging and finally the distribution set-up necessary to service all the record shops around the country. I also learned about imports and exports of product through E.M.I's international counter-parts. But what fascinated me most was that all of this was totally dependent upon the receipt of the finished masters emanating from E.M.I Studios. What was it that contributed to being classified as a finished master? In fact what was the real definition of the word 'master'? That intrigued me. I really wanted to know!

On returning to East Castle Street I thanked George sincerely for arranging for me to go to Hayes. I had learned a great deal that would really help me in the future especially if I was lucky enough to get more involved with the actual production of a record.

I thought this was the moment to present him with my only finished sample of the re-constructed catalogue. He was so surprised and impressed I thought he was going to have a heart attack! He immediately phoned L.G.Wood and sent it up to him. Two days later I was sitting in front of L.G in his office with my work in front of him. For a moment there was silence and I felt once more like the naughty schoolboy awaiting his fate.

"What I like is the amount of time, thought and initiative you have obviously put into this project. I am going to send it down to the appropriate department asking them to think about revising our record catalogues using your innovative ideas as a guideline," he firmly said.

That was certainly more than anything I'd expected. Then he said

"John what do you see yourself doing within the company?"

"Well I really want to work with music itself. I've noticed that Norman Newell has just acquired an assistant in John Burgess. I was wondering if any of the other label managers would be doing the same" I said inquisitively.

"I will have a word with Norrie Paramor and see what he feels. In fact I will ring him now." He did this and then with a smile said to me,

"Well you heard. Norrie says he will certainly consider it and would like you to go up and see him now."

I thanked L.G accordingly on both counts and had to stand outside his office for a minute to collect my thoughts. Everything was happening so fast. It seemed only like yesterday that I had received that long awaited letter from E.M.I and now suddenly having worked in the Sales Office for

EMI Recording Managers and their respective labels.

*(Left to right) George Martin (Parlophone), Wally Ridley (HMV),
Norrie Paramor (Columbia), Norman Newell (All Labels)*

practically a year and the factory as well, I was now on my way to the inner sanctum so to speak, for an interview with the great Norrie Paramor! I thanked god that I had done some homework on all the recording managers and their artists.

As I approached Norrie's office I told myself to calm down and not to count my chickens!

I was greeted by Norrie's secretary who introduced herself as Felicity. She seemed to be very pleasant and very charming. As she knocked on Norrie's office door she whispered "Good Luck!"

I had the feeling that Norrie and I clicked as soon as we started talking. I think he was impressed that I knew so much about his Artists and also how desperate I was to make music my career. I told him briefly about my education and that I had done five years classical piano, won the school music cup and had formed and played in two bands during the last couple of years.

He came across so endearingly and laid back that I truly felt I knew him before I knew him! Strange though it may seem, I honestly felt I could have been his son! He looked at me; sort of sizing me up. Then there was that awful pause again before he said

"John. Welcome to the Columbia label. You are now officially my assistant. You will have to look after me and I will look after you but it won't be an easy ride. You will have to be prepared to work all hours but I think between us we can make this label even more successful." With a smile of gratitude I said

"Norrie you won't regret it. This job will be my life and I have waited a long time for it!"

"I will inform L.G. Wood. You go down and tell George Dawson and I will see you at nine o'clock tomorrow morning," he said with a reassuring smile.

On my way out I said to his secretary

"Thanks Felicity. I'll be seeing you in the morning. I am now officially Norrie's assistant." I said proudly. She was genuinely pleased for me.

As I left Norrie's office I didn't know whether to dance or cry with joy. My dream had actually come true. Nothing else in the world mattered now.

I could never ever thank George Dawson enough for his personal concern and fantastic support that ultimately led me to this moment!

Christine and I were still together but it wasn't marital bliss by any means! Christine for some antiquated reason still maintained she should not have to work! There was no justification for it. She knew we were struggling financially. She could never tell me what she did during the day! There was one time when she was smitten with the idea of getting into modelling. I agreed to pay to have some professional photographs taken. Seeing the result I thought she really looked the part, very attractive and sophisticated, but unfortunately nothing ever came of it. She had to make some effort in approaching the right people but the determination and belief in herself to do it were just not there. Photographs alone were not enough!

Christine was never a great lover of music and so there was no common ground between us in that respect. In fact my burning desire for a career in the music industry now seemed to incite jealousy. I could never talk to her or share anything with her and she wasn't particularly interested to hear about my first day at E.M.I, George Dawson or working down at Hayes, or even my greatest achievement in attaining the position of being Norrie Paramor's assistant! In the end I just gave up.

However, in spite of all this there was a part of me that felt sorry for Christine since unfortunately she had no real idea and nor did I at the time I first met her, of the tenacity of my obsession with a career in the music industry. Once in it I realised to be really successful you needed to eat, sleep and breathe it. It was totally demanding, so much so that your personal life and your professional life literally became one and the same thing. And that exactly was what was happening to me!

However during all this turmoil and out of guilt more than anything else Christine suddenly found herself pregnant. In my present mental state this initially came as a surprise and a shock but then I realised it might be a blessing in disguise as it would occupy Christine's mind and give her something worthwhile to love and live for. We named her Michelle and Christine turned out to be a good mother but shamefully I was a lousy father because I was already married…to the music industry!

Sunday night I couldn't sleep at all. I was just too excited.

It was déjà vu in that all day I was worrying about what to wear. I felt like a dithering old woman. However, it didn't take too much dithering because I came to the conclusion that it must be a suit, and all I had was one grey one. Grey was a good colour because there wasn't much that didn't match with it so I could change the tie every day and it would make me look different! I was concerned about the creases so I carefully folded the trousers and laid them under the mattress. The following morning they looked like they had just come out of the cleaners. I ended up doing this meticulously every night.

One day a music publisher who had seen me on a couple of previous occasions surprisingly said,

"You always look so smart, John. Things must be good. Just how many suits have you got?"

That complimentary remark more than made up for all the time, trouble, and effort, night after night but I wasn't about to tell him the truth!

I arrived at Norrie's office just before nine o'clock on Monday morning. Norrie wasn't in yet so I had a good talk with Felicity.

"You've come at the right time," she said "we're desperately busy because we're having so much success at the moment. Norrie doesn't seem to be able to stop producing Hit records!"

"Well that's fantastic. I'm lucky to be joining the label at this time. I have a feeling you like the job." I said.

"I love it. You meet all kinds of people and Norrie is a fantastic boss. He is so kind and thoughtful. The only problem we have is that the offices are far too small and too cramped but there is a rumour that we could be moving very soon." she said.

At that moment Norrie walked in.

"Good morning. We are going to be a bit short of space but as a temporary measure we'll get a small desk and chair for you John, and have them put in my office. We are all waiting to move to a brand new building in Manchester Square. You will be able to have your own office then. Felicity, could you get us some coffee please? John, come in to my office and we'll have a chat."

Strangely, I did not feel one ounce of nervousness or anxiety being with him. At first I thought, here we go, master and pupil again but it was nothing like that. He made me feel totally at ease. He knew from the first time we met just how much I respected him. He was my boss but he never talked down to me. In all the time I worked for him we never had one argument or disagreement. We only exchanged opinions which could justifiably be called 'team work'!

As I sat there with him in my true capacity as his assistant, I felt I was now in the music industry properly and professionally. It was hard to believe!

Norrie began, "I want you to look, listen and learn as quickly as possible. I will introduce you as my assistant, to every person that comes in to see me, and I'll tell you exactly what they do, and what they are here for. Take a note of their names, who they work for and the position they hold. Their phone numbers and addresses, often personal and otherwise, are kept methodically by Felicity. I want you to familiarise yourself with every artist we have under contract and when you have the time look at those contracts checking as to whether the terms and conditions have been fulfilled by us. Usually E.M.I Records dictate that if an artist has not been successful after three single releases, then that artist should be dropped. There may obviously be some special circumstances, whereby we feel this policy should not apply. I want you to control my appointments diary in conjunction with Felicity. This will allow her more time to concentrate on her other work. Try and spend as much time as possible with her as she is very conversant with the mechanics of our label and our record releases."

"I think that will do for the moment. In a while we will have another session."

The anticipated move to Manchester Square came suddenly, with little warning. Our new office looked like a huge square glass house, impressive but certainly not beautiful. However, it was conveniently located in the vicinity of Marble Arch which was definitely the right area to be in. The entire fourth floor was allocated to the recording division. The HMV, Parlophone and Columbia labels all had their own suite of offices. Ours were nicely situated in a corner overlooking Manchester Square. Norrie's office was large and spacious whilst mine was a comfortable size and perfectly adequate. Felicity was sandwiched between us which was either very thoughtful or luckily convenient. Having my own office and virtually my own secretary for the first time in my life made me feel very important.

Once we had got settled in and Norrie was getting himself organised, Felicity sensibly suggested that I should start looking at the Artists. In doing this, I soon realised that Norrie was very good at spotting potential talent in a prospective Artist. He was also good at putting the right song with the right

Artist. On listening carefully to the current records made by our Artists, it occurred to me that every one of them had an immediately identifiable voice, and that I felt was a very important factor. I was proud to discover that all our current Artists had had Hit records. Felicity confirmed that Norrie was highly respected and envied in the music industry, not only as the Label Manager for Columbia but also as a producer, composer and arranger. The success of the product undoubtedly proved that. It had Norrie Paramor's stamp all over it!

It wasn't long before practically everybody in the industry knew Norrie had an assistant. I was soon meeting and getting to know managers, agents, music publishers, arrangers and of course our artists. Whilst Norrie was unavailable, on many occasions working from home, I became very available and very busy, which was exactly how I liked it. Felicity put almost all calls for Norrie to me. It became difficult to get to Norrie Paramor without coming through me first and that made him more elusive, which was what he wanted and I certainly had no objection! We were in touch with each other throughout the day so we both knew exactly what was happening.

I sat quietly through almost every meeting Norrie had in his office, listening and learning. Norrie had many personal friends in the music industry and I began to take a note of who they were. Bunny Lewis who was a manager/agent, Johnny Wise of the Lawrence Wright Music Company, and Martin Slavin, an excellent arranger, were just three important names that come to mind out of a very long list.

Surprisingly, after a very short time, Norrie wanted me to use my initiative and start to make appointments to see people in my office, on his behalf or the label's behalf. He particularly mentioned music publishers and advised me that they must be treated with the utmost respect. Our job was to assess their new material in relation to our Artists and at the same time evaluate a new song's hit potential. I soon realised how very difficult that was. Through personal experience, Norrie pointed out to me some of the things that needed to be addressed when evaluating a song's potential, apart from one's own intuition. It was totally impossible to be one hundred per cent certain about a hit record because there were ultimately too many unknown factors which could make or break it, such as little or no airplay. However, if the song was not right or strong enough to begin with then nothing else would be.

It wasn't long before I was inundated with appointments with music publishers. The reason was simple. We were a very successful label and we had a roster of very successful artists but now they discovered they had to go through me before getting to Norrie. Perhaps easier for some and harder for others!

Personally, I loved seeing music publishers. They were so different and so interesting since they came from all walks of life. They always had a good story to tell and most of them had many invaluable years of experience in the music industry. I made some very good friends and apart from mutual respect I had the opportunity of imparting my evaluation on all kinds of songs. This became a very good exercise for me in the art of assessing a song's potential in addition to marrying the right song with the right Artist.

Music publishers also provided an open door to undiscovered talent as they often had demos sent to them of new bands, male and female Artists and most important of all, self penned material. I made them aware I was very open to listening to or even going to see new Artists at any time, especially if they wrote their own material. It wasn't long before I was also in the position of being able to offer them a recorded audition at E.M.I Studios, which was very much a big plus.

After only a short while I felt Norrie and I became very close. He seemed to trust me implicitly, giving me more and more responsibility and opportunity to use my own initiative.

One day out of the blue he said that if I was not doing anything socially that evening I should come round for dinner and meet his wife and family. I said I'd be delighted.

The Paramor family resided in Bishops Avenue. The Hampstead area was very up-market and Norrie certainly deserved to be there. It was a stunning

The Bishops Avenue, Hampstead garden suburb

house and outwardly impressive with a driveway and wrought iron gates. It was deceptively large and the inside did more than compliment the outside. It was beautifully and tastefully furnished. There was, without a doubt a feminine touch involved there somewhere. Oak beams, Persian carpets and French drapes gave the whole house a feeling of warmth and friendliness. There was love in that house, which felt very noticeable. Norrie's wife Joan was attractive, very charming yet quietly assertive. There were three children, Caroline, Jane and David, aged between three and ten years old, all very polite and well behaved.

I had a great evening and afterwards over coffee Norrie and Joan gently started to question me about my domestic life. Because I was somewhat uneasy and not too forthcoming, they guessed I was married and I felt they knew I was not that happy. I believe Norrie also suspected I was struggling somewhat financially. His next remark, I felt confirmed it.

"Upstairs in the attic I have an extensive library of all the scores I have ever written. The trouble is they are in a diabolical mess with no logical filing system whatsoever. Consequently I am having a tough time in finding anything. Would you be prepared to come over two or three evenings a week and sort them all out for me and start a simple filing system? I will, of course pay you for doing it," he said hopefully. This request sounded familiar. I distinctly remembered doing the same thing for Graham Hill when he first set up Speedwell Performance Conversions.

"That should be no problem and I'd be pleased to do it," I said.

I felt Norrie had the perfect home, but there was one final and even more perfect touch that made me feel not just envious but outrageously jealous. A brand new Jaguar XK 140 convertible, in glorious bright red, with beige tan leather upholstery, sat ostentatiously in the driveway. It was a dream of a car. Something I could easily die for! *One day*, I thought, *my dream will come*!

Seeing that, immediately made me think the relationship with my current car needed some serious attention. Without seeming to be flash, something more up market would be nice since I was now a certified assistant A and R Manager! I would have to give that some serious thought.

Norrie had made it clear from the start that he wanted me to attend every recording session but so far we had not been anywhere near the famous front door of E.M.I Studios!

One afternoon in the office, when I was least expecting it Norrie took me through, with careful and deliberate explanation, the basic format and the necessary meticulous attention to detail in setting up a recording session. I hung on to his every word as if it was my life. It was and more!

"First and foremost," he said "you have to be positive in your belief with the material you have selected to record with the Artist in question and ensure that the Artist is equally happy with the material. Obviously in recording material that the Artist does not really believe in, you are not going to get his best performance. However, it is very rare indeed for an artist to disagree with his producer, who after all is his mentor and virtually has the power to make or break the Artist's career by what he ultimately produces on record.

Once the material has been agreed, the artist is then given time to learn and live with the song or songs or tune or tunes. A suitable arranger is selected which is often myself or Martin Slavin. There are others of course, and you will get to know them all in good time. Following this, we set a routining session in my office with the artist and arranger where the keys are set and the basic musical formats for the songs in question are agreed upon. This would include the rhythm patterns, the intro, solo breaks, the tempo, key changes, backing musicians and backing singers and anything else that might be applicable.

As far as I am concerned there must always be a routining session whether it is material for a single or album, a song or an instrumental. It is vitally important because the final arrangement is virtually based upon it. Lastly a mutually agreeable date and time to do the session is established obviously subject to studio and musician availability. You will find most Artists prefer to record in the evening rather than during the day. It is much more relaxed and better for them vocally. I personally prefer the evening, although instrumental projects are fine in the morning or afternoon. E.M.I has a studio booking office and it is their job to aim to please which they do very well. Session musicians are booked through two 'fixers' namely Charlie Katz, who is also an excellent violinist, or Harry Benson. Both are very capable and helpful. They will always do their best for you. You will discover the session circuit has some incredible musicians in it. There is a choice of drummers, bass guitarists, lead guitarists, strings, woodwind, backing singers etc, and over a period of time you will certainly get to know them, probably personally and by first name. As you begin to recognise their individual talents you will be able to select who you prefer for the session in mind. If you cannot get them for the envisaged date then Charlie or Harry will recommend some one else as equally competent. I might add that to be a session musician requires a great deal of ability and talent. The standard of musicianship required is extremely high. They have to be able to sight read immediately and correctly and deliver a performance often within a very short period of time. They are all members of the Musicians Union and are paid according to Musician Union rates relating to recording. Harry or Charlie will pay them cash at the end of the session.

There are two types of session, a full session and a half session. The full is three hours in time and the half is two. You will find you are always fighting the clock but in both you are able to go into overtime for which there are special M.U rates. Remember also you are not allowed to start a new title in overtime. There must also be a compulsory break of fifteen minutes on a half session and twenty minutes on a full session." He paused for a minute hoping I was taking it all in.

"This basically is what happens in setting up any recording session. Oh and Felicity will collate a list of the musicians and she'll send it to E.M.I so the engineer whom you would have previously selected and booked can set up the studio accordingly. As to what happens in the studio itself you will see, learn and find out very soon." Norrie looked at me with that certain smile as if to say, "well?"

Words failed me. I was totally mesmerised by all that he had said.

Norrie at times could be very unpredictable and full of surprises. He stormed into work one morning and said to me

"Leave everything. It's time I took you to the studios and showed you around your other place of work where you will shortly be spending a great deal of time." There was a pause and then he remembered something

"I have just two calls to make before we go and whilst I'm doing that I want you to listen to this demo of a song called *'Stairway of Love'*. I am thinking of doing it with Michael Holliday as his next single but I would like your opinion first. We were rather spoilt with *'Story of my Life'* which I'm sure you know went to Number One and the follow up to that *'In Love'* only made it to twenty six. Now I want him to get back up there. Tell me what you think on the way to the studios."

Realising I was at last going to see the famous E.M.I Studios for the first time and being driven there by my boss in a beautiful XK 140 with the hood down was more than I could ever have imagined.

Norrie looked very anxious. Without turning to me he said

"Well what did you think of *'Stairway of Love'*?

"I liked it a lot and thought it was very much stronger than *'In Love'*. It is absolutely Michael Holliday and with the right arrangement which I know it will have it'll do very well. I think we should go with it. Has Michael heard it yet?"

"I have sent it to him and am waiting to hear. I do feel strongly about that song and thanks for your opinion John. I appreciate it"

As we turned into the studio entrance I didn't know what to expect but I was certainly surprised and a little disappointed. It looked such a drab and ordinary building and disappointingly small too. At that time there was no graffiti on that famous wall but *the* pedestrian crossing in Abbey Road was certainly there. The entrance itself was nothing to shout about either. It was just an ordinary, painted green door with five stone steps leading up to it. There were no signs to be seen on or near the building anywhere.

Once through the front door, the pale apple green paint that was everywhere gave me the distinct impression that I was in a government administration building. I thought it was surprisingly impersonal, after all this was not the BBC.

There were three studios, of which number Three was the smallest, but it really wasn't that small. This studio was used for simple voice overdubbing and for auditions. Norrie said he wanted me to start talent spotting, and if I saw or heard anybody that I thought good enough I should offer them a recorded audition using the facilities of this studio. It should be booked with an engineer just like any session. If there was anybody you thought warranted it, we would have to find a mutually convenient time to listen to the result and discuss recording potential and so on.

Studio Two was *the* star. As studios go at that time, it was one of the best in the business, if not the best. It had an electrifying ambience which you felt as soon as you entered it. It was big, very big with acoustic tiles all the way down the extremely high walls. I reckon it could probably accommodate fifty musicians at one time or even more. It was the busiest studio because ninety per cent of E.M.I's pop product was conceived and recorded there. It had a fantastic reputation and a track record of success a million miles long.

The control room, which was positioned quite high, overlooked the studio via a huge glass window. The console, which was covered with loads of knobs and faders and things, looked very impressive and functional. Over the next few weeks I was to learn a great deal about that console. There were also two large tape machines and two huge playback speakers in each corner of the room facing the console. There were also two small playback speakers sitting on top of the console. As Norrie and I stood gazing down into the studio, you could feel the presence of power and authority over whatever was going on in the studio. I knew one day, that power and authority was to be mine!

Studio One was the dark horse. A huge heavy door allowed us into the studio itself. The size of the studio was beyond imagination, but huge that it was, for me it didn't have the atmosphere of Studio Two. There was a stage, the size of a theatre stage at one end that could quite comfortably accommodate the entire Royal Philharmonic Orchestra. This studio was devoted almost entirely to classical recording and had its own team of classically trained producers and outstanding technical staff. The control room and console were equally as impressive. After a period of time I was to realise that this studio had produced some of the finest classical recordings in the world. I also found out that the studio was extensively used by Film Companies to record movie sound tracks. Only once during my entire career with E.M.I did I have the opportunity of experiencing recording in Studio One. Thinking of the front of the building and the enormous size of this overwhelming studio let alone the others too, it seemed a miracle that the building was able to accommodate any of this at all!

Norrie then showed me one of the cutting rooms where I witnessed the capabilities of the incredible disc cutting machine and the skill of the engineer using it. This was where the masters were cut and consequently sent down to Hayes. Norrie couldn't emphasise enough how important this process was. Basically, the master tape having been mixed and approved by the producer was then sent to the cutting room. Since the equalisation could be altered when transferring from tape to disc the engineer would cut sample acetates of both the A and B side of the record for the producer's approval before cutting the masters themselves. Little did I know it then but I was to spend quite some time in cutting rooms during my career.

Of course luckily for me I had had the opportunity of working at Hayes, E.M.I's manufacturing plant. I had seen the records being pressed and had actually operated a pressing machine myself. I had also seen the labels being manufactured and I had seen the finished product packaged and dispatched to the shops. Now I knew what was actually meant by 'the masters from E.M.I Studios'. Everything began to make sense.

Our last call at the studios was meeting the Manager of the studios, the booking office and of course having coffee in the restaurant. This place was as important as the session itself especially to the musicians who took their well earned breaks there.

We were lucky to find all three recording engineers having coffee in the restaurant at the same time. Norrie had told me previously how important it was to get on with these guys since I would be working with all of them at some time or other. Norrie introduced me to Stuart Eltham, Peter Bown and Malcolm Addey. All three were highly qualified, and had the technical power to easily make or break a session. It was easy to see that they had tremendous respect for Norrie which in turn thankfully rubbed off on me. Norrie used them all with different Artists bearing in mind their individual musical tastes. Norrie finally reminded me that on every recording session, the producer always had the last word. He was in charge of the session and ultimately had to answer for its success or failure.

On our way back to Manchester Square Norrie said he had spoken to Michael Holliday who had confirmed how much he loved '*Stairway of Love*'.

He was now expecting a call from me to fix a mutually agreeable date and time for the routining session.

E.M.I. Recording Studios

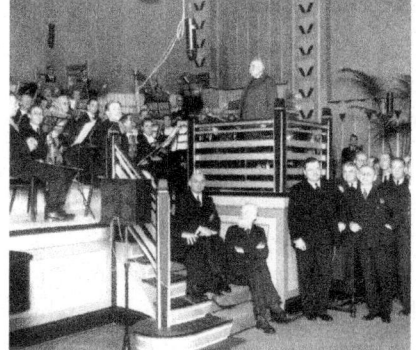

Sir Edward Elgar launched Abbey Road in November 1931

Studio One

The First Mobile Recording Studio

Studio Two

CHAPTER TWO

At Norrie's request, I contacted Michael Holliday, introduced myself and arranged a mutually agreeable date and time that suited all of us for him to come in to routine the song.

I found him to be the perfect gentleman, very polite and sort of casually laid back.

I congratulated him on the amount of TV coverage and the amount of records he had sold. He couldn't really believe or understand his success which to me was rather sad. I asked him what he thought of *'Stairway of Love.'* He said he loved it and thought it was much stronger than *'In Love.'* I totally agreed and confirmed that I felt it would do surprisingly well.

The routining session with Michael went exactly stage by stage as Norrie had previously explained and described to me. He encouraged me and wanted me to air my views on the anticipated arrangements of the songs and in actually doing this and listening to what he had in mind made me realise and really appreciate just why the meticulous attention to detail at the routining session was so vital.

A mutually agreeable recording date was fixed and we decided it should be a full session being 7.30 to 10.30 in the evening.

Norrie sensibly always stayed away from the office to write the scores at home. On completion he gave me the combination and the names of the musicians he particularly wanted to use including the backing vocals, namely The Mike Sammes singers.

I phoned E.M.I Studios and as the date was fine I confirmed the booking and requested Peter Bown as the engineer. I then phoned Charlie Katz giving him the date, the combination and selected named musicians. I mentioned the Mike Sammes singers and Charlie said as it was my first session he would book the backing vocals with Mike Sammes. I thanked him for that and then gave Felicity the combination which she sent to the studios for Peter Bown's attention.

Thankfully I had had no problems and then I suddenly realised I had in fact booked my first session and the dream of actually working at Abbey Road Studios was about to become a reality. This was so unbelievable I actually felt nervous and I was certainly wondering what my role on the session would actually be. Norrie, as perceptive as ever knew what was troubling me. He told me to be myself, act calmly and introduce myself to the musicians as being his assistant and then carefully listen to his instructions. He would indirectly look after me, and as such, I would be in the driving seat with Peter Bown as he would be taking care of things in the studio. He assured me that I should not be frightened to say how I felt about anything as he truly respected my opinion. That meant a great deal to me.

The day of the session arrived, and that evening I went straight from work to the studio getting there twenty minutes before the start. Peter Bown was already in the studio setting up the mikes so I went down and had a chat with him. He explained how necessary it was to be very careful as to where the mikes were placed, especially on certain instruments such as drums. I watched him as he miked up the drum kit. As the musicians and singers drifted into the studio I introduced myself to them and found them all extremely pleasant. It was very obvious they had great respect for Norrie and were even happier to learn that the Artist was Michael Holliday.

Norrie arrived and made his way to the conductor's platform which was positioned in the centre of the studio. He then gave me the band and vocal parts and told me to distribute them accordingly at the same time saying

"When you have done that, go up to the control room and take the control sheets for each song with you. They will tell you briefly what is happening throughout the arrangement. Sometime when we get back in the office I will show you how to read a score. Meantime, work with Peter up there as I have asked him to explain things and guide you through the session as much as possible."

I was now sitting to the left of Peter enjoying the luxurious leather comfort of the producer's chair with that impressive piece of equipment in front of me known as the Console. An amazing feeling of power suddenly came over me as I looked down at all those incredibly talented people in the studio realising they would soon in effect be under my control.

Peter pointed out the multitrack tape machine behind us and introduced me to Brian, the tape operator, someone who also played a very important role in the project. Peter told me everything would be recorded on multitrack, to be specific on three tracks. The voice would be on one track, the backing vocals on another and everything else on the third track. He then said it was vital that the balance of the instruments on the third track was what we had in mind. There could be no going back changing anything once the master track had been accepted. I thought that was pretty frightening because there was no second chance. You had to get it right!

He then pointed out the studio talkback switch on the console.

At that point Michael Holliday entered the control room, said hello to everybody and then went down to the studio and conversed with Norrie and the musicians.

The clock showed 7.30pm. Norrie called for 'hush' and it was time to begin. Peter told me via the talkback to ask Ronnie Verrol, the drummer, if we could hear some drums on their own. Inwardly nervous I pressed the talkback switch and said

"Ronnie, could we have some drums please." To my surprise those words came completely naturally with no nervousness at all. And then like magic Ronnie immediately obliged whilst Peter wrestled with getting a sound out of the kit. Peter asked me to ask Ronnie if we could have the snare drum on its own and then the bass drum on its own. Ronnie Verrell obliged again and Peter soon got a really nice sound on the overall kit. We then went through every instrument on its own after which Peter told me to ask Norrie to run through the rhythm section from the top, then the string section, then the backing vocals. Norrie then put his head phones on and I made the request to run through the number with everybody from the top except Michael. The sound through those huge control room speakers was just amazing. Peter checked and double checked the individual and overall sound, especially on the backing vocals but Mike Sammes, always the professional had meticulously ensured the group was properly internally balanced. Peter then asked me what I thought of the instrumental balance on the third track. I said I liked it but thought there could be more bass and the keyboards could have a touch more reverb. Peter adjusted them accordingly and then suggested a run through with Michael. Michael was in an open sided vocal booth facing Norrie and the orchestra. I asked Norrie if he could now run it through with Michael from the top.

This he did having first had a word with Michael. Peter checked everything again but this time concentrated on the vocal sound. However, as this was on a separate track the finer details could be dealt with later. We were now ready for the first take.

This was a magical and memorable moment for me as for the very first time on my very first session I announced "*'Stairway of Love'* Take One."

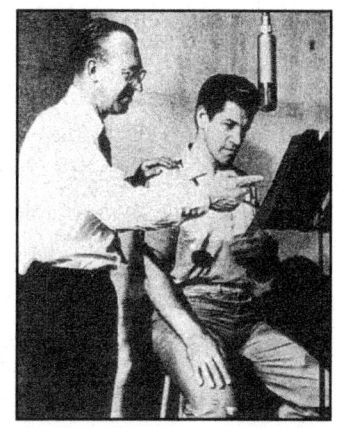

The control sheet was easy for me to follow but the take broke down because of a wrong chord which Norrie rectified. Take Two was complete after which Norrie and Michael and some of the musicians came up to the control room to listen to the playback. Norrie thought it wasn't a bad take but suggested a little more lead guitar and a touch more acoustic rhythm guitar. He then looked at me. I said it hadn't quite got the magic for me as I thought the tempo could be a fraction up and Michael could be more relaxed. Michael agreed and knew he could do better. Peter was quite happy. We were very near it. I announced it again.

"*Stairway of Love.* Take three."

Norrie increased the tempo marginally but it was not until the fifth take that the overall magic was there. It was *so* together and Michael's performance was faultless. On hearing the playback it sounded a hit. We all took a well deserved break feeling pretty pleased with ourselves. Norrie took me to one side and asked me how I got on. I told him it felt and I felt absolutely fantastic. Peter was a gem. I thought I would be nervous but I didn't feel that at all. What mattered was what he thought.

Norrie answered quite emphatically,

"You did far better than I thought you would and your observations were spot on. My guess is that you have the makings of a good producer once you get more confidence and experience. Be patient. It will take time."

"With due respect, I was wondering how on earth you managed to cope in the past with everything on your own and so successfully too." I said inquisitively.

"It was very difficult because I was both the conductor and producer so I had to keep going up and down from the studio to the control room all the time and that's one very good reason why you're here", he answered. Then noticing the time, he said

"We'd better go and do the 'B' side. I would like you to come down to the studio and listen to the track from the studio floor as we run it through. I want you to listen carefully to each instrument and section including the backing vocals. Once we have run it through go back up to the control room. Peter will have already got a balance".

It was incredibly enlightening hearing everything live down in the studio.

Norrie had given me a *very sound piece* of advice. Amazingly as I stood there I found myself being able to shut everything out except the instrument I was listening to. I was then able to assess the sound and what was being played by that instrument in relation to everything else. If it was right or wrong in the studio it would be magnified enormously through the playback speakers in the control room. Although they could easily 'blow your mind' with volume creating amazing excitement they tended to be deceptive and I was subsequently caught out on several occasions.

I found myself in future automatically going down to the studio before a session and listening to what was happening live on the studio floor. This little exercise became totally invaluable and methodically adhered to.

We got the session wrapped up without going into overtime. Charlie Katz arrived at the finish and paid the musicians. Then Michael's wife arrived. She was strikingly beautiful with long flowing blonde hair, short skirt and very sexy leather boots. I thought if only …!

We listened to the playback of both songs and were very pleased with what we had achieved. Michael's wife nodded her head in approval so we felt pretty sure we had a good chance of another hit on our hands.

Now my first recording session was over. It had been an amazing experience. I felt mentally drained and I couldn't sleep at all that night. I was re-living every beautiful minute of it!

The following morning back in the office Norrie's first words were – "Well?"

I replied very emphatically "Norrie, *I absolutely loved it*. It was one of, if not the most, exciting and creative experiences of my life."

Norrie agreed the session had gone extremely well and so it was decided to tentatively set a release date of mid to end of April. He then said,

"Now comes the most important part of all and that is mixing the tracks to create *the* sound that will hopefully be played on radio stations and which ultimately will sell enough to give us another Hit record, that is of course if we were right about the song in the first place."

"I want you to book a couple of hours in Studio Two with Peter Bown. It could be a morning, afternoon or evening".

I booked an afternoon, but I noticed Norrie never ever invited the Artist along to the mixing session. Funny when after all, it was his record. On questioning Norrie he said quite bluntly,

"Frankly Artists can be a pain in the bum. They become too emotional which puts everybody on edge and it is then hard to concentrate. Mixing is mentally very stressful. It can initially be the making or breaking of a record. You, as the producer have to get it right which means you have to be happy with it. Remember you and only you are responsible for the end result".

Once again on the afternoon of the mixing session I had my eyes opened to a whole new spectrum. It amazed me how much the recorded sound could be changed on the mix. You could add top, add bottom or add reverb individually on each track. You could even mix two tracks together and then overdub other instruments or whatever on the free track. Norrie was happy with the balance on the music track although at this stage we couldn't have done anything about it. The slightest amount of reverb on the lead vocal gave Michael's voice that silky smooth laid back tone which enhanced the emotion of the overall performance even more. The backing vocals were a big part of the arrangement of this song and much depended on them being carefully placed in the right perspective with the other two tracks.

It took just over an hour to mix *'Stairway of Love'* to the point where everybody present on hearing the mixed track smiled and nodded their heads in approval. It took three days to receive the lacquers from the studio which were now awaiting our approval. Norrie and I heard them first and we were very pleased with the result. When Michael got to hear them he appeared to be even more laid back than usual which meant he was pretty excited as was everyone else connected with the promotion and distribution of the record. The record was released mid April and by May 16th *'Stairway of Love'* was standing at number three in the charts.

I was very happy!

As promised Norrie took me through the arrangement of *'Stairway of Love,'* showing me how to read and follow the individual instrument and vocal parts. He then told me to cast my mind back to the routining session reminding me of what had been discussed and agreed upon between the three of us. He then showed me how and where it all sat in the score. Once it was written he had to make very certain that there was nothing missing in the score and that it made complete musical sense before handing it over to his copyist who would then create the parts for each instrument transcribing them from the score. These were the parts Norrie had asked me to give out to the respective musicians in the studio. The copyist would usually bring the lead sheets and the score to the studio before the session was due to start or get them to the arranger prior to the session.

Norrie was blessed with an incredible knowledge of music and the talent to putting it cleverly to such good use. This talent never ceased to amaze me.

Unfortunately my knowledge of music by comparison was limited but since the music industry was my life I decided to continue having music lessons twice a week at the Ivor Mairants School of Music in Denmark Street. Norrie thought this was highly commendable and gave me a lot of extra help and advice when time allowed. However, I could never ever see myself as an arranger, hearing the individual instrument parts in your head and writing everything down and creating a musical picture at the same time. It required a specialised talent but now thanks to Norrie I could at least read a score.

Right from the start of our relationship Norrie had indicated he wanted my presence on every session and this he got right up until the time I was to leave E.M.I. As time went on we seemed to work closer and closer together, in fact I distinctly felt we made a great team. I found myself really confident about ideas and making decisions and suggestions solely because Norrie always encouraged it. We had a natural telepathy in the studio. I found all the studio staff extremely helpful and I regarded the recording engineers with utmost respect. I went out of my way to befriend session musicians because I strongly felt one day I would definitely be depending on them.

Subconsciously I had one burning question on my mind – would Norrie ever let go of the reins and allow me to do a session completely on my own?

Perhaps the answer was never, since I was officially employed as his assistant and nothing more!

Norrie and I were quietly pleased with ourselves for managing to sustain the success of the Columbia label which of course also meant the personal success of the Artists that we had contractually committed to it. I suddenly realised I was not aware of one Artist that was or had been under Norrie's care and supervision that had not achieved success of some kind.

Without a doubt success breeds success!

When George Ganjou, a respected Agent, and Franklyn Boyd, a well known music publisher, walked into our office one day in June 1958 and played a rough demo of a young rock 'n' roll band called Cliff Richard and The Drifters Norrie and I were both surprised and impressed because they were not only so different to any Artist we had but they were extremely good at what they did. We knew rock 'n' roll was just beginning to take hold of the younger generation's imagination. Dictated by America it was quite definitely here to stay. The 2 I's coffee bar in Soho was fast becoming *the* rock 'n' roll venue because young Bands were being given the opportunity of playing live.

Cliff Richard and The Drifters had built up such a following there that even a fan club had been set up.

Harry Webb alias Cliff Richard, as he was professionally named, had the looks, the boyish charm, sex appeal, movement and a voice to die for, especially as there was a hint of Presley about it. The Drifters were equally as talented and this was to be clearly demonstrated in a few months time.

It was a memorable occasion when one day they all descended upon us in Manchester Square. By everyone's reaction you would have thought they were already super stars! We realised just how devoted they were and how much they lived and died for rock 'n' roll music. They seemed to be a little bewildered by the speed of what was happening around them, especially when Norrie told them they were about to join the Columbia label on the strength of their recent studio audition. We knew we had a hot new property on our hands and it was very obvious to me that Norrie, not being as apparently laid back as usual was genuinely excited, in fact he could hardly contain himself with such a find.

In no time at all the first single was planned with the intention of the 'A' side being a song called *'Schoolboy Crush'* which Franklyn Boyd had unearthed. The 'B' side was to be a song called *'Move It'* written by Ian Samwell who played rhythm guitar in the group at the time.

Norrie forewarned me that to produce a self contained band was totally a different ball game to producing a voice with session musicians, except that likewise, it was essential that you had a very good idea beforehand of what you wanted to achieve. On a recording session emotional feelings between individual members of the band often ran high and sometimes even out of control. You had to be a bit of a psychiatrist and learn how to cleverly manipulate them into making them feel *they* were providing the musical inspiration and creative input but realistically you were getting them to do what you wanted and had in mind.

The more I worked with Norrie the more amazed I became. Was there nothing he was incapable of?

Malcolm Addey was the youngest of the three recording engineers at Abbey Road and therefore Norrie asked him to engineer Cliff Richard and The Drifters since it was felt that he perhaps had more understanding and feeling for this type of Artist. As a safeguard, and because Norrie also thought it astute, he arranged to have two session musicians, namely Ernie Sheer who played lead guitar and Frank Clark who played bass, on standby just in case...

On the night of the session, Malcolm divided the studio in half by using a huge curtain. As usual we had three available tracks whereby the voice went on one, lead guitar on the second and drums, bass and rhythm guitar on the third.

There was obviously nothing to conduct so Norrie could run things totally from the control room.

In the studio and without the adulation of an audience, Cliff Richard and The Drifters were a thrill to both watch and hear. They performed as if they were doing a gig. There was so much conviction about it and Cliff so obviously had the potential of a superstar. Both songs had been well rehearsed before the session and the arrangements were spot on but Norrie ultimately decided that Ernie Sheer should play the guitar intro on *'Move It'*.

When the group heard what we and they had done through the studio monitors they were like everyone else, momentarily lost for words, and then as if in one voice they said incredulously – Is that really us?! – and repeated it three or four times.

Mixing the tracks was also an education with no member of the band being allowed to attend. With no disrespect to Malcolm Addey who had got a great sound, nothing seemed to bother Norrie. He knew exactly what the finished tracks should sound like. He had brilliantly captured the excitement and rawness that was rock 'n' roll. Cliff Richard and The Drifters were on the road to stardom but we had an immediate problem.

The record was released with *'Schoolboy Crush'* as the 'A' side but it was met with a disappointing reaction, that is until Jack Good decided to include *'Move It'*, the 'B' side in his national TV show 'Oh Boy'. With the amazing sales reaction resulting from this there was no question that *'Move It'* should be the official 'A' side so the record was flipped, with the result that *'Move It'* stormed up the charts reaching number 2 on the 12th September 1958.

This event focused massive media attention on the band who found themselves inundated with all sorts of offers. Cliff acquired a new Manager in the form of Peter Gormley, a charming Australian who also managed Frank Ifield who was eventually also signed to Columbia. It was fate that Peter Gormley had arrived on the scene just at the right time.

Whilst all these things were happening so fast Norrie and I found most of our time had to be devoted to progressing Cliff Richard and The Drifters' recording career. I told Norrie I was somewhat concerned for our other Artists, some of whom I had heard on the grapevine were feeling a little 'pissed off' or possibly jealous. Norrie said as far as Cliff was concerned we had to strike while the iron was hot so he had no option but to put any problems with our other Artists back in my court. He felt I was quite capable of dealing with the situation and reminded me that we had recently just had two hits with the Mudlarks namely *'Lollipop'* and *'Book of Love'* and we had the current single *'Girl Of My Dreams'* with Tony Brent at present looking pretty good. In fact the Tony Brent record made it to number 16 on the 5th September, one week before 'Move It' made it to number 12 the charts.

During the next few months Cliff, the Band and Norrie practically lived in the studio making further single and album product. I went to all the sessions but became deeply involved in handling all the administrative hassles in putting it all together. The follow up to 'Move It' titled 'High Class Baby' made it to number 7. 'Livin' Lovin' Doll', 'Mean Streak' and 'Never Mind' all made the Top Twenty, but it was the next single release that produced a musical explosion. 'Living Doll' was written by Lionel Bart and featured in the musical 'Serious Charge'. It was a very simple catchy song with lyrics and a melody that were immediately memorable. Bruce Welch who played rhythm guitar made the rather ingenious suggestion of slowing down the tempo which became one very good reason that contributed to producing an incredibly successful Number One record. This record had amazing appeal to both young and old and it was to become an ever lasting memorable mile stone in Cliff Richard's career. The date was the 10th July 1959.

This achievement immediately increased our already overstretched work load since Cliff Richard and The Drifters, by public demand, required a new single release almost every two to three months let alone the thought of an album at the same time. Every release made the charts somewhere with

Cliff and the Shadows In the Studio

(l/r) Norrie, Myself, Cliff, Bruce Welch, Malcolm Addey, and Hank Marvin

'Travellin' Light' the follow up to *'Living Doll'* making number one again with many more number ones to follow at various intervals over the years.

In January 1960 Cliff decided to digress slightly by accepting a tempting offer to appear in a musical film entitled *'Expresso Bongo'*. I remember we made an E.P of the music from this film. Cliff Richard was fast becoming a superstar solely through an unprecedented appeal across the board, in other words captivating the hearts and minds of young and old as well as Mums and Dads.

I could see Norrie was beginning to suffer with the heavy pressure required in handling the every day work load and the lack of time to do it. Norrie needed space, space to think, space to write, space for personal things so sensibly he decided to work from home which would lessen the rat race and allow him to have more freedom. He came to rely upon me, putting the day to day running of the office firmly on my shoulders, with Felicity finding herself often working late and having a lot less time to herself. This arrangement worked well as I was in constant daily contact with Norrie. It was a tough call but I had no qualms about doing it. A personal life? This was it!

CHAPTER THREE

The Eurovision Song contest (1959) was in its fourth year and England's entry was *'Sing little Birdie'* to be sung and performed by Pearl Carr and Teddy Johnson. At the time they were managed by Dennis Preston, who was responsible for the foundation of the Lansdowne Jazz Series. This found its way onto the Columbia label through a deal which Norrie successfully put together. Norrie, having been the pianist with Harry Gold and his Pieces of Eight obviously loved jazz and The Lansdowne Jazz series represented the best of British jazz with musicians of the calibre of Tubby Hayes, Ronnie Scott, and Bill Evans etc

'Sing Little Birdie' didn't win the contest that year but it did come second which more than justified it being recorded and nationally released as a single. Norrie negotiated another deal with Dennis. The next thing I knew I was booking the musicians and the studio time for this session. It was an evening session at the usual start time of 7.30 pm somewhere around the end of January. In view of Eurovision a routining session was not necessary.

I got to the studio fifteen minutes before the start. Norrie's copyist arrived and handed me the scores and band parts for both songs which I then distributed to the respective musicians. At half past seven there was no Norrie. At twenty five to eight there was no Norrie and twenty to eight there was still no Norrie. Something had to be done and quickly. Inside I was panicking and I could feel the tension building with everyone getting more and more restless. All eyes were turned to me. With visible determination I pressed the talkback button and asked Kenny Clare to give me some drums, then the snare drum on its own and the bass drum on its own. Peter Bown was once again the engineer but this time there was no smile or look of encouragement coming my way. I felt incredibly lonely as I went through the orchestra one by one so Peter could get the sound which as always he did very professionally. I did have the advantage of knowing the arrangement of the song because it was virtually based on what was done for the Eurovision Song Contest. Even so Norrie teaching me to follow a score was a distinct godsend.

Resigned to the fact that the session was now my responsibility I decided to take more positive control and casting nerves aside, I pressed the talkback again and said, pleading strongly

"Could I have some quiet please? I would be really grateful if I could get some help from all of you since Norrie isn't here. Kenny can you do the honours and count it in from the top with Pearl and Teddy. Thanks." They ran it through from the top and whilst Peter meticulously got a balance I hurriedly went down to the studio and listened to everything very carefully from the studio floor. I realised what a nightmare it must have been for Norrie having to do so many sessions totally on his own.

With the advance of technology we now had more tracks to play which made things a little easier especially as this was quite a large backing. Peter, having sorted out the tracks looked at me inquiringly. I said I would like a little more lead guitar and more bass. I then asked him

"Do you think the woodwind should have more reverb on them?"

He was abrupt and quick to answer.

"I don't know. You're the bloody producer." That remark took me aback and shut me up but only for a minute. It wasn't called for, but undeterred I pressed on.

"O.K everybody let's go for the first take. Kenny can you count it in please?

'*Sing Little Birdie*' – Take one"

Following this, many of the musicians were interested enough to come up to the control room to hear it and thankfully they all thought it was pretty good. Jacques, who was leading the string section was very helpful and pointed out a couple of discrepancies to me which he would rectify. I told Kenny that the tempo was good and should stay the same but we needed to make it a little lighter and happier in its overall feel. Kenny knew exactly what I wanted and so did Jacques. Before the next take I asked everybody if we could have a few bars from the top to check everything again. This we did and then we went all out for the master take.

"*Sing Little Birdie*. Take Two"

The magic was there! It was exciting and I felt happy! Everyone agreed it was the one. I thanked everybody for their patience and their help as without it I probably could not have done it. Whilst they were having their break Peter Bown came up to me and said

"John, I'm sorry to have appeared a bit off and somewhat abrupt. It was deliberately done to make you work it out on your own. You really did well in a very difficult situation. You'll be ready for anything now! Norrie should be well pleased. He should be here in a minute"

Moments later Norrie appeared and looking directly at Peter said smiling profusely but with an element of distrust.

"Well let's hear it, let's hear how you managed to cope on your own"

Peter played the track, looking smug. At the finish there was silence and then with the look of pleasurable surprise Norrie turned to me and said

"Sounds pretty good to me. You can now have the honour of mixing it."
I answered with relief

"Thanks Norrie. The whole scenario was one big shock. I just didn't expect it and I called you a few names under my breath."

"I think you'll find you'll know exactly what you want to hear from now on. You've made a big step forward and I will be giving you more responsibility in the studio."

I had managed to complete the mix by the end of the following week. At first it seemed a mammoth job and somewhat overwhelmed me. Once I had managed to get myself relaxed enough to know what sound and internal balance I was striving for everything seemed to fall much easier into place. Peter was now my best friend and did everything and more that I asked for. This was, after all, my very first attempt at being a producer on my own thanks solely to Norrie's trust and ingenuity and of course not forgetting Peter's invaluable input.

The lacquers for my approval of the A and B side arrived on my desk and I now had to wait for the right moment to play them to Norrie. They finally came and I said with obvious excitement in my voice.

"Norrie listen to this!" He smiled during the playback of *'Sing Little Birdie'* and then said quite casually,

"Do you not think the woodwind are a bit too forward?"

I answered feeling somewhat unnerved

"Frankly, no."

"That's fine," he said. "It's your record. Well done."

The record was released with some heavy promotion behind it. On the 20th March 1959 it made it to number 12 in the charts and stayed there for 8 weeks. In spite of the circumstances I was proud of the achievement even though it was really only Norrie who knew what I had actually done. It had taught me a lesson making me feel much more confident in my own ability.

After the *'Sing Little Birdie'* saga I felt I had earned my wings and reached another plateau in my career. Norrie too seemed to have put me on a higher pedestal by giving me considerably more responsibility in the studio. Amongst the madness of everything else, we were desperately trying to complete some tracks with a new group. Norrie got me seriously involved with it asking me to handle a fair amount of the work on my own subject to his final approval of course. There was one particularly strong song but we just couldn't get the feel right. On each of the following two sessions we gave the song two or three takes more to try to get it right. After the third take on the third session everything suddenly fell into place and we unanimously agreed that it was at last *the* one.

Being honest as always and informing Norrie of the problem with this song having so far attempted six takes he advised me to forget about pursuing it as it was using up valuable studio time and costing money but against my better judgement I went with the flow and decided to persevere with it. It was such a strong song. Now, after ten takes or so we all felt we had a possible hit on our hands and we were looking forward to hearing the playback. We made ourselves comfortable in the control room and the tape was running. We waited... and we waited... and we waited... but there was nothing but silence. We all turned towards the tape machine and of course the tape operator. He stopped the machine and went bright red, admitting he had accidentally put the machine into record mode when it should have been in playback mode! As we were hoping to listen to the result of everyone's three day effort the machine was in fact wiping the master track off the tape! There was silence and total disbelief lasting a good two minutes. The session came to a sudden end and everyone went home totally gutted, disheartened and frustrated. Malcolm Addey, our engineer was furious and couldn't apologise enough. That must have been that guy's worst nightmare but Malcolm Addey reckoned that a worse nightmare than that was about to come his way!

I was in deep shit too as I didn't know what I was going to tell Norrie after he had told me not to continue with the recording in the first place!

I got on very well with Eddie Calvert and his manager, Max Diamond. They both had a remarkable sense of humour. Like me, they loved dirty jokes and Eddie always kept a couple of glasses and *other goodies* in his golden trumpet case. He was of course, a very successful Artist having had at least six hit records before I had the pleasure of meeting him. Two of those, namely *'Oh Mein Papa'* and *'Cherry Pink and Apple Blossom White'* were both number one records. Unfortunately and not for the want of trying, he had not had a sniff at the charts properly since *'Mandy'* in February 1958 which made it to number 9. Now Norrie had come up with the idea to record that great old standard called *'Jealousy'* but they hadn't got anything for a 'B' side. On coming up to the office one day Eddie and Max asked me if I had ever written anything and I remembered the short but sweet inspiration of two tunes when I was living at my parent's house. *Ma's Tune* was definitely not right but the other one – for a trumpet lead? Possibly. It would be worth a shot. Since Norrie was out of the office I took the liberty of playing it to them on Norrie's piano. To my surprise they loved it and suggested I put it under a pseudonym and agree to it being published by Max Diamond Music but saying nothing to anybody about it not even Norrie. Inwardly, I felt somewhat guilty about that but Eddie and Max insisted so I agreed. Anyway at this stage of my career I was totally ignorant of anything about the mechanics of something like this. All that mattered to me was that at that moment I was flying high with the thought of Eddie Calvert, who let's face it, was still quite a big name at the time, actually going to record one of the only two tunes I had ever written.

The pseudonym I chose was Chris Sturm which was Christine's maiden name, and because of Eddie's fond memories of the place I was more than happy to agree to call the piece *'Malta G.C'*.

It was ironic that Norrie wanted to do the arrangements of the two tunes without knowing his assistant had written one of them! Norrie never found out, but the day we recorded them became my own enjoyable nightmare. I was truthfully shitting myself with a mixture of fear and bravado. When I heard Eddie play the tune for the first time in the studio it was *more* than magic and I heard myself inwardly and proudly saying – I wrote that! When I witnessed Norrie mention to Max and Eddie how good the tune of *'Malta G.C'* was I smiled in total agreement and bit my lip accordingly!

1960 proved to be one of if not the busiest and most productive years of my career. Although at first I was particularly worried that Cliff Richard would wipe out the thought of anyone else, Norrie and I did somehow manage to find time for the rest of our talented commitments even to the extent of adding some new faces.

We virtually finished 1959 off with two hits. *'Seven Little Girls Sitting in the Back Seat'* by the Avons made it to number 3 on the 13th November and *'Living Doll'* re-entered the charts at 26 having previously been at number 1. Amazingly on the 1st of January 1960 we found ourselves again with two chart records. Cliff Richard's *'Living Doll'* re-entered the charts incredibly for the second time at number 28 and my dear friend Michael Holliday went to number 1 with *'Starry-eyed,'* which was truly a fantastic achievement.

Columbia's success rate remained unscathed due to careful planning in producing a consistent flow of chart singles. Without a doubt Cliff Richard became our most successful artist, always good for a laugh and easy to work with. We were very proud of witnessing him develop into such a class act with seemingly unending star quality. He had such an incredibly wide audience primarily created by the success of *'Living Doll'* which captured the hearts of both young and old. This continued with the success of *"Voice in the Wilderness"* which made it to number 2 on the 22nd January 1960, *"Fall In Love with You"* which made it to number 2 on the 24th March 1960 and *"Please Don't Tease"* which made it to number 1 on the 30th June 1960. By then we had had 13 chart singles with him including three number 1 records. This was an amazing track record that was to continue throughout the sixties, the seventies and well into the eighties!

The Swingin Sixties was a name created by the British media to describe the dramatic changes in the younger generation's outlook on life with regard to music and especially clothes and fashion. It was the time of Biba, Carnaby Street and Mary Quant amongst many other things. Musically speaking it was a period that was so exciting due to the success and acceptance of so many different types of Artists. America as usual contributed with such phenomenal talent in the form of Buddy Holly, The Drifters and Brenda Lee. British groups such as The Hollies, The Rolling Stones and especially The Beatles with their songs, their image and their music were to change and influence the world for ever. The Sixties were undoubtedly the best years of my professional and personal life.

During 1960 one of the greatest honours bestowed upon me was to produce The Norrie Paramor Orchestra. Norrie, being my boss, made it such an occasion for me and the pressure to make it successful was so enjoyably stressful. It was a big orchestra made up of the crème de la crème of British session musicians and cleverly featuring the beautiful voice of Silvia Adano. It really was a major music challenge. The project was a single, the 'A' side being 'Theme from *'A Summer Place'*, a truly gorgeous piece of music. The big kick for me was that Norrie was the Artist and he was allowing me the freedom of being the producer. I felt the adrenalin flow making me feel strangely powerful in telling Norrie what I thought he needed to do or change, and what was more, him doing it with no objection whatsoever!

Much to our delight, the record made the charts to just outside the top thirty in March 1960. Being the Artist this time around, Norrie looked like the cat that had just got the cream.

Producing an orchestra of this size made me feel and realise the incredible emotional strength that strings were able to portray. Like the sound of the wind blowing softly and delicately and then suddenly strongly and passionately they could transport your mind with no resistance at all into a world of fantasy.

It was Barry Mason, a good songwriter friend of mine who first told me about Tommy Bruce who was a Covent Garden porter at the time and lived in the same block as him. He had a habit of always singing in the bath. Barry said he had never heard such an amazingly awful voice but there was just something unusually striking about it.

I had always respected Barry so I suggested I could either arrange a recorded audition in Studio Three but without the bath or that he came up with a demo and if I thought the same regarding potential I would do a number on Norrie. And that is exactly what happened. Barry made the demo and I agreed with him that Tommy's voice was seriously hilarious, seriously awful and at the same time seriously great and totally unique.

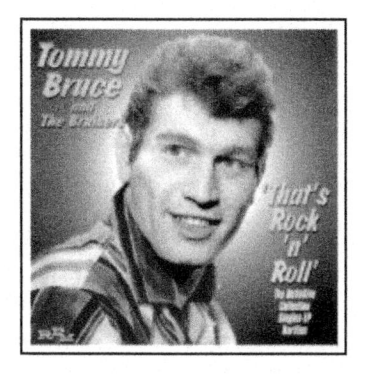

I found just the right moment to play it to Norrie who with his usual laid back sense of humour thought it was one big joke and then suddenly realised I was deadly serious. After some passionate persuasion I got him to agree to a record deal. We discussed material and Norrie bless him, came up with an idea. Lo and behold we were to have three hit records in succession. Not bad for singing in the bath! But Norrie and I hoped the world would sing in the bath too. And they did when they heard *'Ain't Misbehavin'*, the first release, taking young Tommy to number three in the Charts on May 26th 1960.

It was pretty obvious to both Norrie and I right from the start that the Drifters, Cliff Richard's backing group who were subsequently re-named The Shadows to avoid confusion with the American soul vocal group called the Drifters, had the talent to be recording Artists in their own right. Norrie deliberately did not take this further at the time but astutely decided to wait until they had gained more experience in recording and performing technique. He knew that at the same time they would be expanding their own fan base by riding on the back of Cliff Richard's escalating success. Norrie signed them to Columbia around June 1960. When their first single entitled *'Apache,'* written by a young talented songwriter called Jerry Lordan was scheduled for release, the pre-sales practically put the record in the charts straight away. Suddenly we had another time consuming hot property on our hands when the record shot up to number 1. This group's recording career was to become as big and as successful as Cliff Richard's, having more number one records to their credit than any other instrumental act in the World.

One memorable day in the studio sticks in my mind. Norrie had asked me to do a couple of tracks with the Shadows for their album. On two occasions they turned up late for the session and I had previously warned them about this. On the third occasion I am afraid to say I emphatically lost it. I gave them a fair old bollocking, saying they were in breach of their contract. They were wasting valuable studio time, money and my time and if they continued to act this way they would not only be jeopardising their contract, we would have no choice but to charge them for the studio time and the loss of finance, deducting it from their forthcoming royalties. In other words they might very well not get paid anything for a very long time to come! That really put the shits up them and for some unknown reason it never happened again!

Sometimes we would find a song that we thought shouted hit but we had no Artist. This was the case with *'Tell Laura I Love Her,'* which was brought to Norrie's attention by Johnny Wise, a close publishing friend. Norrie played the American version to me and I totally agreed with him that the song had hit written all over it. As we had no Artist and we really wanted to do it I suggested that I go through the audition tapes I had done in studio Three over the last three or four months. I came across Ricky Valance, whom admittedly I had passed over as having an interesting but rather average voice. However, on listening second time around I had no doubt that he would be perfect for this song. Norrie totally agreed and left it to me to get in touch with Ricky Valance to give him the news. Having tracked him down, I said

"Ricky, its John Schroeder. I have some good and some bad news for you. Norrie Paramor and I would love you to record a song that we both think could be a huge hit. The bad news is that the song, which by the way is high in the American charts at the present time, could be classified as a 'sick' song but it is just the sort of thing that is happening at the moment." He answered

"I am really thrilled that you want me to make a record but I don't like sick songs. I just hate them." I replied

"Sick songs are very much in at the moment and I advise you not to give up on this one because it will give you a recording contract and could make you feel *very well indeed,* especially financially. Sick and hit are a good team at the moment! Come up to the office and I'll play you *'Tell Laura I love Her'* and we'll take it from there. What have you got to lose?"

Fortunately Ricky saw the sense of it all but still took the advice rather reluctantly. However, the song proved to be tailor made for him and he performed it brilliantly. Amazingly the record made it to number one on the 25th of August 1960! How sick is that? Very sadly, Ricky joined the ranks of other Artists as being classified as a one hit wonder. However, it really was a good record and well worth the trouble of putting together. I amazed myself in my ability with powers of persuasion.

CHAPTER FOUR

Ever since Norrie had given me carte blanche use of Studio Three for recorded audition purposes I had become so endeared to it that I regarded it as being *my studio*. I loved its intimate atmosphere which unquestionably helped all those I had the privilege to audition over the past six months. But there was nothing amongst them that had really excited me or that I felt was that different. Ricky Valance was the only exception and that was because we had found a great song which we didn't want to pass up. Sometimes it's worth remembering that a singer is only as good as his song.

However, there was a certain audition I held in Studio Three that was destined to become one of if not the greatest discoveries of my career and was to result in world wide success for that Artist spanning many years to come.

The scenario began with a personal phone call to Norrie Paramor from Maurice Burman who ran a school for music and voice training in Baker Street. Norrie advised Maurice to call and ask me if I could spare the time to come and listen to some of his pupils, giving them advice, in particular with regard to recording. I of course agreed and Maurice ultimately selected seven pupils. I suggested that each one sings one song of his or her own choice with piano accompaniment in a room by themselves, after which I would list my comments with any helpful or constructive advice. Maurice was really grateful for this and then casually mentioned he thought that there was one pupil who stood out from the rest but he wouldn't say who.

Having heard four of them on the designated afternoon, the door opened and she confidently walked in, gave the sheet music to the pianist and launched into '*Birth of the Blues*'. I say launched because the performance was truly amazing. There was a touch of jazz and soul about her phrasing as though she had been singing for years. She sounded so professional and she was blessed with a voice that was totally incomparable, so deep and rich in tone and so full of emotion. The most astounding thing of all was that she was only thirteen and a half years old! I found it very hard not to show how impressed and excited I really was. Quite frankly I truly thought she might be the answer to Brenda Lee.

I had coffee with Maurice after the event having given him my notes. Before he could say anything I said

"Helen Shapiro." He smiled knowingly. "I want her to come to E.M.I Studios for a recorded audition which I will arrange. I want her to sing the same song but not to come before she feels one hundred per cent happy about her performance and interpretation since this time it will be recorded. I do not want her to fail this audition! If it is as good as I know it will be I will personally play it to Norrie Paramor at an opportune moment. I hope to give him a big shock and for both you and Helen to have a nice big surprise. Is that a deal Maurice?"

Maurice was over the moon especially as it was very clear how proud he felt having singled out Helen Shapiro as being the one. After a short while he phoned me and said Helen was ready.

I booked Studio Three and couldn't wait to do this audition. It had been on my mind constantly since I first heard Helen sing. We met on the day and she seemed just as confident as the time before. I did think the studio bothered her a little but leaving her alone with the pianist for a while did the trick. It only took one take because it was so damn good. She just made that song her own. I told her how pleased I was and I promised her I would discuss the matter with Norrie Paramor, but it was he who had the final say with regard to a recording contract.

I had to wait three frustrating days before receiving the acetate of what we had done. I nervously put it on the turntable. Thank God it sounded just as unbelievably exciting, if not more so, than before. What I had to do now was to pounce on Norrie at the right moment when I could capture his total attention. I carefully monitored his moves throughout the day and then about 5.30 pm I saw my chance. I said trying not to show my excitement.

"Norrie I want you to listen carefully to this. It is the result of an audition I did a week ago." I put the acetate on his machine and watched his every expression.

When it had finished there was yet again that awful pregnant pause. My heart sank, thinking for a fleeting moment that perhaps I was wrong. Then Norrie said quite slowly and emphatically, and looking straight at me

"He is good isn't he?

I smiled to myself and thought now it's my turn for some dramatics. I answered emphatically and very slowly indeed.

"*He* is not a *he*. *He* is a *she* and *she* is thirteen and a half years old. Her name is Helen Shapiro." He was speechless but his reply said it all.

"That is the most amazing thing I have heard for a long time and you should be proud of yourself. Arrange for Helen and her parents to come in for a meeting with us as soon as possible. You must tell me the whole story."

I did, in detail.

I arranged the meeting, and Helen's parents were very sweet but somewhat taken aback by the speed of events. Helen was too, but being the age she was she had that intangible air of confidence which I felt was so endearing and so much part of her. Norrie said he was really impressed with the audition and would love her to join Columbia as a recording Artist keeping company with Cliff Richard and The Shadows and others. On hearing that name, none of them could believe it and Helen was totally in another world!

Helen finally leaving school

The subject of the recording contract came up and as Helen was a minor it was necessary for her parents to sign the agreement. Norrie explained that it was a standard company agreement which all artists signed. He tried to explain in simple terms the most important clauses such as royalties. With no disrespect I don't think Helen's parents really understood it or even cared at the time but as everybody else had signed it they agreed to as well. It was natural that they were all in a state of shock, especially as their daughter was only thirteen and a half years old and still at school.

As time went on Norrie and I found ourselves with a big problem. We could not find a song strong enough or suitable enough for Helen's debut single. The word had gone out to all the music publishers and we were soon inundated with songs but a song for someone so young was just not written. Lyrical content was the big problem.

At one of our weekly meetings when we reviewed our Artists individually Norrie said "I am desperately worried about Helen Shapiro. We are now six months into her contract without a record. If we are not careful we will lose her. I know we've not found a song for her or come anywhere near, even though we have heard hundreds of songs. How about you John? Couldn't you write something for her? You know her better than anybody." I replied

"Well I have never really written anything (Malta G.C flashed across my mind!) but I will certainly give it some thought." Norrie answered

"You will never know unless you try. The opportunity is there for you"

"Thanks Norrie. I will certainly have a good think about it" I answered with a considerable amount of uncertainty.

I did give the matter a great deal of thought but never really believed I would be able to come up with anything. What I did have was Helen's voice and phrasing firmly logged in my head and I felt it and heard it very strongly day and night. Sometimes it drove me crazy as it was a little like having a headache but a nice one!

I was always messing about on the piano and then one night inspirationally out of nowhere the melody line and 'hook' suddenly came to me. Although there was no lyric or title at this stage I could clearly see and hear Helen singing it. Sensibly I had continued with my music lessons at the Ivor Mairants School of Music in Denmark Street which Norrie also agreed was commendable. In view of my job I considered it to be very important, so just for the hell of it I decided to play my masterpiece to Eric Gilder, my teacher to get his opinion on what I had conceived. To my surprise he thought it was pretty good, primarily because it was obviously inspired. He said inspiration was a natural phenomenon, not giving any real clue as to how, when, why or where it occurs. Some have it and some don't. He suggested changing a couple of chords and pointed out that it would need the right lyric. Giving that some thought and not being a lyric writer as such myself I decided to play it to Mike Hawker, my lodger at the time since he was a journalist and good with words.

I knew exactly what I wanted to hear but could I present Norrie with a finished song that had all the ingredients and potential of being a hit song? That was what I had to do. I felt I needed Lady Luck to do more than just smile on me!

A short while before Norrie had asked me to think of something for Helen Shapiro, Mike Hawker had joined the promotion department of E.M.I. Records having been working as a freelance journalist for Jazz News, Jazz Monthly and Melody Maker.

We became friends since we found we had mutual interests. Mike had decided to take up my offer of staying with me as a lodger until his newly acquired apartment was ready to move into.

I told Mike the story of the discovery of Helen Shapiro and that Norrie and I had found it impossible to find the right song for her first record. The problem was that no one at the time was writing songs for someone of her age because there just wasn't anyone of her age, apart from Brenda Lee perhaps. I then played him the acetate of the audition I had done with her in the studio at E.M.I. Although the song was *'Birth of the Blues'* he was of course initially as amazed as I was. I then played him on the piano the melodic piece of inspiration that had come to me. In fact I played it to him several times and I have to admit I was getting quite excited about it. Mike was non committal but felt it had potential. He also felt that Helen being a teenager, something to do with rebellion lyrically might be a good idea!

Mike moved from E.M.I to work for Larry Parnes but he took the tune with him because it stayed in his head which was a good thing. Incredibly inspiration once again played its part and he came up with the idea and title of *'Don't Treat Me Like a child.'* whilst returning home on a train from visiting his parents. He told me the hammer-blow chords (his quote) that I had written into the last line of each verse reminded him of someone banging their fist on a table in frustration or anger!

Gritting my teeth, the right moment finally presented itself for me to approach Norrie with the finished masterpiece.

"Norrie, I have managed to come up with something for Helen. I don't know how strong or good it is. It's called *'Don't Treat Me Like A Child'* but in view of Helen's age it sounded right."

He answered.

"That's a good title. Are you going to let me hear it?"

"I'll do my best" I said nervously. For some unknown reason, I have never been as frightened in my life as I was at that moment. Maybe it was because he was my boss and musically he was brilliant. I was relieved when it was over.

Again the Norrie Paramor pregnant pause. He then said quite calmly

"I believe that's what we've been looking for. It's really strong both melodically and lyrically and it's right for Helen. Great title!"

I answered

"Norrie I live with Helen's voice in my head night and day. It's like a drug. She's become part of my daily existence."

Maurice Burman and Helen were thrilled with *'Don't Treat Me Like A Child.'* and couldn't wait for it to be recorded. Maurice then approached me about the B side. He said he had the skeleton of a tune and if I would like to work with him on it Norrie might agree to it being used as the B side. When I told Maurice that I worked with a lyricist called Mike Hawker Maurice confirmed that he had no objection whatsoever to having the addition of Mike Hawker's involvement.

When we had finished the song, both Helen and Norrie agreed that it would make a good 'B' side. I also thought it would be a nice way of saying thank you to Maurice Burman for all he had done. The song was called *'When I'm With You.'*

Norrie decided to use the talents of Martin Slavin to do the arranging. The songs were routined with Helen in exactly the same way as everybody else except we now had ideas from two highly skilled arrangers and one novice songwriter! Martin's ultimate ideas for the arrangements, taking into consideration suggestions from both Norrie and I, seemed to me to be in the right direction. I particularly liked what he had in mind for the three girl backing singers.

As Studio Two was not available I booked, with Norrie's approval, a full evening session in Studio One with Malcolm Addey as the engineer. As Studio One was so huge and intimidating, Malcolm arranged for curtains to be fixed to shut off a large part of the studio leaving us with something much smaller and providing much more of an intimate atmosphere. This recording session was going to give me such a special buzz as I really couldn't believe it was my song that was going to be recorded.

Witnessing seeing and hearing the transition of my playing *'Don't Treat Me Like A Child'* on the piano to what I was hearing at this moment, although just the rhythm, was absolutely amazing. I was shaking with excitement and had to keep on asking myself – "did I really write this?"

The moment came when Norrie asked Martin to run the song through from the top with Helen. What a moment that was! As soon as she had opened her mouth and sung the first line I had goose bumps all over me. I was mesmerised and I had never heard anything like it. Not only that, it was plainly obvious that the song and the Artist were made for each other. Norrie and everyone else in the studio that night were 'blown away'. It was sensational.

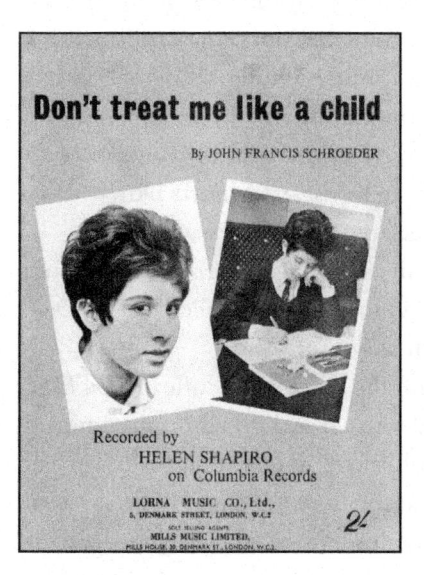

I remember Norrie and I having an in depth discussion just prior to us deciding on a release date for *'Don't Treat Me Like A Child'*. Funny enough, the problem was Helen's name – Shapiro. Norrie didn't particularly like it but after some deliberation we decided that that was her name and that was how it should stay. I pointed out, if nothing else, it was a name that would certainly stick.

The initial response to the release of *'Don't Treat Me Like A Child'* was a little strange and disappointing, although it did manage to make the charts at number twenty eight. The turning point for Helen was her inclusion in the first programme of 'Thank Your Lucky Stars' thanks to Jack Good, the producer. After this the sales started to escalate, finally putting the record in the charts at number three. It was a very proud and unbelievable moment for me. The sudden respect I had gained at Abbey Road and Manchester Square was amazing. There were" good mornings" coming from all over the place!

Being so young was very much in Helen's favour. There was so much interest in her, publicity-wise from so many sources. The biggest problem of all now faced Norrie, myself and Helen, and that was the follow up single!

To follow a hit record is one of a record company's and producers worst nightmares. It is particularly crucial since an Artist's career could be at stake and all the concerted effort and hard work initially put in by so many people could be a waste of time if the follow up single failed to make it.

To follow *'Don't Treat Me Like A Child'* was no different to anything else. Norrie was always astute and did not believe in breaking up a winning team so my input together with Mike Hawker's talent as a lyricist were an essential combination with regard to future Helen Shapiro material if there was to be any! Norrie was more than amenable to giving us the opportunity of a follow up before looking at material from other sources.

Mike and I discussed the whole thing again and again but the problem always remained the same. If the follow up single did fail then you would be hearing the 'ones in the know' implying that the song was too similar to the hit or that if it was totally different then it should have been more similar to the hit. What ever you did would be wrong but our gut feeling was more inclined to gamble with something totally different. But what? It is not usually possible to write a hit song to order. I was having trouble writing a song let alone a hit song. Inspiration had totally deserted me but then… I remembered *Ma's Tune!* I played it again and again before convincing myself it would be right for Helen if of course it had the right lyric! In my heart of hearts I knew it was absolutely right. It was Helen and it was different.

By this time Mike Hawker was living in his flat in Victoria. I put the tune on to tape, called him and told him I was sending him the follow up to *'Don't Treat Me Like A Child.'* I was that confident about the song.

It wasn't long before Mike came up with the lyric and the title of *'You Don't Know.'* He said it was the best thing I had written and it had inspired him to write the lyric based on the uncertainty of his love affair with Jean Ryder who was one of the Vernons Girls vocal group at the time. He thought he stood no chance with her but she eventually became his wife maintaining ten years of marriage with two children! That song certainly had something special for him too!

Norrie and Helen loved it and Martin Slavin once again did the honours with the arranging. The session itself was a very emotional experience. Tears came to my eyes thinking of my mother and how much she adored that tune, saying it deserved to have some beautiful words. Mike Hawker, bless him, had managed to do just that. It is one of the best songs, if not *the* best, I have ever written and to this day even Mike would condone that. I loved everything about that record and I distinctly remember witnessing Norrie playing the acetate for the first time to his much respected friend Bunny Lewis. Of course Mr. Lewis had a vested interest in the record since he and Norrie wrote the 'B' side which was called *'Marvellous Lie'*. Norrie was worried about a breath noise from Helen on the words 'how hard'. Bunny emphatically said

"You don't worry about a little thing like that Norrie, not when you have a certain Number One record on your hands. That record, believe me will go to Number One!

Unexpected success at only fourteen years old

Adoring fans

CHAPTER FIVE

Due to extreme pressure of work I was guilty of not having found the time to go down to see my parents since just before the discovery of Helen Shapiro. My mother loved to be kept up to date on everything and became very dependent on my giving her every little detail, good or bad, of *'the story of my life'*. I gave her a full version of the Helen Shapiro saga which of course included the inspiration of *'Don't Treat Me Like A Child'* and the writing partnership with Mike Hawker. She clung on to every word, totally enthralled but couldn't resist rather frequent interjections of 'how wonderful darling' whilst my father most of the time shook his head in disbelief.

A few days after the release of the record, Ma called me and very excitedly said, "Darling they played your song on the radio today and I felt so proud. I am going to the local record shop to buy a copy so you will earn some money. I am also going to tell all my friends to bloody well buy one as well, including your father." No matter what, she was always there for me!

When the follow up single, *'You Don't Know,'* had been recorded and mixed and I had got my hands on a promotion copy, I wanted my mother to be the first to hear it. After all it was *Ma's tune,* and I knew it would be a totally unexpected and fantastic surprise. On arriving at the house, I was in a way disappointed to find my father not there. Everything was so strangely quiet. I called, a little concerned

"Ma, you're on your own. Are you all right? The old boy's away then?"

"The old boy's been away a couple of weeks now", she replied, her voice coming from behind a high backed armchair in the lounge.

"Has he gone on one of his clock tours?" I asked.

"On one of his *cock* tours more like. God knows what he gets up to or who! He's a dark horse, your father," she retorted with a nervous laugh.

"He's probably just innocently enjoying himself," I said with kind of tongue in cheek reassurance.

"Oh he's enjoying himself all right, but innocently…I'm not so sure," she answered with a hint of loving resignation.

I felt rather sorry for her. I gave her a big hug and said

"Don't worry Ma. I know how much you love the grumpy old sod. He'll be back soon. I have a surprise for you. Just listen to this."

I put the record on. Witnessing her changing expressions whilst the record was being played was a sight for sore eyes. By the end, she was literally crying with joy and disbelief. It took a while before she was able to control herself. She said it was the most beautiful thing in the world I could ever have done for her. The words were as perfect as the melody. And Helen's voice was so strong and emotional and so right for the song. How could the record fail to be a hit?

Well of course the record did not fail to be a hit and as Bunny Lewis had predicted, it went to Number One and stayed there for six weeks. It was also in the charts for twenty three weeks! To this day *'You Don't Know'*, with due credit to Mike Hawker for the amazing lyric, remains at the top of my list as being the best song out of everything I have ever written, particularly as my mother helped to put it there!

With a number one record, the attention given to Helen by the media was phenomenal but well deserved. Helen, at only fourteen years old was a natural, whether it was T.V, Films, Tours, interviews or whatever.

Norrie was approached by Rank Films with regard to their currently successful series of programmes entitled 'Look at Life'. Each programme took the format of a ten minute feature film which was shown at every Rank cinema across the country in conjunction with the current 'A' film. In this instance the idea that Rank wanted was to portray the making of a hit record, namely Helen's next single from the time the song was initially conceived to it being recorded, released and promoted, and finally being bought by the public.

One Friday evening Norrie sat me down and explained the whole Rank proposition. He said

"John, you need to come up with something even more outstanding for Helen's next single as this feature film will provide us with the biggest form of promotion ever. There is nothing to compare to it. If the record were to fail with this sort of promotion it would be highly embarrassing and probably very difficult for us to get Helen back into the charts again. What do you think?" I replied

"Well, we were under heavy pressure with *'You Don't Know'*, but this is even more exciting and even more frightening. What can I say? I'll say my prayers and pray for a miracle."

Norrie replied.

"Right now Helen is red hot and every publisher wants to get in on the act. I am leaving the door open for you because of what you have already achieved. We haven't got much time because I have got Rank breathing heavily down my neck and we do need the follow up single." He paused to let it sink in and then with an almost apologetic smile said "Good luck. I'm sure you can do it."

I went home that evening inwardly shaking with nervous excitement and my mind going crazy over such a ridiculous situation. On the one hand it was a one in a million opportunity, whilst on the other, to follow *'You Don't Know'* with something as strong or stronger under such pressure needed much more than a miracle. I contacted Mike and gave him both the good and the bad news. His immediate verbal reaction said it all but after the enormity of the true value of the request had sunk in we both agreed that any pre-planned activities for the next few days had to go on hold and we had to give ourselves totally to coming up with a song, or to be more correct – *the* song.

Mike could do nothing until I had come up with a melody. Once again we were following a hit but this time a number one record which was a far worse scenario. My creative instincts went into logical mode and I was sure the new song had to be mid to up tempo since *'You don't Know'* was a ballad.

I was convinced that the song we were hoping for, taking 'Look At Life' as an additional consideration, had to be happy, singable and danceable to. It needed to be extremely melodic from start to finish, every bar had to count to its ultimate strength and it had to register on its first hearing. Somewhat of a tall order!

Each day went by with nothing worthwhile coming to fruition and I was getting a headache and getting rather fed up. I needed a break and so I went for a walk but before going home that evening decided to have a drink in a local pub. I often get inspiration from studying people, their expressions their movements even their relationships. It didn't matter if I was right or wrong it was how I musically translated it. On looking around me the entire melodic content of the song suddenly came into my head. I left immediately as I was frightened I was going to forget it!

Once on the piano the whole thing fell into place very quickly and very easily but I was really stuck with an idea for the intro. My mind for some reason wandered on to some of the great standards of all time, songs like *'I Get A Kick Out Of You'* and *'I've Got You Under My Skin.'* They all had long colle voce intros before the main melody came in so I said to myself "why don't I write a colle voce intro?" It would certainly be different and it would kick start the main melody and that is exactly what I did. I then recorded it and sent it to Mike Hawker with an appropriate explanation. I was pretty excited because I felt it was strong and I couldn't wait for Mike's reaction. He must have felt the same because Mike, as brilliant as ever came back with a simple, catchy, message of love type of lyric with the fabulous title of *'Walking back to Happiness.'* Once again he had hit the nail on the head by coming up with the perfect lyric, to dare I say, the perfect melody! The intro was a dream too – 'Funny but it's true what loneliness can do.'

Ironically Mike had developed the title from a bad day at the office. Whilst feeling depressed and walking several miles home to save fare money (we had not as yet received anything financial from our previous success) he remembered that Jean, his by now live-in girl friend was coming back from a concert tour and would be waiting at home. Thankfully for us the combination of actually walking back to something happy provided Mike with the necessary inspiration.

It is an interesting fact that *oop bah oh yea yea* was not initially part of the lyric but envisaged as a musical riff possibly using brass. Mike had indicated this on his copy of the lyric to me by scribbling in something like *ooh bob bob doodle bah.*

The song was complete and once again I was holding my breath whilst playing it to Norrie and of course anticipating the bloody pregnant pause at the end. It came but this time there was actually some excitement in his voice

"What rhythm feel do you have in mind? This? or this? or this? He played three different patterns and I endeavoured to demonstrate and verbally describe what I roughly had in my head." I then said

"I feel there should be something Latin about it. That's what I'm hearing."

"It's a strong song, very commercial and absolutely right for Helen. You and Mike have surpassed yourselves and I am sure Rank will go for it. Fix the routining session, book the studio and make sure we get Malcolm Addey."

And then with a smile and as an after thought he said

"I suppose we should let Helen hear it."

This time Norrie had decided to do the arrangements himself probably because of the importance of Rank but I was thrilled and felt very secure in having his additional input. Helen loved the song and sang it with seemingly such little effort because once again it was tailor made for her. On the routining session Norrie didn't particularly like the idea of the brass riff and suggested it should be replaced with something vocal. Noticing and bearing in mind what Mike had initially scribbled down and from the top of my head I suggested *ooh bah oh yea yea,* subconsciously remembering 'You Don't Know'. Everyone immediately condoned it and it became virtually as strong as the chorus of the song itself even being taken as part of the chorus itself.

The recording of *'Walking back to Happiness'* was certainly one of the most exciting highlights of my career. There was magic in the air that night in the studio and I cannot find the words to describe how I felt. Everyone involved had such a great time enjoying every minute of the recording of that song and I don't think there was anyone who didn't go home singing it!

I had to smile to myself when I discovered that Norrie and Bunny Lewis had once again written the B side which was entitled *'Kiss 'n' Run.'* It's what you call keeping it in the family! It was a pretty good song and there was a time that Helen thought that it was in fact stronger than *'Walking Back.'* No one else agreed I'm glad to say.

Rank was thrilled with the record and suddenly within the next two days we had to re-enact the entire session again. No one complained as everyone was getting paid all over again without having to play or sing a note! It all came off brilliantly, even re-enacting the painful moment of me playing the song on the piano to Norrie and Helen for the first time. The film was obviously incredible promotion for the record since it virtually sent it storming up the charts to Number One with it eventually selling a million records!

Studio Playback
"Times I shall never forget"

Don't Treat Me Like A Child
(L/r The Mike Sammes Singers,
Helen, Martin Slavin & Norrie)

You Don't Know
(Helen, Norrie and me)

Walkin' Back To Happiness
(Me, Norrie, Helen & Malcolm Addy)

There were two incidents connected to *'Walking Back'* that I shall always remember. The first was one of those very rare occasions when I genuinely felt my father was proud of my achievement. There was a record shop near his office and according to Ma he used to come home from work each day and with the excitement of a little boy said

"Joy it's gone up another five places. Joy it's gone up another ten places."

When I did see my father he said, smiling and a touch begrudgingly

"Well I see you have done something right at last."

"Gotcha", I thought to myself.

The second incident was very different and it happened some years later. I had driven into a garage to get petrol and in those days you had this done for you. Surprisingly the young attendant was whistling *'Walking Back to Happiness'* as he filled the car up. It made me feel *really good* that I had helped to make his day happy. He came up to me and said

"That'll be five gallons madam"

This time long hair and a change of image hadn't done me any favours!

Whilst I was thoroughly enjoying all this sudden personal success with interviews, write-ups and pictures in various papers and magazines, Norrie unjustly received a gentle nudge from the powers that be questioning him as to why he was allowing himself to being so 'upstaged' by his assistant. Norrie being Norrie emphatically declared that as his assistant was writing the songs and doing the work so well he justifiably deserved the success that followed and he was not in a position to stop it. The company should be more than grateful for the additional input in helping to keep Columbia as the Number One label.

I thought that was bloody nice of Norrie and it showed just how much respect there was between him and myself. However, with all this attention on me I couldn't help wondering about my future. Since it was just a fleeting thought I decided to ignore it for now and concentrate on my work.

On my travels I came across a very likeable and talented young Northern artist named Jimmy Crawford. Norrie liked him and the first single entitled *'Love or Money'* was a minor hit but the follow up single entitled *'I Love How You Love Me'* made the Top Twenty. It was truly a fabulous song and it was one of those songs that I really wished I had written myself.

At one of our weekly meetings we discovered that Frank Ifield's recording contract was about to expire but he was still owed a single record release before we could consider dropping him. Norrie wasn't too interested and handed the problem over to me to find something that would be good enough to record as a single. Frank Ifield was Australian and a really charming guy. He was managed by Peter Gormley who was also Cliff Richard's manager at the time. Frank was in a Club show in London and I decided to go and see him. I thought his act was excellent but there was one song that had the audience giving Frank a standing ovation. That song was *'I Remember You'*, but it was Frank's vocal rendition of it that was so awesome. He had managed to incorporate a yodelling effect in the voice that was so different and effective and that it virtually' blew the audience away' and me for that matter!

I told Norrie about it in detail and suggested we should seriously think about recording that song, after all we had nothing else. Norrie did eventually agree even though perhaps a little half heartedly. By the time Norrie had got the session together I was unfortunately not there to participate in it. I had in fact handed in my resignation, subsequently sadly having left the employment of E.M.I Records, Norrie Paramor and Columbia some time before.

I was more than pleased that *'I Remember You'* made it to number one the week of July 5th 1962 since I had originally suggested doing it. The record was in the charts 28 weeks, and following that, Norrie and Frank Ifield enjoyed two further number one records with *'Lovesick Blues'* and *'Wayward Wind'*. It was ironic that an Artist we were about to drop ended up having three number ones in a row!

Well it was on the cards. With *'Walking Back to Happiness'* standing at number one in the charts it wasn't long before I received offers from two other record companies, namely Philips Records and Oriole Records.

Obviously I told Norrie and he said that I was experienced enough and talented enough to be a Label / A&R Manager and Producer in my own right. He guessed what I was thinking and with a smile assured me he had no intention of vacating his position! He said he had expected it and advised me to go with my gut feeling, and so I had to seriously consider the two offers in question.

Phillips was a very successful major record company and I knew I would have security there but the offer from Oriole Records was unusual as it was something very different and very challenging. Morris Levy, the Proprietor and Managing Director, had built this family business up virtually single handed from a record shop in Aldgate to the only facility in the country whereby you could record your own personal message for an occasion such as a birthday. Now it was a company that had its own recording studio, its own offices in New Bond Street, its own distribution and its own pressing plant at Aston Clinton. It also manufactured and distributed Embassy Records, the Woolworths Label. It was in fact the only Independent Record Company at the time and what Morris Levy had in mind was to re-launch the Oriole label with its own roster of Artists and put it in direct competition with the majors. It would be a mammoth task, but if I could pull it off and he was able to financially support it, it would be an amazing achievement. A challenge like this got my adrenalin going and for me it was just too good to pass up.

Norrie gave me his blessing and confirmed he thought I had made the right decision. He said he would have done the same, which was encouraging but I am sure I detected a slight hint of reservation.

The day I actually left E.M.I Records, saying my good-byes, was a very sad day indeed. I was leaving behind some great friends and some incredible memories that will stay with me forever. I shall never forget George Martin, Wally Ridley and Norman Newell, the other label Managers, their assistants, the promotion and publicity teams, everyone at the factory at Hayes, E.M.I. Studios and especially Stuart, Peter and Malcolm, the engineers, Norrie himself and our lovely secretary Felicity, L.G. Wood, the Managing Director who got me to Norrie Paramor in the first place, and last but not least George Dawson who did so much for me in my early days at E.M.I There are so many more that I would love to personally thank for making my time at E.M.I. so happy and unforgettable. I was speechless when Cliff Richard himself presented me with a Ronson cigarette lighter with the words 'Thanks John' inscribed on it. I was also thrilled to have an inscribed gold Parker biro from Norrie Paramor, who was really sad to see me go. We truly had had some great times together.

There was a part of me that didn't want to leave. It had been my home for nearly four years and to be truthful, I was nervous of going out there on my own.

I accepted the position at Oriole Records and with an agreed release date from E.M.I the start of my employment with Oriole was to be December 4th 1961 which gave me a short but welcome break.

Little did I realise how much the sudden success of the Helen Shapiro songs was about to change my life. Since I knew nothing about the mechanics of music publishing, Norrie introduced me to Alan Paramor, his brother who successfully ran a music publishing company called Lorna Music. Once again there was nothing like keeping it in the family but Alan was totally straight and honest.

He helped me become a member of the Performing Rights Society which was an absolute necessity. Since initially all my songs were published by Lorna Music, Alan was responsible for paying the royalties due. Having struggled financially for so long I now suddenly found myself with what I felt to be a considerable fortune.

Obviously changes were about to take place.

Heathway Court

How my marriage to Christine managed to stay together I'll never know, although the birth of Michelle obviously had a lot to do with it.

Christine and I decided to sell the house and move to a rather nice large apartment we had found in Heathway Court, Childs Hill near Golders Green which we rented. Needless to say as was originally agreed, any profit from the sale of the house went to my father. Apparently Ma had to call the doctor when my father finally received the cheque from the buyer's solicitors!

At last I felt I was out of my father's clutches. I was grateful for the past financial help even though it was conditional, but now my life was solely down to me.

It was fortunate that Mike Hawker's new accommodation was also ready and he could now move in. Mike was more than grateful to us for helping him out as it had unexpectedly created an extremely successful writing partnership between Mike and I which we fully intended to develop.

Now that life was easier financially and we had moved to Heathway Court I decided I deserved to update my rather neglected love affair with the motor car. The Speedwell A.35 was fantastic and I shall never forget Graham Hill, but I had grown out of it, so I changed it for a Morris Minor Traveller, a very pretty estate car in black with part wooden body. Needless to say it was 'schroederised' and ended up with curtains round the side and rear windows. 'Be Prepared' had always been one of my favourite mottos!

It wasn't long before I had my eyes focused on what I considered to be a proper sports car. I fell in love with a red Triumph TR4.

It certainly had the looks and it certainly got the looks! I had no problem seeing myself with the hood down, dark glasses and the blonde sitting beside me with *gorgeous* long flowing locks blowing in the wind. A little voice whispered in my ear

"You wish…dream on!"

CHAPTER SIX

THE ORIOLE RECORDS STORY

It was very nice to see that my forthcoming move to Oriole Records had created genuine interest throughout the Music Industry and initiated some excellent press. It always upset me to read the usual concluding remark of 'well let's wait and see what happens'. I tended to take it far too personally since I assumed it pointed a finger at me!

As I walked into the Oriole Records offices at 104 New Bond Street on that Monday morning I felt exactly like I did walking into the E.M.I offices in East Castle Street for the first time, but this time I was praying I had made the right decision about the job. I consoled myself by remembering I had four years experience with a major record company behind me and I had had the best tutor in the world so there was no reason why I shouldn't feel confident. Even so, it was a daunting task to put a small and virtually un-established label in direct competition with the majors. The financial cost, let alone anything else, could be crippling. Inwardly I was truthfully scared stiff. To make matters worse, I had now put myself face to face with my old boss. What Norrie didn't know was that he would more than likely be sitting on my shoulder whispering in my ear on many of my forthcoming decisions.

I certainly thought New Bond Street was a strange place to have a record company. It was without a doubt a prestigious address but the front entrance could have belonged to any one of the shops in the street.

E.M.I and Oriole Records were like the giant and the dwarf and to go from working for the giant to working for the dwarf was a lot more difficult to adapt to than the other way round. As for my office, it was half the size or less to what I had been used to. However, my new secretary Debs or Debbie made up for all other deficiencies and provided a very worthwhile attraction, or was it distraction! She was obviously highly thought of in house, and confidently introduced me to everyone. I did feel the welcome I received to be very genuine, and this did much to ease my state of mind.

Reg Warburton, who was in charge of the Woolworth's Embassy label kindly offered me his help anytime I felt I needed it. Fred Dennis who looked after label copy, artwork and copyright clearances, and Ronnie Bell, the promotions Manager, were eagerly waiting to offer me their services as soon as necessary, both having confirmed that there was now a real purpose for them being there. Having such support from everyone helped to fuel my incentive to make Oriole into something really successful.

Since we had not spoken for a while I needed Morris Levy to once again confirm the following, which he gladly did.

1. Would I have complete authority to sign and drop
   any artist I wanted?   The answer: Yes

2. Was there finance to cover recording costs for both
   singles and albums for unlimited time?   The answer: Yes

3. I believed it was imperative to have our own
   Luxembourg programme two or three times a week.
   Was this feasible?   The answer: Yes

4. I had in mind to re-design the Oriole logo.
   Was this acceptable?   The answer: Yes

5. To show how serious we were, we also needed
   American product. Was this acceptable?   The answer: Yes

With a positive response like that, I had to respect and admire Morris Levy's ardent determination. The challenge was there. The company's support was there and he had personally given me the key that hopefully would open the right doors. I could only do everything in my power to make it work. However, I was sure I had heard that word 'miracle' whispered behind my back more than once! I remained undeterred.

Having at last managed to squeeze a piano and an extra chair into my office, my first task was to go through all the Artists that were currently signed to Oriole. I did this with certain reservation and reluctance and finally decided to keep just three, Jackie Lee and The Raindrops, Clinton Ford and Maureen Evans. They were all experienced, blessed with identifiable voices and had already enjoyed some minor success, a good example being Clinton Ford's rendition of *'Old Shep'* which did in fact chart at number twenty seven and Maureen Evans *'The Big Hurt'* at number 26. With the right material and promotional support there was no reason why I shouldn't be able to develop their potential. I asked Debbie to fix up individual appointments for me to see them.

My next job was to re-design the Oriole logo. After some thought I came up with a design using yellow and black as the basic colours incorporating straight black lines running down between each letter of the word Oriole. The type set would be in silver. Seeing the sample, I felt it was right. It looked business-like and impressive. Thankfully everyone agreed, giving it their blessing. It only left the industry to accept it.

It was now time to check out my biggest fear and worry, the Studio. If it was not able to produce product equal to the quality of E.M.I there would be no point in starting to compete at all!

The studio was situated a little further down New Bond Street with a similarly unimpressive entrance. Jacques Levy, the studio manager had obviously been primed by Morris Levy beforehand of my impending visit. He was ultra polite and said he had been expecting me. He introduced me to Geoff Frost, the senior balance engineer and John Wood, the chief technician. I liked them both and they were thrilled with the prospect of this new venture, but they also appreciated the magnitude of the task. Geoff, whom I would consistently be working with, was quite adamant that with the right producer the studio could match anything coming from a major record Company. I appreciated his confidence but hearing was believing, so he suggested I spent time with him in the studio checking out everything before attempting to do a fully blown session. I did this and discovered the studio did have a very nice ambience. It was also not too large and yet not too small and I came away feeling very much more secure, but I knew I would only be feeling really comfortable once the first session was over.

The Method Behind The Madness

I believed the correct strategy was to not to say anything to anybody, particularly the Press, as to what was happening at Oriole until we had everything one hundred per cent in place before we launched the product and could realistically justify our intentions to the industry as a whole as far as present and future policies were concerned. This needed a lot of thought and a lot of input from a lot of people, and I was determined it could and would be done. I had to come up with a strategic game plan that was both realistic and feasible.

Quality and quantity of product were my first concerns. True, we needed hit records to attract positive attention but we also needed a solid number of records for the first release that would surprise the industry. About four weeks after the announcement of the initial releases I envisaged a 'New Era' launch party to be held in the Studio, inviting about three hundred people who would be beneficial to us now and in the future, such as The Music Press, Radio and T.V presenters, Music publishers, programme producers, Artist management and certainly retailers. At the function, two of our Artists would perform their current single releases. I would introduce Morris Levy and then he or I would outline the Company's future plans and policies.

If this promotional launch proved to be as successful as I hoped it would be, then the industry and the other major players in it might well realise that Oriole was determined to be taken as a serious player and one to watch.

I asked everybody in the company to look out for new talent and to let me know if there was anybody worth auditioning. I asked Debs to notify as many music publishers as possible, making them aware that we were looking for new artists and new material. The response was pretty overwhelming.

Debbie made an appointment for me to see Jackie Lee and The Raindrops. I asked them how they felt about entering the Eurovision Song Contest with a song that I would write for them. If nothing else it could create very much needed publicity for them, for Oriole and for me. They all thought it was a great idea, but a lot depended on the song. I got together with a lyricist called Peter Pavey and we came up with a song called *'There's No-one In the Whole Wide World'*. It was a very catchy mid tempo ballad that the group thought was very strong and stood a good chance. I got Frank Barber to do the arranging but I was very nervous on the night of the session, since it was my first serious session in the studio. Unbelievably there were no problems and it sounded pretty good, even better when we had mixed it. It was submitted to Eurovision and it made it to number sixteen in the final top twenty. This created some very promising sales and the record became part of Oriole's first release schedule.

The second record focused on the talents of Clinton Ford. He was an amazing Artist who vocally wore two hats, the first being his love for comedy and fun songs whilst the second was a love for serious country music. Clinton brought a song to my attention called *'Fanlight Fanny,'* which was truly hilarious. I loved it and decided we should go for it as a prospective single, but how was I going to capture the sheer hysterics of it on record? I had no worries about Clinton, but I came to the conclusion that the answer I was looking for lay totally in the very careful selection of the musicians involved. Clinton suggested George Chisholm, who not only played trombone brilliantly, but had a fantastic sense of humour and loved to have musical fun. On contacting George he said he would be honoured to do the arranging, and knowing what I wanted, to leave the selection and booking of the other musicians to him. The session was booked for a 7.30 p.m start.

I arranged to discuss this session with Geoff Frost, my engineer, an hour before start time to tell him what I had in mind. I needed him to initially get a sound and balance on each instrument and Clinton, without having to do a full run through of the song. I then intended to send everybody into the pub for an hour. On their return we would hear a few bars from the top and then go all out for take one.

Everyone arrived at 7.30 and by 8.15 Geoff had got the sounds and balance and everything was set up. They were all so surprised, including George Chisholm, when I told them to disappear to the nearest pub for an hour. No one objected, but when they returned they were so very, very happy. A few bars from the top and then I almost shouted

"Settle down. Quiet please. "*Fanlight Fanny*" – Take one"

From the first note to the last it was so hilarious that another take was totally impossible. Once over, everyone fell about laughing and on hearing the playback did the same thing again. *'Fanlight Fanny'* was released exactly as it happened in the studio. As a double act Clinton and George were made for each other!

The third record to be scheduled was a new find called The Gary Edward's Combo, with a fun piece of musical charm, maybe sacrilege to some called *'The Franz Liszt Twist'*. Remember *'Liebestraum'*. Dancing to the classics was what it was about and probably ahead of its time, but the potential was interesting. I was not unhappy about its release.

The fourth single to make up the first Company release was Maureen Evans. I adored her voice and it inspired me to write a song for her entitled *'Tomorrow Is Another Day'*. It came off well and was considered to have stood as much chance as anything else. I was one hundred per cent sure that we would eventually get that hit record with Maureen Evans even though it might not be this record and that it might take a little time.

Those were the four singles making up the first release and intentionally released four weeks before the launch party so by that time, a proportion of those invited would certainly have been aware or even have heard or played the records in question, hopefully.

That was part of the strategy.

The Big 'O' Show

I was usually busy in the studio most evenings recording material that had been already pre-planned. During the days I was seeing music publishers, seeing Managers with prospective new Artists, working on routine sessions, booking musicians, listening to demos and so on. I was also involved in meetings with Morris Levy and Ronnie Bell, our promotions manager with regard to setting up our own Radio Luxembourg programme. This was an absolute must, since we would never be able to compete without this promotional facility. I felt for Morris Levy because it was a very expensive necessity. We approached Alan Keene, the Head of Radio Luxembourg and he came back with an offer of two fifteen minute shows to be produced and presented by Paul Holingdale and Chris Eaton who both had a much respected reputation. We accepted this and at the same time agreed that the show should be called The Big 'O' Show. Ronnie Bell would be in charge of the admin and supply the producers with the respective product and any other information for each week's show.

The Oriole Record

Since promotion was the lifeline to success and everyday existence, Ronnie Bell, Fred Dennis and I thought it would be an innovative idea to have our own house journal, named The Oriole Record. This was envisaged to contain reviews, write-ups, adverts, photographs, information relating to new Artists, ideas and policies, new releases etc. It would be compiled by the three of us but printed and edited by Ronnie and Fred. It would be sent out fortnightly to those that mattered in the industry, but most importantly to the retail trade. The Big 'O' Show and The Oriole Record would be announced at the launch.

"Oh what a night it really was"

The 'New Era' launch party was planned for the evening of February 7th 1962. The invitations, which we agreed would be worded that they had come from Morris Levy himself, were sent out by Ronnie Bell two weeks before the launch date. The four singles had been announced two weeks before that, or to be precise, four weeks before the launch date. A bar was set up in the studio and a small stage built at one end of the studio. Ronnie Bell did a great job making everybody feel welcome and pointing them towards the bar. After an hour the place was full, and Morris Levy opened up the proceedings, thanked everyone for coming and handed me the baton. I told everybody the reasons for my taking on such a challenge, how I admired Morris Levy's determination to make it work, outlined present and future policies, informed them of the Big 'O' Show and the introduction of the house journal, The Oriole Record, how the pressing plant and distribution company were geared to handle the influx of new product, and last but not least, the studio, which had been technically updated and was very well managed by Jacques Levy with production in the very capable hands of Geoff Frost. I then introduced the four Artists with current single releases, and both Maureen and Clinton performed their songs with backing tracks. They were very well received, especially as the product had already been reviewed and was receiving airplay. I then introduced three of the new Artists, who had not yet recorded, namely Susan Singer, (Helen Shapiro's cousin), Brett Ansell, and The Dowlands who were produced independently by Joe Meek. Finally I said it was encouraging to have such a dynamic team behind me who believed implicitly that Oriole was able to achieve being up there with the other major players. I thanked everyone for their time and for any future help they might be able to give in helping us to realise our ultimate goal.

All in all it was a great evening, said a lot for Oriole and made Morris Levy a very proud man.

What they actually said
We were all over the moon that the hard work and effort that had gone into the presentation of the launch had been so worthwhile, by the response it had received. It had achieved all that we had set out to do and more.

The following are extracts from some of the write ups in the Trade press:

Things are Swinging

BIG TRADE
REACTION TO NEW
POLICIES

Orders for the first 'New Era' Oriole singles released last month were the biggest in the label's long and colourful history – a positive reflection of the faith placed in the revitalised company by dealers and wholesalers. To cope with the increased demand, Oriole's factory has been geared to greatly accelerated production and the A and R department under the control of that progressive young man of music, John Schroeder – is bristling with new ideas.

The Launch Party
Oriole chief Morris Levy (seated centre)

NEW LOOK FOR ORIOLE
Policy changes will streamline label

MAKE WAY FOR a "new look" Oriole label! Sweeping changes in policy – plus the introduction of a new recording manager and several promising new Artists – have revitalised the company, and an all-out attack on the best sellers is launched this month. Distribution has been streamlined, and monthly releases have been scrapped in favour of a new batch of discs each week.

Eager to meet the increasing demands of pop music fans, Oriole's chief Morris Levy's first step in establishing Oriole as a major force on the disc scene has been to appoint talented John Schroeder as artists-and-repertoire manager. Formerly at Columbia where he was assistant to Norrie Paramor for three years, John is nationally known as the composer with co-writer Mike Hawker of such song hits as "You Don't Know, " "Walkin' Back to Happiness" and "Don't Treat Me Like A Child."

John's first move on joining Oriole last December was to design a new, strikingly different Oriole label – an eye-catching yellow and black trademark that makes its debut in the shops this month. Already he has signed several new Artists and has retained such established favourites as The Raindrops, Clinton Ford and Maureen Evans.

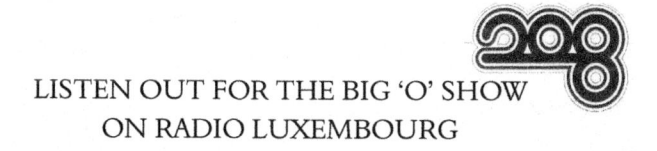

LISTEN OUT FOR THE BIG 'O' SHOW
ON RADIO LUXEMBOURG

Exposure on Radio Luxembourg is one of the finest methods of bringing a record to the attention of the public known to the pop music profession. And bearing the popularity of Luxembourg shows in mind, Oriole will launch their own twice-weekly disc series this month.

Introduced by disc jockeys Chris Eaton and Paul Hollingdale, the 15 minute programmes will commence on February 7th and will thereafter be heard at 9 p.m every Wednesday and Friday. Known as "The Big 'O' Show," the programmes will remain on the 208 airwaves for an indefinite series.

Exploitation chief Ronnie Bell said "Even when the policy changes were only in the talking stage, a Radio Luxembourg series was one of our major aims. We feel that it is vitally important towards our objective – the establishment of Oriole as a major force in modern recording."

TALENT A-PLENTY AT ORIOLE
"And there's more to come"
- A & R CHIEF

Britain is packed with undiscovered talent, and Oriole – encouraged by the success of the "New Look" campaign launched in February intend to offer every opportunity possible to the country's youngsters in their bid for stardom in the pop music world!

Since the beginning of the year, recording manager John Schroeder has built up a roster of 25 promising new Artists on the label.

"All of them have a sufficiently strong impact on the pop scene to face the future with confidence, and I'm convinced that some of them will emerge as major stars." he says.

CHAPTER SEVEN

JUST A MONTH AFTER the launching of the "New Era "Oriole label, Clinton Ford's "Fanlight Fanny" – one of the first discs recorded by a-&-r manager John Schroeder – entered the nation's best sellers. Demand for the disc continues, and in the meantime, two more Oriole records are hovering on the fringe of the charts – Gary Edwards' "The Method" and "The Franz Liszt Twist"

"It's a wonderful start," was Schroeder's reaction to the news. "It proves that the public, as well as the trade, are aware of the sweeping policy changes recently introduced at Oriole, and are taking much more than passing interest in our recordings. But we've still a long way to go," Schroeder added, 'And now my aim is to put more and more Oriole discs in the hit lists." Commented exploitation chief Ronnie Bell: Our new policy of top talent and top class-class songs is clearly paying dividends."

(NME – March 1962)

'Behind You, There's a Piano'

Following the unanimous success of the 'New Era' launch I became totally committed to pushing the label forward looking towards longevity and the future. Apart from successful singles I had album product in the back of my mind. *'Fanlight Fanny'* and the hour in the pub had paid off! I now had good reason to focus my attention on our first L.P with Clinton Ford as the Artist. It was of course another hilarious affair with George Chisholm once again in the driving seat providing some serious musical frivolity and Clinton as always rising to the occasion. The pub round the corner once more provided the necessary ingredients to enable us to produce another hysterical affair with sales that surpassed all expectations.

Truthfully the piano was my musical weakness and how I wished I had the gift of playing it really well. Oscar Peterson was my idol.

The BBC aired a programme entitled *'Younger than Springtime'* featuring a young talented pianist named Johnny Pearson. I was so impressed that I asked Debbie to track him down. He apparently gave his first concert at three years old, was blessed with perfect pitch, was classically trained and like me loved jazz.

We put an album together entitled 'Piano Sweet Piano Wild' which contained some incredibly exciting and innovative arrangements of such classics as 'Baubles Bangles and Beads.' I was to discover that every piece of 'ad lib' he played he wrote down so that he wouldn't forget it! Obviously I didn't know it at the time but Johnny Pearson and I were to have some incredible success together a few years later.

Susan Singer was in her late teens and had a good voice but strangely reminiscent, maybe too reminiscent of her cousin Helen Shapiro. Mike Hawker and I wrote *"Hello First Love"*, *"Johnny Summertime"* and *"Lock Your Heart Away"* for her, all strong songs and I really couldn't understand why none of them didn't do it especially *'Hello First Love'*. We were close though with good air play and sales that ultimately made the effort worthwhile even though somewhat disappointing.

Other signings followed – Brett Ansell, Jackie Trent who by my introduction and blessing was produced by, and eventually became, Mrs Tony Hatch!, The Dowlands who were independently recorded by Joe Meek and Tony Sheveton who had a minor hit with *'Million Drums'* but nevertheless a hit, and there were more young hopefuls to follow.

One day Debbie came into my office extremely distraught. She told me she was being pestered by a guy who kept on and on phoning, day after day, wanting an appointment. He said he had all the answers to make us successful and that it was only a matter of fooling everybody. He said we needed him as much he needed us.

For Debbie's sake, and feeling annoyed about it on her behalf I told her to make an appointment for him. I then said half heartedly

"Oh what's his name?"

"Jonathan King," she replied

On the day I was duly prepared. He came into my small office like a bolt of lightening. He was wearing a pin stripe suit but with trainers! There was an unusual aura of arrogance about him and he couldn't stop talking, with a University type accent.

"You know you need me and I need you. I want you to make a record with me and you won't regret it. I have studied the Music Industry for the last three years and it is one big joke. Anyone can make it if they're clever and can fool a few people. I know the names of all the A & R guys in the big companies but I chose you because you are small and I admire what you are trying to do. I'll give you a hit record. I play a bit and write a few songs too."

As he entered the room he had not seen the piano behind the door, so I said

"Behind you there's a piano. Let me hear something," feeling certain that now I'd got him!

He did momentarily change colour but soon had an answer.

"Well I am too excited to do that because I want to tell you about the song I want you to record with me. It is not one of mine; in fact it is a Goffin/King song and is on the latest Bobby Vee album. It is definitely a hit song."

I must admit by now he had unnerved me a bit so I thought I'd call his bluff again and quiz him about the business in general. I asked him names of Label Managers, producers, promotion people, what Artists belonged to what companies and so on. He did not make one mistake. He said it was a piece of piss because it was all such a big sham. I then said

"O.K. Jonathan (note Christian name now) I have to know what your voice sounds like before I can consider anything."

"I appreciate that. I will do a demo for you of me singing the song in question. That will kill two birds with one stone. You won't be disappointed," he said excitedly.

I sort of hoped I wouldn't see him again but four weeks later he was in my office with the demo. I put it on the turntable and just couldn't believe it. It was great and it sounded a hit. I said

"How did you do that?"

"I overdubbed my voice on top of Vee's so it was perfectly in sync." He said smiling conceitedly.

God knows why but he had won me over and I was prepared to give him a chance. Very unusual was the fact that I did not do a routine session with him because he said the key was the same as Bobby Vee's and he *expected* the arrangement to be virtually identical as to what was on the album. Quite casually all he said was "Give me a ring. Tell me the time of the session and I'll be there".

As usual it was an evening session and it was a big orchestra with a cost that was a little embarrassing. For some reason I was feeling nervous that night but Geoff, my engineer, assured me all would be well. Jonathan arrived totally overwhelmed by the fact that all this had been especially put together for his benefit. Frank Barber had done the arranging. I went into the studio, had words with Frank and some of the musicians. Frank then ran it through from the top whilst I had a good listen to what was going on. Meanwhile Geoff in the control room was busy getting a rough sound and balance. I then went up to the control room and between us we got the balance and sound of the musical background that I was finally happy with. I then asked Frank to run it from the top but this time with Jonathan. In the next few seconds it was a choice of me being buried or cremated because what we were all about to hear gave me much more than a major heart attack! I instantly died of embarrassment more than a thousand times. Jonathan King could not sing a note in tune. Basically he could not sing, period! He had only attempted sixteen bars when the whole studio could contain themselves no longer and burst out laughing including me and Jonathan too! It wasn't at all funny but my God, what was I going to do about the cost and telling this story to Morris Levy! More annoying was the fact that Jonathan was thoroughly enjoying himself and was even joking with the musicians! The session had to be abandoned but under severe stress and feeling quite ill I managed to get two very good but useless backing tracks. The only salvation would be to find someone who could handle that song but it had to be in that key. All in all a pretty hopeless mess!

After everyone had left having, at my expense, enjoyed a better comedy show than anything currently on TV, Jonathan unemotionally said

"I told you how easy it was to fool people in this industry. It was a marvellous experience and I will always remember it. I am sorry it happened to you. Morris Levy can afford it"! I thought to myself "You clever little bastard. I could lose my job over this". Geoff and Frank were totally lost for words and totally upset for me but really it was my own bloody fault. I should have set up a routining session which would have stopped Jonathan getting any where near the studio. A lesson learned and a well deserved bollocking from Mr. Levy is what I got. But it was ironic, that five years later Jonathan King had a number one record with *"Everyone's Gone To The Moon,"* which was self penned. I was not totally wrong, just way ahead of my time! Believe it or not over ten years later Jonathan phoned me and took me out for an Indian in Bayswater. He said he felt very guilty that he had not thanked or re-paid me for the huge favour I had done him in those early years.

I was so taken aback that the surprise was as much as the first time I had heard him sing!

Maureen

I knew she could do it if I could only find the right song. Unfortunately after considerable air play and good reviews *"Tomorrow Is Another Day,"* which I and Mike Hawker wrote didn't do it for us. We were all disappointed but then you can't win them all.

One afternoon a Music Publisher brought my attention to a well known classical tune which had a very attractive lyric written for it by Dick Manning. It was titled *"Like I Do"*. I really believed it had chart potential and immediately Maureen Evans came to mind. Having listened to the demo several times I had a very definite arrangement and rhythmic pattern in my head. Maureen heard the song and loved it and I got Debbie to fix a routine session with Frank Barber. We discussed and agreed the arrangement, the routine, the key, the rhythm and the musicians which I got Debbie to book for the evening in question. Everyone, including Maureen, arrived as usual right on time and I asked Frank to run it through from the top. When I heard what was being played I shouted at poor Geoff banging my hand on the desk in despair

"It's wrong, it's wrong, it's fucking well wrong! The rhythm is all wrong! Now what the fuck am I going to do?" Geoff reacted by trying to laugh which aggravated me more.

I immediately stopped everything and told the musicians to have their break now while I sorted out some problems. I asked Frank to come up to the control room where I told him in no uncertain terms that the rhythm feel was not as I envisaged, so much so that I wanted to scrap the session, re-arrange the song and book it all again. Frank was really taken aback but had no choice but to agree to just record the 'B' side. Maureen bless her went with the flow and was quite happy with whatever I decided to do. Of course I was in the shit again by throwing away a few more hundred pounds. I thought this time it would be best to say nothing to anybody at all. I couldn't muster up the courage anyway after the Jonathan King affair.

Frank came up to the office and I emphatically explained to him how I felt the rhythm of the song should be. He would now re-arrange it and put the matter right.

The session was re-booked and on that evening it went off like a dream. Frank and Geoff agreed that it sounded fantastic and that I was absolutely right about the rhythm. Maureen sang her heart out, obviously loving every minute of it. It had everything going for it as a potential Hit record.

When it was subsequently released it received the following review in Disc:

Oriole's Record of the Month

Maureen Evans
Like I do/Starlight, Starbright
45 CB. 1760

The very likeable Maureen Evans stakes a powerful claim for chart honours with this very melodic modern treatment of a well known tune. The song is very direct and sincere and Maureen's performance highlights the Charm and tenderness of this very appealing record.

"Like I Do" – That memorable session – Just another little problem! Maureen Evans, Frank Barber, myself and Geoff Frost

On the 29th of November, *"Like I Do"* made it to number 3 in the charts and remained in the charts for eighteen weeks. Morris Levy was ecstatic because he always had a *very soft spot* for Maureen Evans. I prayed the drama surrounding the session would now be buried, forgotten and remain undiscovered forever!

Frank Barber

This very talented person deserves a special mention. He was a brilliant arranger and musician and I loved working with him. He had undoubtedly contributed to the success of many Hit records.

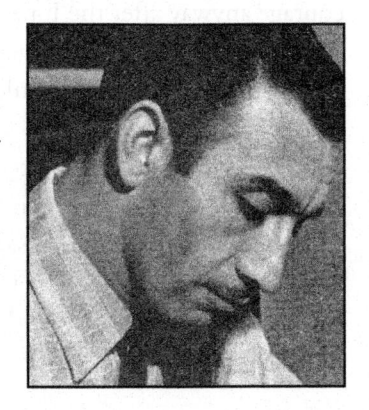

He was easy to work with, being quiet and unassuming. Due to my past association with Ricky Valance it was particularly satisfying to know that he was responsible for the arrangement of *'Tell Laura I Love Her'* which went to Number One and now the unforgettable *'Like I Do'* which went to Number 3.

The success of Maureen's *'Like I Do'* brought about one of the greatest joys of my career, that being a very personal letter to me from Norrie Paramor himself. I found it extremely touching and very thoughtful. It said:

> Jan. 23. 1963.
>
> Dear John,
>
> Sincere congratulations on your big hit with Maureen Evans. In spite of the enormous difficulties you face, you've made it and, I guess, after the year of hard work and worry, this must be the best thing in the world.
>
> Both Joan and I hope that this is the forerunner of more successes for you — (please leave a little room on the charts for me!) Sincerely Norrie.

Sweden calling

One day Debbie said there was a call from Stockholm Sweden from a guy called Roland Ferneborg. I took the call wondering what to expect.

He said that he had been watching the progress of the Oriole label with interest and all that it was doing and achieving. He had also been listening to the Big 'O' Show on Luxembourg and reading the British trade press. He then said he managed an instrumental group called The Spotnicks who were doing extremely well in Sweden. He had the feeling that I was always hungry for good, new talent, and because I was developing a young and exciting label, he felt I would be interested in a young and exciting new group. I said he might well be right but I needed to hear something first before any further consideration could be made.

He sent me a copy of a Swedish recording and it was brilliant. It reminded me of the Shadows but it had its own positive identity. I subsequently called Roland and said I would come over to Stockholm to see them and catch a live gig if that were possible. He was more than pleased to hear this and when I got there he treated me like Royalty and that was an understatement! The gig, which was at the famous Tivoli Gardens, was amazing. The group were so tight, and Bo Winberg, the lead guitarist had fingers like lightening. At one point in the set the whole band walked off stage except drums, and mingled with the audience but the sound was still coming from the stage!" What a great gimmick," I thought to myself "I will have to bring this group to England."

I had a long talk with the boys and Roland, saying how very impressed I was and that I would certainly love to release the product in England. We did a deal and from the material I heard I decided to go with their version of *'Orange Blossom Special'* as the first single release.

SPOTNICKS FOR BRITAIN

British debut on oriole for the "Swinging Swedes"

Television concert and radio dates in August

Spotnicks
Orange Blossom Special/ The Spotnicks Theme
CB. 1724

FROM SWEDEN come The Spotnicks with one of the most exciting discs of this or any year – the urgent compelling "Orange Blossom Special". This is beat music at its extreme best and British groups will have to pull their socks up quickly if they want to keep pace with this truly remarkable group. The background choral effects employed on "Orange Blossom Special" greatly aid the success of the disc, and the technical brilliance of the nimble-fingered solo guitarist Bo Winberg on this title will hit you right between the eyes.

Job Well Done

I was pleased. I had done my homework properly this time, and due to the initiative and effort of Ronnie Bell, The Spotnicks appeared on 'Top of the Pops' looking sensational dressed in space suits. We had done it again with another hit record, but this one dispelled any thought of The Spotnicks being here today and gone tomorrow.

"*Orange Blossom Special*" made it to number 29 in the charts. "*Rocket Man*" followed it and made it to number 38 but "*Hava Nagila,*" the following single, made it to number 13 and remained in the charts for ten weeks. All in all a very pleasing result, but The Spotnicks deserved to have been every bit as successful as The Shadows. They were so very talented and unquestionably underrated.

Prestigious Award

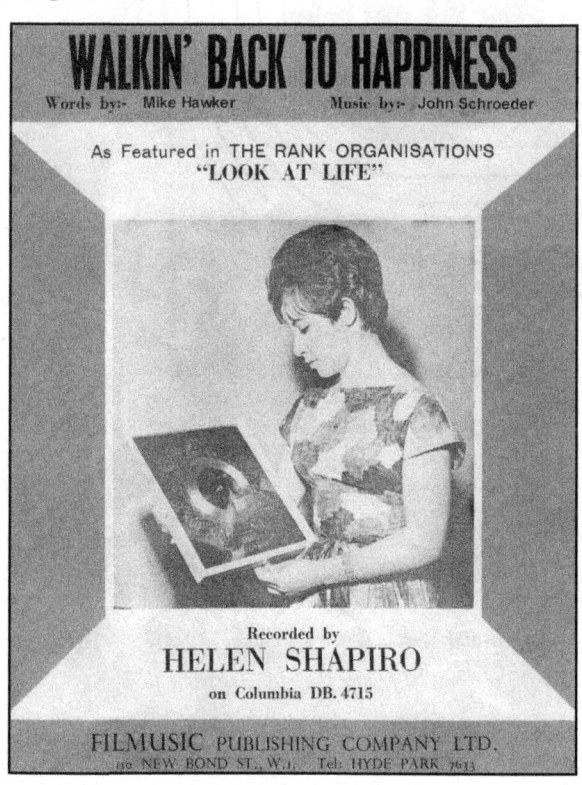

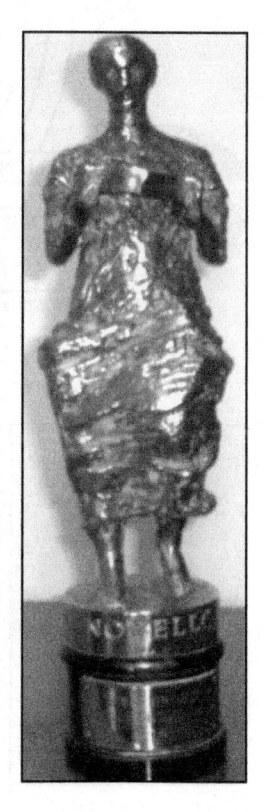

The news came as a shock and totally unexpected during one of my busiest weeks at Oriole. Mike Hawker and I were informed that we had been nominated for **The Ivor Novello Award**, which is the most prestigious award a songwriter can achieve. This was to commemorate *'Walkin' Back To Happiness'* being voted the biggest and most successful song of 1961. The Award was presented to us at the Savoy Hotel in London and I remember following John Lennon and Paul McCartney up to the rostrum. What an occasion and what an honour!

The Oriole roster begins to grow –

Ronnie Bell
Head of Promotion

An incredible asset to Oriole's
sadly short-lived success

SUPERON!

CHAPTER EIGHT

THE TAMLA MOTOWN STORY

Now that Oriole was well on its way to being accepted by the industry as a serious player, having had some substantial success to prove it, my gut feeling was that we needed American product to consolidate the present situation.

I have always been interested in the American market and in particular the importance of it. On avidly reading Cash Box, the American trade journal, I noticed that there was a label called Tamla Motown which constantly had six or seven singles in the Cash Box Top 100 every week. I became quite excited since I was not aware of any outlet for this product in this country. I realised it was a Soul or R and B label, and with the amount of hits they were consistently having they must have some phenomenal Artists and writers. I felt I was hooked on the music before I had actually heard one note of it.

Berry Gordy
A genuine pioneer

I had a hard time with Morris Levy and virtually begged him to make contact with Motown and suss out the current situation. Eventually he did this and discovered the President was Berry Gordy, and they had at present no distribution deal in England. He made the offer to him of coming over to England to discuss and work out a viable proposition. Mr Levy suggested that I should do the entertaining, at the same time informing Berry Gordy of our current and future plans and policies, and to impress upon him how strongly we felt about the importance of American product being part of Oriole's concept.

The evening I took Berry Gordy, Barney Ales, Motown's vice president and Ester Edwards out to dinner at the Talk of the Town was unforgettable. Fortunately Berry Gordy and I had something in common; we were both successful song writers and that made good conversation. This led to my understanding of their united dedication to achieve the dream that had been initially envisaged by Berry Gordy. They became really excited as they related the fascinating Motown story. For some unknown reason I felt what we had achieved at Oriole to be somewhat inferior. The apparent incredible talent of their Artists, writers, musicians and the reproductive brilliance emanating from their studio was so obviously powerful. I then realised it was wrong to make such comparisons since circumstances and situations were totally different and besides we had moved some mountains ourselves which should not at all be underestimated.

Talk of the Town

(l to r) Ester Edwardes, Motown's company head secretary, Barney Ales, Vice President Motown, Berry Gordy, President Motown, myself and wife Christine

We must have done something right because Morris Levy managed to clinch an exclusive distribution deal with Berry Gordy. He then passed the whole thing over to me, emphasising rather strongly that as I had now got what I wanted I should get on and do something about it!

After Motown had despatched the first masters to me and I had had the chance of hearing some of this amazing product I was convinced that the initial release should be at least three singles. The press must be given the story and the product must be heavily featured on our Luxembourg Big 'O' Show. I knew we had a mammoth task ahead of us, but I also knew the sheer talent featured on this label could not help but eventually register. It was only a matter of time.

SEPT. 14th ON THE ORIOLE-AMERICAN LABEL

3 SMASH HITS

FROM THE U. S. CHARTS

1	**YOU BEAT ME TO THE PUNCH**	Mary Wells	
	OLD LOVE (LET'S TRY IT AGAIN)	CBA-1762	
2	**DO YOU LOVE ME ?**	The Contours	
	MOVE, Mr. MAN	CBA-1763	
3	**BEECHWOOD 4-5789**	The Marvelettes	
	SOMEDAY, SOMEWAY	CBA-1764	

ORIOLE LAUNCH NEW LABEL
AND ACQUIRE IMPORTANT AMERICAN CATALOGUES

A NEW SERIES – Oriole-American-makes its first appearance on the British disc scene this month. It will be the outlet in this country for material from the powerful U.S independent Motown, Gordy and Tamla labels, all of which are now represented on this side of the Atlantic by Oriole.

Oriole recording manager John Schroeder, who initially set machinery in motion to acquire the British rights, comments "This is an extremely important development and I heartily welcome Mr Levy's efforts in gaining access to American catalogues for Oriole. I'm sure the labels will produce many hits in Britain".

Sore Thumb

Although we had conjured up a lot of ideas to support and promote this product, we were finding things rather difficult. The prime reason being that there was little or no support for this kind of music. It was so different that it was hard to establish, because no Radio Station or radio programme would gamble by including it, even taking into consideration the outstanding success the product was enjoying in America. Certain presenters really wanted to include it but their programme producers would not allow it.

I remember Alan Freeman (Fluff) apologised to me personally for not being able to play this material. "My producer said it would stand out like a sore thumb even though I personally am hooked. You have my word I will do everything in my power to help you guys get this label the recognition it truly deserves."

We had the same cool reaction from the Trade papers all except one and that was The Record Mirror. Peter Jones, bless him, almost every week dedicated a two page spread featuring the Tamla Motown artists and product. He was a gem to have done this but then he too was an ardent believer, and like me knew it was only a matter of time before it happened.

All of us at Oriole had worked our butts off for practically two years before we came through with our one and only hit which was *'Fingertips' part 2* by Little Stevie Wonder. We then, due to the contract expiry date, lost the label to E.M.I and immediately Mary Wells charted with *'My Guy'*.

Personally I felt totally gutted and still do to this day. However there was one consolation for me in that I personally had been responsible for giving the British public the opportunity of having the initial access to the incredible talent and amazing product that had and was to emerge from the Tamla Motown Record Label for years to come.

Tamla Motown – The Beginning

Mary Wells
(You Beat me to the Punch)

Little Stevie Wonder
(Fingertips Pt 2)

The Home of Tamla Motown

The Marvelettes
(Beechwood – 45789)

The Contours
(Do You Love Me?)

Photos courtesy of Motown Records Archives

TAMLA MOTOWN and all that it stands for in relation to the World's History of Music
WILL LIVE FOREVER

I am proud to have been part of it!

Motown's 40th Anniversary

*An international mixture of 'Motownmen' gathered together to celebrate and mark the 40th Anniversary of the Tamla-Motown Revue held at Redferns Music Picture Gallery London W.10. in June 2006.
(l to r) Daryl Easlea (Universal), Keith Hughes, Jo Wallace, Me, Chris Jenner, Adam white (Universal)
John Lester, Bob McGuire, Harry Weinger (Universal), Paul Nixon*

LIVERPOOL – *The Cavern Club and more*

The Beatles had arrived and were causing musical chaos across the world, but Liverpool, their home town, became the centre of attention. All eyes were on Liverpool, especially mine. It was particularly satisfying to know that all the Artists emanating from Liverpool especially, including The Beatles, were familiar with the Tamla Motown label, its Artists, its songs and its records. The reason for this was the docks, because this music was carried from America across the sea. Often Liverpool groups were playing the Motown songs before I had even heard them. As I became more familiar with the Liverpool music scene I was surprised to learn just how much respect there was for the Oriole American label since we had clinched the distribution deal with Berry Gordy.

My first ever contact with anybody to do with Liverpool was through a phone call from Bill Harry who told me he was the editor of a music trade journal in Liverpool called Mersey Beat. He said very affirmatively

"I've been watching you and I have been admiring what you have done and what you are doing with the Oriole label. The acquisition of Motown was a brilliant move. Since the discovery of the Beatles, Liverpool is where the action is and you should get your arse up here. The talent is like a beehive. There are so many fantastic groups, and I pretty well know them all because we do the advertising for the venues and so on. The paper is tied up with Nems, a chain of Northern record shops owned by Brian Epstein, the manager of the Beatles." I replied obviously interested

"I would love to come up to Liverpool as soon as possible and check everything out. If you could show me around that would be just fantastic."

It meant a lot to me when what I had been trying to do had actually been noticed, and with a concerted effort from all concerned had almost unknowingly ultimately proved itself.

I went up to Liverpool almost immediately and Bill was as good as his word. I was amazed to discover just how phenomenally knowledgeable he was about the local scene. We got on well together and I came to respect him immensely.

Our first stop was The Cavern club and that really blew my mind.

Amazingly, lunch time gigs at the Cavern were all the rage and the queues to get in stretched all the way round the building. Very narrow steps took you down to a cellar complex, very hot and very quaint. There was a stage at one end of a large stone square floor area accommodating room for stand up listening only. On each of the other sides there were the curved arches of three cellars. There was deliberately no sit down areas. You came for the music, the ambience was electric and the sale of alcohol was not permitted.

When Bill and I finally managed to get in, it was packed and heaving with sweaty bodies. You could hardly move and you were hit with the feeling of being drugged by the music, the heat and the condensation dripping off the walls. No wonder every band wanted to play this incredible gig. The thought of a fire down here didn't bear thinking about!

Bill also took me to the Iron Door Club which was a little more refined. However it still featured a hundred and one local bands playing music that initiated 'hooked on listening' and gyrating sweaty bodies. Unfortunately someone literally got stabbed on the dance floor there one night during my stay, which was a bit disconcerting. Bill assured me this was very unusual. It was music that gripped the city not violence.

We visited a couple of Nems record shops and went to the Mersey Beat offices where we had a very in depth talk about the Liverpool music scene. Bill told me about so many groups and their individual music styles. He also said as far as he knew there had been no contact from any of the major record companies whatsoever, except of course what Brian Epstein had done with the Beatles. Certainly no one had been up to Liverpool before me and he wanted me to be the first to witness the scene for myself. Admiring what I had achieved at Oriole he thought I was the right person to find a way of giving a break to all this frustrated talent before the major record companies had a chance of a sniff or had got wind of it.

On my last night he took me to the Blue Angel Club which stayed open to the early hours. This was a drinking club and its main purpose was that it provided a place where musicians, artists and members of groups could relax and congregate after doing their gigs. It had a very laid back atmosphere but its proprietor, Allan Williams was truly a larger than life character. I was lucky to meet Brian Epstein there who introduced me to Priscilla White alias Cilla Black. Brian enjoyed talking about the Liverpool music scene and particularly his discovery of the Beatles. In fact one night I found myself sitting next to John Lennon and we were talking about art. He grabbed a serviette and drew a caricature of Alan Williams who was standing at one end of the bar with his usual 'I'm in charge' look on his face and gave it to me. I remember it was very life-like but as it was on a serviette I threw it in the waste bin on my way out!

Having thanked Bill Harry for his wonderful hospitality I said I would have a good think about it all and come back to him.

What I had seen and heard in Liverpool was constantly on my mind night and day during the next week and then... I had a brainwave! I called Bill and said excitedly

"I have an idea to put to you. Supposing I could get the studio to come to the Artist instead of the Artist coming to the studio. By that I mean if it is technically feasible, I will bring a mobile recording unit up to Liverpool, set it up somewhere with space like a cinema or a ballroom and invite as many groups as possible to record two tracks. We would have the right to issue whatever I thought fit on two proposed albums entitled 'This is Mersey Beat Volume 1 and Volume 2.' We would pay no royalties, but any Artist who participated could use the tracks as demos and we will supply the copies to activate a recording contract with whoever, or use them as an ad. to get work and gigs. Once the records were released they would have a showcase anyway." Bill replied without hesitation

"That is a fantastic idea. I will organise it and put the word out everywhere to as many groups as possible via Mersey Beat, explaining the deal. I will find a suitable venue and firm up a mutually agreeable date with you providing of course that it is technically possible. I really hope that it is because I think this is a fantastic opportunity, and will also enable them to realise what they really sound like for the first time. Please let me know as soon as possible".

I put the idea to Geoff Frost and John Wood, our engineers, and they told me they would love to design and build the mobile recording unit themselves. They reckoned they would have it up and running in two weeks.

The venue Bill had in mind was the Rialto Ballroom, and Geoff and I arrived with all the gear one weekend in July 1963. Bill met us there and we spent the next two to three hours setting everything up. Bill had also painstakingly lined up an uncountable flow of groups. He had all their details and the titles of the songs they were going to perform. The response to the whole thing had apparently been amazing because it was the first time anybody from London had taken the trouble of checking out the Liverpool scene. Bringing the studio to the Artist was considered an ingenious idea. Consequently, all the participants had willingly agreed to the terms which they considered to be fair, since they would all walk away with samples of their work which would be a great asset in hopefully furthering their careers.

I don't know exactly how many groups we recorded in the two days we were up there. I have to admit there was no time for perfection and usually I

The Control Room – The Rialto Ballroom

accepted the first take. I would have loved to have spent more time and done re-takes with many of the groups but the session was not designed that way.

The final result would hopefully produce two albums that would paint an overall picture of the vast musical talent that Liverpool had to offer.

We went back to London pleased but very tired, and I had a lot of listening to do and ultimately a lot of mixing and editing too. I think Bill was very happy and helped to console everybody that it was intended to be an in and out type of gig even though we would all have loved to have spent more time in getting things really right. It was not possible to please everybody.

Geoff and I were to spend many hours and often into the early hours, meticulously putting the two albums together. It was a labour of love but it was well worth the trouble. It certainly opened our eyes and ears to the incredible music scene that was continuing to erupt in Liverpool. *This is Mersey Beat Vol 1 and 2* were released in September 1963 and Vol 1 made it into the L.P Charts.

Every Artist represented on these two albums had a wide spectrum of music stories to tell. One interesting fact stood out above all else and that was the inclusion by most groups in their repertoire of a great deal of Tamla Motown's incredible material. I took that to be a compliment to our efforts at Oriole in endeavouring to put Tamla Motown where it should rightly be but I knew Berry Gordy wasn't at all happy about many of the covers of his material which in many cases he considered were sacrilege to the original!

My experiences in Liverpool and all the wonderful and talented people I was lucky to have met will all always be with me. It was an incredibly worthwhile project and my personal and special thanks go to Bill Harry and his lovely wife Virginia as without their input this piece of musical history would never have been achieved.

Virginia and Bill Harry

"Crazy Liverpool" Faron's Flamingos

The Sounds of Mersey Beat

Sonny Webb & The Cascades

Faron's Flamingoes

Ian & The Zodiacs

The Del Renas

'Earl' Preston

The Nomads

Volume 1 Oriole PS 40047 Mono

Rory Storm & The Hurricanes

Volume 2 Oriole 40048 Mono

I knew it was only a matter of time before my marital *existence* came to some sort of conclusion. It could not go on like it was for much longer because it was strained beyond breaking point. I had willingly committed myself to being married to the music industry and I was certainly to blame for always being too busy and working late. Michelle was now practically two years old and I was truly worried for her.

Moving to Heathway Court Golders Green was sensible. It was a spacious and comfortable apartment in a good location and of course Michelle was born there. One night as Christine and I were, unusually, quietly having coffee at about 11.30 p.m there was a God Almighty crash. My reaction was very quick and I rushed outside to find a coach with its nose deeply buried inside the off licence building next door. The engine was still running and there was glass everywhere and the smell of all kinds of mixed up drink was diabolical and sickening. There were only three people on the coach and I quickly got them out through the back door. I then went down to the front of the coach and switched the engine off and then I realised there was no driver. Seconds later to my horror I saw his leg sticking up through the floor with his head and body crushed between the near side front wheel and the mud wing. That was some shock! It made me feel quite ill!

Christine made tea for everybody and it wasn't long before the police and ambulance arrived. Apparently the traffic lights had gone berserk registering green in both directions and the coach had tried to avoid a car coming from the other direction. Ironically it was a show biz coach dropping Artists and staff off after a show. The star was Julie Grant and I believe she was in fact one of the remaining three on the coach. It was not a pleasant experience and unfortunately I shall never forget the stomach churning sight of that poor guy's face.

For some time, one single thread had held the fragile relationship between Christine and I together, and that was Michelle, but the final curtain came when I arrived home one night from the studio and walked straight into the aftermath of what looked like an 'anything goes' party fuelled by excessive alcohol. I felt sick at what I saw and immediately drove down to my parents'. The following day I found the courage to go back to the flat and realised Christine had left, taking Michelle with her. There was no note but I inwardly knew that she had gone back to Germany. This was shortly confirmed when she wrote a letter to my mother saying that the marriage was a farce and that she was now going to live in Germany but would obviously take good care of Michelle.

Eventually a divorce was filed and ultimately granted so I presumed I had lost custody of Michelle. There was more tragedy to come.

Christine had got married again. I suppose to whoever had been writing to her, but this time the relationship became violent, apparently very violent with alcohol again being the instigating factor. Sadly it ended with Christine committing suicide and Michelle finding her mother in that state. Thank God my mother and Christine had kept in touch because the German Authorities found the letters and contacted my parents accordingly. They told them what had happened and that before they found a foster home for Michelle they wanted to know if my parents would like Michelle to return to England since it was quite legal that she could. Christine had also not signed the custody papers! Of course there was absolutely no question about it and I remember going to the train station with my father to meet her. She was a lost little girl with no mother and as such no father. She could not speak a word of English! I felt so gutted and so guilty at that moment more than at any other time I can ever remember.

We came to an agreement. My mother desperately wanted to bring her up and for her home to be with her and my father. I had to agree that this was in Michelle's best interests because of my work situation and its demands. I would see Michelle as often as I could. My mother found herself in seventh heaven because she now had a real purpose in life and she had a precious and valuable weapon to counteract my father's often untactful and uncalled for remarks and attitude. Over the next few years he was to mellow considerably without even realising it. I knew he loved Michelle very much.

Even though my personal life had been very traumatic and had now as such come to an abrupt end I found it hard at first coming home to emptiness and even loneliness. I also found myself missing Michelle.

As I settled into a bachelor type of lifestyle I felt I needed to give myself an uplift which as always resulted in my changing my present mode of transportation. I rather fancied a saloon car but one with a bit of 'pizzazz'. So I traded in the Triumph TR4 for a Jaguar 3.4 Mk 2 with metallic paint and chrome wire wheels. She looked the biz so much so that after two weeks of having her I went out one morning to go to work and she was gone, stolen from under my nose! The next time I saw her was on the front page of the Evening Standard wedged in between two police cars. She had been used in a robbery and taken off the road for nine weeks apparently being prepared for it! There was considerable damage done and the radio had been taken. As the police refused to release the car, the insurance company had no option but to pay me the equivalent price of a new car plus the hire of a car whilst they were looking for mine. No more Jaguars for me at the moment!

I fell in love with the Mercedes SL 250, a fantastic 2 seater sports

Jaguar Series II 3.4 Saloon   *Mercedes 250 SL*

convertible in white with a curved black roof. It was a dream of a car. I had heard a rumour that this car was adored by high class ladies of the night in certain German cities who loved to use it for curb crawling since its image conjured up some really good business. It did me proud, attracted a lot of attention and some good business too and I didn't even have to curb crawl!

Although nearly two years of my contract with Oriole were complete I knew things could not go on for much longer and it was worrying me a lot. The vast financial outgoings to keep Oriole Records alive as a major competitor could be nothing short of crippling. I felt for the Company and its dedicated staff who had achieved so much in such a short time. I especially felt for Morris Levy who had bravely and conscientiously supported what he had determined to prove and set out to do in the beginning. The Luxembourg programmes were the first to go. This move obviously seriously affected the promotion of the product. Ronnie Bell became very frustrated and I was beginning to worry about my future. Geoff Frost and John Wood and the studio were in danger too.

    The very last appointment Debbie arranged for me at Oriole Records was with Galt McDermott, a charming Canadian. All he wanted was a chat because he was so impressed by the talent and pianistic skills of Johnny Pearson. He was smitten with the album *"Piano Sweet Piano Wild"* as he loved jazz and orchestral music. I said I thought it a great shame that the younger generation had not had the chance to really appreciate this music and it was on my mind to find a way of achieving it.

    He asked me if I would do him the honour of listening to one or two of his compositions. What I heard was amazingly good and very different. He was obviously a very competent pianist with a tendency towards jazz. I loved the melody lines and rhythmic feel of the songs. I wished him all the luck in the world and I was sorry I was no longer in a position to offer any constructive help. However I told him I really felt the songs needed some sort of showcase.

Five years later the musical *Hair* had taken London by storm. The music and songs were on the radio night and day having been recorded by so many different artists. I was having problems placing where I had heard this music before. It was a long time ago and then it suddenly came to me – Galt McDermott. I remembered saying to him that the songs needed a showcase. Well what bigger showcase was there than *Hair*?! I was very pleased for him, a little inwardly jealous maybe, dreaming that one of my ambitions was to write a musical that was good enough to make the West End of London but then he had created some wonderful material and deserved the long awaited success. I was to join the long list of Artists who had the honour of recording such fabulous tunes as *Aquarius, Good Morning Starshine* and so many more.

Fortunately what I had personally achieved at Oriole Records had not gone unnoticed and I received a job offer as the A & R Manager of the Piccadilly Label at Pye Records. Pye's offices were nearby, located in A.T.V. House in Great Cumberland Place Marble Arch. Pye also had its own Studios in Bryanston Street. I subsequently had a meeting with Louis Benjamin, Pye's Managing Director and Les Cocks, his personal assistant. We all got on well and we negotiated a mutually agreeable contract. The company was very successful at the time and they had already employed Alan Freeman and Tony Hatch as producers. Little did I know it but Tony Hatch was to be my biggest worry, providing me with some fierce inter company competition.

As Louis Benjamin wanted me to start as soon as possible I had to tell Morris Levy and give him the reasons why I wanted to move. He understood perfectly and made no objection to my leaving when I wanted to. We were both understandably upset and wished the Oriole venture could have gone on but it was not meant to be. We both knew we had given it our all. Eventually Oriole Records was sold to CBS primarily I believe for its pressing plant at Aston Clinton. However, apparently CBS were very surprised at the financial solvency of the company. Hopefully my time at Oriole had helped to contribute to this.

CHAPTER NINE

PYE RECORDS

ATV HOUSE – Gt Cumberland Place Marble Arch London W.1

Pye Records was to be the third Record Company I was to work for and it proved to be my luckiest. As I walked through the front doors of A.T.V. House taking the lift to the fourth floor, I felt nervous as usual but also strangely confident.

Les Cocks, the Assistant Managing Director was full of smiles and made me feel very welcome. He showed me to my office which was quite adequate in size, introduced me to my secretary Sue and to Tony Hatch who was in the next office. Tony was very polite but came across with the confidence of someone who knew exactly what he was doing. If the truth be known I was actually rather scared of him. His knowledge of music was far superior to mine and he had already enjoyed success as a producer. He became my greatest challenge, so it was from now on very important for me to prove my credibility if only for the sake of some good *friendly* competition!

I had my old faithful Brinsmead piano moved into the office, but they gave me a desk chair with the springs hanging down underneath it and they gave me a tatty old waste paper basket which should have been committed to a waste bin itself!

Of course I was also given The Piccadilly label! I had heard that it was rumoured to have the reputation of being Pye's junk or down and out label. Why, I am not too sure since doing some research on the matter I found that the Piccadilly label had been responsible for a vast quantity of single releases which included some high profile names such as Jackie Trent, Johnny Keating, Vince Eager, Jackie Lynton and so on. However, the label had no direction, too many people were involved in it with a hit and miss attitude and the only real thing going for it was its logo which was impressive in red, black and yellow.

The challenge before me was to turn the label around giving it some sort of musical direction and identity and consolidating it hopefully with some chart success. I was forced to clear it of all its Artists unless I particularly wanted to keep any of them. I remember doing this once before – my Oriole days had come back to haunt me!

I dropped all the Artists, but some like Joe Brown who was produced by Alan Freeman and had sold very well, were moved to the Pye label.

I had now got a clean slate and I set about building up a new Artist roster.

Whilst I was seriously thinking how I was going to do this I decided to check out the studios and introduce myself to all concerned.

The Pye Recording Studios – Bryanston Street London W.1

By taking the lift to the basement you could get to the Studios without going outside the building which was very convenient. The outside entrance was situated in Bryanston Street which was on one side of ATV House.

There were two Studios and they had proved themselves beyond any shadow of doubt capable of delivering some amazing product. Unlike E.M.I's studios at the time, Pye Studios encouraged outside bookings. Studio One, the larger of the two, had achieved such a reputation internationally that it had attracted Artists of the calibre of Burt Bacharach, Nancy Sinatra, Sammy Davis Jr, Udo Jurgens, Francoise Hardy plus many more, and of course it also catered for all of Pye's home product.

Both studios were very well equipped with the latest technology and there were also two cutting rooms which was a major plus. Studio One's control room was fantastic. It was positioned above the studio itself and it stretched almost the width of the studio which provided an amazing view of everything going on below. Alan Florence and Ray Prickett were the very capable engineers handling most of Pye's pop repertoire. I had a good talk with them and they were both pleased I had joined the Company and looked forward to working with me. I was introduced to Pat Godwin, the Studio Manager, the girls who took the bookings and those very important cutting room engineers.

On returning to my office I felt totally confident about the studios and its entire staff. There was a great atmosphere down there and I was looking forward to my first session.

Benjie

Time was getting on and all eyes seemed to be focused on me, especially Management's eyes, wondering what the new boy was going to do and when! This was a bit disconcerting because I felt I hadn't been there five minutes and they were looking for a return on their investment already! I could feel the pressure building!

Louis Benjamin, the Managing Director, or Benjie as everyone endearingly called him, ran a very tight ship. He was a human dynamo, small in stature with unbelievable energy. The first time I met him you knew *he was* Pye Records and through his ingenuity and talent had made the company what it was. However I found him to be extremely intimidating. Benjie's almost obsessive policy, probably due to pressure from those above, namely ATV and Sir Lew Grade, was *'Money Money Money.'* That meant making lots of it as quickly as possible. Quick turnover – that seemed to be all that was important. However, as I got to know him better I eventually came to really respect him.

At first he made my life a nightmare, particularly with the strange habit of never acknowledging my existence. Whenever he saw me he would never say hello, good morning or how are you? If I was passing him in the corridor he would walk straight past me even though I always acknowledged him!

"How bloody rude," I thought to myself. He had a direct line to my office. I would pick up the phone and with no introduction whatsoever he would say quite aggressively whatever was on his mind.

"When can we expect to have something from you?"

"Soon" I said a little frustrated and angry. Then he'd abruptly put the phone down.

"Fucking hell, this all a bit much," I thought to myself.

He often had the habit of doing this right in the middle of an important meeting. I got some really strange looks. It was embarrassing and often wrecked my train of thought but apparently that's how he was with everyone in the Company, no matter who they were.

I was determined he wasn't going to beat me so I learnt how to deal with it by speaking back to him in a similar tone of voice and putting the phone down as abruptly as he did. He seemed to appreciate that!

One unfortunate morning I found myself in the lift with Benjie and Sir Lew going up to the fourth floor. Mr Grade always had a large cigar in his mouth. Benjie turned to him and said "This is our new boy on the production team. We are expecting great things from him"

Sir Lew looked at me and took a great big drag on his cigar and virtually blew it in my face as he stepped out of the lift. The message was clear. "Make money – or else!"

Benjie was clever. He had built a very good team around him, all very capable, very professional, very trustworthy and very reliable in carrying out his wishes. They might not have always shown it but they did respect him and even loved him. Benjie knew what he wanted and he knew how to get it!

The success of Pye Records as a company proved just how good he was at it.

The Executive Team

Louis Benjamin – Managing Director

Les Cocks
Executive Director

Tom Grantham
Marketing Director

Tony Hatch
Producer Songwriter

Madeline Hawkyard
Company Secretary

Johnny Wise
Head of Promotion

Geoffrey Bridge
Company Director

The dreaded A&R meeting

It seemed to be the norm for every major record company to hold a weekly A&R meeting – every producer's nightmare! The idea being that at this meeting each producer would present his new product to be evaluated and assessed as to what level of promotional support by the Company it should receive. This was fair enough if the producers respected all parties present at the meeting of having the ability of being able to assess the potential of all the various types of product. I did appreciate that sometimes due to the amount of material presented some records would have to be assessed as having greater potential than others and would therefore receive more intense promotional support. The final decision to my mind should have been left in the capable but unenviable hands of The Head of Promotion because that was his job. It was the nature of the beast that some one would always get upset especially when internal competition was running so high.

Present at Pye's A&R meetings were Louis Benjamin (The Managing director), Les Cocks (The Assistant Managing director) Tom Grantham (The Distribution Manager) Madeleine Hawkyard (The contracts Manager) Johnny Wise (The Head of Promotion) and often other executive staff and of course any producer that was unfortunate enough to have new product to present!

Thankfully it wasn't long before word had got around and the music press had got hold of the story of my joining Pye Records. Sue had her time cut out with phone calls and making appointments for music publishers, managers and agents etc. One of those calls was from Maurice King who managed the Walker Brothers. He presented me with a demo of a group from Birmingham called The Rockin' Berries, and the song they had demoed was *"I Didn't Mean To Hurt You"* because apparently this song always received great response on their gigs. I was very impressed with what I heard so I made the trip to Birmingham to catch a gig. The group were well turned out, had slick routines and looked good on stage. Geoff Turton, the lead singer had a wonderfully commercial and identifiable voice with a great falsetto and Clive Lea provided excellent entertainment value with a particularly brilliant impression of Norman Wisdom and *"Don't Laugh At Me"*. They had quite a following and were spot on about *"I Didn't Mean To Hurt You"*. The audience response was excellent.

I had no doubts at all about signing them but I had no idea what to do with them. Time was getting on so after much humming and ha-ing I decided to go with *"I Didn't Mean To Hurt You"* as the first release (a) because I didn't have anything else and (b) because the song always received such a great audience reaction it could only help the sales of the record. It would have to do until I could find something stronger.

As luck would have it, and almost immediately after the release, a Music Publisher came to see me and played me a song called *"He's In Town"* by an unknown American artist. He said that as this was climbing the American charts very quickly, if I had anyone to cover it I would have to move very fast before the American record had any chance of being scheduled for release here first.

I told him I felt the song was so right for the Rockin' Berries that nothing was going to stop me or deter me from losing this opportunity. The Publisher was thrilled with my reaction and assured me he would do everything in his power to help with the promotion of the record.

I called Maurice King immediately, putting him in the picture and sending him a copy of the American record. I told him I was emphatic about my wanting the group to do it and they had one week to get it together, but it had to be good enough to go into the studio and I would come up and help them if they needed it. I emphatically pointed out to him that I wanted them to keep as near to the original arrangement as possible.

Maurice called me back and said the group loved the song and would have it ready to go into the studio within one week.

When I finally got to hear it just before the end of the week, it was brilliant. They had done exactly as I had asked and yet managed to make the song their own. I was really looking forward to recording it.

I designated Alan Florence to engineer the session and I gave him an in depth musical picture of the group explaining what I ultimately wanted to achieve. Double tracking the lead vocal was one thing we totally agreed upon. The group were very tight and very confident in the studio. The atmosphere was electric and when they heard themselves back through the big speakers they were blown away which made them perform even better. The master take screamed hit but everything depended on the mix.

I hated anybody else other than myself and the engineer being present at mixing sessions for obvious reasons. It needed more than just concentration and this track was not at all easy to mix as there were so many things going on. From past experience, as the producer you had to have a very positive mental picture of what you were striving to achieve. After several hours, and at last Alan and I being happy with what was to be the final mix, everyone unanimously agreed that we had a really strong record on our hands. Maurice King and the Berries were ecstatic.

I was thrilled with the whole thing but what would the comments be at the dreaded A&R meeting?!

The meeting had begun. All eyes were on me as it came to my turn. It was painfully obvious they were eagerly waiting to hear whether they had made the right investment in their new boy!

Confidently I made everyone aware of the situation regarding the song and this record, and what effect its release would have on the first record released by The Rockin' Berries only two weeks ago.

There was anticipation in the air as they listened to *"He's In Town"* for the very first time. I was watching every one of their faces and they were all expressionless! When it had finished there was that awful momentary silence

Johnny Wise, the Head of Promotion was the first to speak and said very emphatically.

"There is absolutely no doubt whatsoever in my mind that that is quite definitely a hit record and in view of the situation should be released immediately."

Les Cocks, looking in my direction with a big smile on his face then agreed, saying that the Company should give me and this record one hundred per cent promotional support. It was truly a great record.

I noticed there was just a faint hint of a smile on Benjie's face as he listened to the comments and then he nodded his head in approval. I felt a huge sigh of relief.

After the meeting, Johnny Wise categorically told me he would do everything in his power to make that record a well deserved Hit. I had known Johnny Wise for a long time, in fact since my Norrie Paramor days when he was working for The Lawrence Wright Music Company. I respected him enormously and of course he was one hundred per cent true to his word. *"He's In Town"* made the charts at number 3 on October 15th 1964 but strangely *"I Didn't Mean To Hurt You"* also made the charts at number 49 on October 1st 1964. They charted two weeks apart.

Maurice King and the group were over the moon, and of course so was I.

The Rockin' Berries

I walked (or was it strutted) around the offices of Pye Records, inwardly congratulating myself, and deliberately waiting for the well dones and the question of how I was feeling, even from Tony Hatch believe it or not! I said I was feeling relieved and happy as I had now passed the initiation test and I could hopefully be accepted as a worthwhile member of the Pye family!

An essential part of the record company producer's job was to discover new talent. One way of doing this was to accept the never ending flow of offers of being asked to judge talent contests virtually all over the country. I had no problem with this, in fact I enjoyed doing it when time allowed.

Just before I went to Birmingham to see the Rockin' Berries I got a call from a Promotions Management Company asking me if I could find the time to be one of the judges for a talent contest to be held in Cardiff. The contest was in fact The Welsh National Talent Contest. I agreed to do this which was one weekend in September 1964.

There were three judges and we were put up in a very nice four star Hotel. They organised a Green Room where we met the contestants before the actual event. There must have been about twenty of them but amongst them was a model called Karen Young.

She was very striking indeed from all aspects and she had already modelled for some of the most prestigious magazines. Apart from every head in the room straining to get a glimpse of her, I noticed, on her being introduced to me that she was holding the sheet music in her left hand of one of my songs, namely *"You Don't Know."* That was quite a shock and in a way I felt rather proud at that moment. After a while on thinking about it she might have been trying to be very clever! Whatever, I was impressed!

The contest kicked off and round about half way Karen appeared looking very stunning indeed and knowing that every eye in the room could not avoid drooling over her ample bosom and hour glass figure, she deliberately made the most of it before singing the song. It's a pity the voice didn't match everything else. It was pleasant and adequate but that was it. In spite of that, hearing *"You*

Don't Know" at any time, being my most treasured composition always put a smile on my face.

Back in the Green Room Karen, or Wendy, which she then told me was her real name, and I had a heart to heart chat. Her vocation had always been modelling and she was certainly in demand, but she had hoped her voice might have been good enough to point her in other directions. Her Agency however, had advised her to concentrate on what she was best at and move to London so she would be nearer to the heart of things and be on short call if necessary. She asked me if I could help her in any way regarding moving to London and I said I would certainly try.

How could I refuse when she was the envy of everyone who looked at her and me for that matter, that being when I was with her!

On my return to London I had a good look around and found a very nice one bed roomed apartment in Craven Terrace, Paddington. She came up, viewed it and decided it was just what she wanted, especially as I was near by. She started to get a considerable amount of modelling work but began to rely on me to vet the jobs before accepting them. Suddenly I realised how much time this was taking and how much my work was beginning to suffer. It had to stop and stop it did eventually, but in a most unexpected way.

CHAPTER TEN

One thing I learnt about being a Label Manager and producer at Pye Records was that you could not afford to rest on your laurels. The Rockin' Berries were happening, so where was my next hit coming from? Louis Benjamin made it painfully obvious that the sole purpose of Tony Hatch and I being employed as record producers was to make money. He enjoyed spelling this out to us at every A& R meeting and I knew it annoyed Tony Hatch intensely because he was a musician at heart and despised Benjie's attitude of having total disregard for the true value of music. I had to agree with him even, though I did appreciate where Benjie was coming from. I still had that burning desire to find a way of having commercial success with something more musically creative.

Tony Reeves was about eighteen years old and worked in the Pye sales office just like I did at E.M.I. He loved jazz, played a bit of string bass and went out of his way to tell me that he had a single in his record collection by Vince Guaraldi, an American pianist, which his friends made him play over and over again every time they came to visit. He wanted me to hear it as he valued my opinion as to why this was.

I cannot remember how many seemingly hundreds of times I had played Tony's record of *"Cast Your Fate To The Wind"*. I asked myself "Was it just for my own pleasure or was it telling me something else?" The piano was magic, the melody was magic, the rhythm was magic, the whole darned thing was magic. There was no question about it, I just *had* to record it and I totally convinced myself that there must be a way to do it that would retain the jazz element and yet culminate in producing an end product that would be surprisingly different, surprisingly tasteful and surprisingly commercial. All in all a rather daunting task!

I came to the positive conclusion that the answer lay in the arrangement, apart from one or two other little things of course, like who was going to play the piano. I thought of nothing else for the next three weeks and it was beginning to drive me crazy.

The basis of the whole thing had to be piano, bass and drums but whoever played piano had to be *so so good*, a born star with a real feel for jazz. Also the musicianship and vibes between all three had to be *shit hot*! I envisaged the commercial aspect of it being instituted by an orchestral sound made up of eight violins and two cellos with the strings being written very high in unison with an arresting counter melody that would provide a musical backcloth to everything else. Norrie Paramor was a good tutor!

All this was fine, but the piano – where could I find that special someone, because without that the whole project was a non starter. Oh God, how I wished it were me! The closest I could get to ever playing it was to find that someone who could emulate what I had in mind.

I became very despondent, as three weeks had gone by with my not being able to think of anybody. I had even gone through all the session pianists. I was on the point of giving up when purely by chance I came across a copy of an Oriole album called *"Piano Sweet Piano Wild"* Why on earth hadn't I thought of it before, especially as I had produced it myself?! Johnny Pearson – *he was so right*. I couldn't believe I had forgotten him. I was certain he'd love it but would he do it for a session fee?

Johnny looked me straight in the eye having heard the Guaraldi record and then he said quite emphatically.

"I'll do it John. I think it's great. I don't get much chance of playing jazz. It'll be fun."

"For a session fee? Unfortunately it's all a bit of an experiment and I shouldn't really be doing it at all" I said feeling very guilty.

"For you John, I'd be pleased to do it" He said reassuringly. He was such a nice guy. I then told him I had worked out an arrangement in my head of how I saw it. I explained this to him in detail and he fully agreed after realising what I was trying to do.

He suggested using Frank Clarke on bass and Kenny Clare on drums, both of whom I totally condoned. He also said writing the strings in unison, using eight violins and two cellos, was a clever idea. The string counter melody would develop naturally. He agreed with me that we should record the piano, bass and drums first and then overdub the strings.

I decided we could do all this quite easily in Studio Two which was blessed with a very intimate atmosphere. I set a mutually convenient date and time but I booked an evening session because the mood of a late night jazz session was more or less what I was after.

I then asked Ray Prickett if he would engineer the session as I felt he would have more understanding for this kind of project.

Having got all this together so far, I thought it only fair to put Tony Reeves in the picture as to what I intended to do. Also, if the result was successful we should come to some sort of arrangement whereby he would get something financially out of it. I had a big shock when Tony replied.

"I don't want anything out of it financially whatsoever. However I do have a request. Would you allow me to play bass on the session?"

That was a surprise. I wasn't expecting that one at all. My mind was racing, saying that I didn't know how capable he was. He might screw the whole thing up. But then I thought if that happened I could re-do the bass part with Frank Clarke. I answered.

"O.K Tony that's a deal. Johnny Pearson will be on piano and Kenny Clare on drums. I'll let you know when the session is. Oh, by the way can you sight read?"

Tony assured me that that was no problem and he was really thrilled to pieces and grateful for me for letting him have this opportunity of a lifetime.

Having made a rod for my own back I now had to tell Johnny Pearson what had happened and what I had agreed to do. Amazingly he wasn't upset at all but seemed rather amused, and he agreed to accommodate the request if we had Frank Clarke standing by.

It was understood that Tony would not be playing bass on the 'B' side which Johnny Pearson and I wrote. We based this on the tune of the nursery rhyme *'Three blind mice'* and called it *'To Wendy with Love'*, Wendy being Karen Young of course.

At last it was all systems go. Everything had been checked and double checked and we met on that memorable evening in Studio Two.

The studio was small, nicely intimate and very right for this occasion. There was anticipation in the air as none of us could really believe that we were here to actually record jazz, something that every one of us was mad about but which seemed totally ridiculous to actually do.

The mood was perfect so it wasn't long before everything was swinging. Kenny Clare was just amazing. How he made that drum kit talk! He had such feel, and swung like mad. He loved every minute of it. Tony was doing really well too. He was obviously inspired by playing with such talented guys but he was right in there. And Johnny Pearson – well I was speechless! He was so meticulous that he wrote down the improvised part so he wouldn't forget it and would be able to play the same thing every time!

It took just three takes to get the master and it was sensational. The only criticism was that Tony was slightly out of tune but we all agreed that it was part of the magic of the track and we shouldn't change a single thing. I know Frank Clarke was very surprised and impressed with Tony's performance.

Johnny Pearson subsequently went over the string parts with me. The strings' counter melodies were beautiful and complimentary to the piece, taking the overall feel away from being so jazz orientated. This was exactly as I had intended as hopefully this would introduce a more commercial aspect to the final picture.

I booked the musicians and again an evening session in Studio Two. When I heard the strings for the first time with the original track I was inwardly overcome with emotion and excitement. They were so right for each other. They fitted like a glove.

Once the strings had been overdubbed and Ray Prickett and I had mixed both titles I didn't really know what we had created. All I knew was we had produced something totally different and totally magical but I didn't have a clue regarding its commercial strength.

After some considerable thought I decided the Artist should be named The John Schroeder Orchestra.

There was a small hole in the partition between Tony Hatch's office and mine. We used to put our ear to that hole and listen to what each of us was up to! Whilst I was playing the finished recording of *'Cast Your Fate to the Wind'* for the very first time, Tony Hatch suddenly appeared and very excited, asked me who and what it was I was playing. I explained to him very briefly and he said it was the greatest thing he had heard for years. He thought it was different enough to be commercial and would in the long run, sell a lot of records. That was indeed a compliment especially coming from him!

I was really dreading the next A&R meeting for obvious reasons!

Something was bothering me the whole of the weekend before the meeting, and that funnily enough was the name – The John Schroeder Orchestra but it just didn't sound right for this project. Luckily, as if from nowhere, I had a piece of genius inspiration. The name of Sounds Orchestral came to mind. I thought to myself "Now that *is* bloody clever!" It sounded exactly right. That was one up my sleeve!

There they were like eagles ready to pounce on their vulnerable prey.

This was my second record and as all eyes and ears were turned in my direction I said.

"As you will hear this is something totally different. I am proud to introduce *Sounds Orchestral* (I emphasized the name very deliberately and very slowly so it would sink in). The track is called *"Cast Your Fate to the Wind."*

As it faded, having fooled them with a false ending, there was total silence, the shock obviously being too much! Benjie then turned to Les Cocks and said with just a hint of sarcasm.

"Surely we're not employing producers to make jazz records. They don't sell do they?"

Before Les could answer, Tony Hatch intervened and said it was a fantastic record and that I should be congratulated on attempting something excitingly different. If it got the airplay he was convinced it would sell a lot of records.

Johnny Wise, being an ex drummer himself and a big band fanatic absolutely loved the record but he did say air play would be extremely difficult.

He went out of his way to give me a day to day run down on the promotion of the record and things didn't look too good until suddenly out of the blue he got a surprising break.

The record was released in October 1964 and the BBC informed Johnny Wise that they had decided to use the track on National TV behind the advertising of their forthcoming Christmas programmes. By 9.0'clock the following morning after it had gone out on air for the first time the night before, there were orders for over ten thousand records!

That morning Benjie stopped me in the corridor and to my surprise said.

"Good morning John. We've got orders for over ten thousand on your Sounds Orchestral record this morning. Umm… you can have a new chair and waste paper basket for your office if you like." He condescended to smile almost genuinely. For him to say that and even acknowledge me was more than unusual and must probably have been a great effort, so indeed it was some compliment.

I was left speechless!

The sales began to grow and grow and I was beginning to feel very guilty about Johnny Pearson. His pianistic skill had contributed so much to the record's success and all he had been paid was a measly £8.00 session fee!

I had a quiet meeting with him and I offered him to go into partnership with me. We would jointly be the Artist, namely Sounds Orchestral, splitting the royalty on a fifty-fifty basis. I would produce and direct the project and he would play keyboards, arrange and conduct it. This amicable arrangement worked like a dream for the entire lifespan of Sounds Orchestral which was to cover many forthcoming years.

I did not realise for some time that Sounds Orchestral was in fact my dream of dreams come true, the dream of bringing orchestral music nearer to the understanding of the younger generation. I knew it could only happen via a Hit record and I had been searching for that magic piece of music for years, so I will always have a special thank you in my heart for Tony Reeves who initially introduced me to *"Cast Your Fate to the Wind."* which of course became the incentive for making this dream come true. My intuition did the rest!

The single was massive, so it was not long before an album was on the horizon.

Truthfully I believed the birth of Sounds Orchestral and the making of the *'Cast Your Fate to the Wind'* album was the greatest achievement of my career, mainly because it proved something I implicitly believed in could be achieved, and unbelievably in a far bigger way than I had ever imagined. My only regret was that it was not me playing that piano so emotively and so beautifully. How many times in my dreams had I made myself believe it was actually me!

The success we had in America with a top twenty album was particularly exciting, but Sounds Orchestral was an International success for many years. All in all Johnny Pearson and I made seventeen albums with Sounds Orchestral. We always liked to use the same musicians and usually if any of them were not available on the designated time and date we would wait until they were and then re-book the session.

Sounds Orchestral –
A dedicated labour of love!

CONGRATULATIONS
AND
THANKS
TO
JOHN SCHROEDER
AND
SOUNDS ORCHESTRAL
FOR MAKING
"CAST YOUR FATE TO THE WIND"
SUCH A
TREMENDOUS SUCCESS

Robert Mellin Ltd.
64 New Bond Street, W.1
Ring MAYfair 3272

Produced and directed by John Schroeder
Arranged and conducted by Johnny Pearson
Piano and Harpsichord – Johnny Pearson
Bass – Peter McGurck Drums – Kenny Clare
Eight violins and two cellos
String leader – Reg Leopold
Engineer – Ray Prickett
Recorded at Pye Studios Bryanston Street London W.1

The Heart and Soul of –
Sounds Orchestral

Peter McGurck

Johnny Pearson

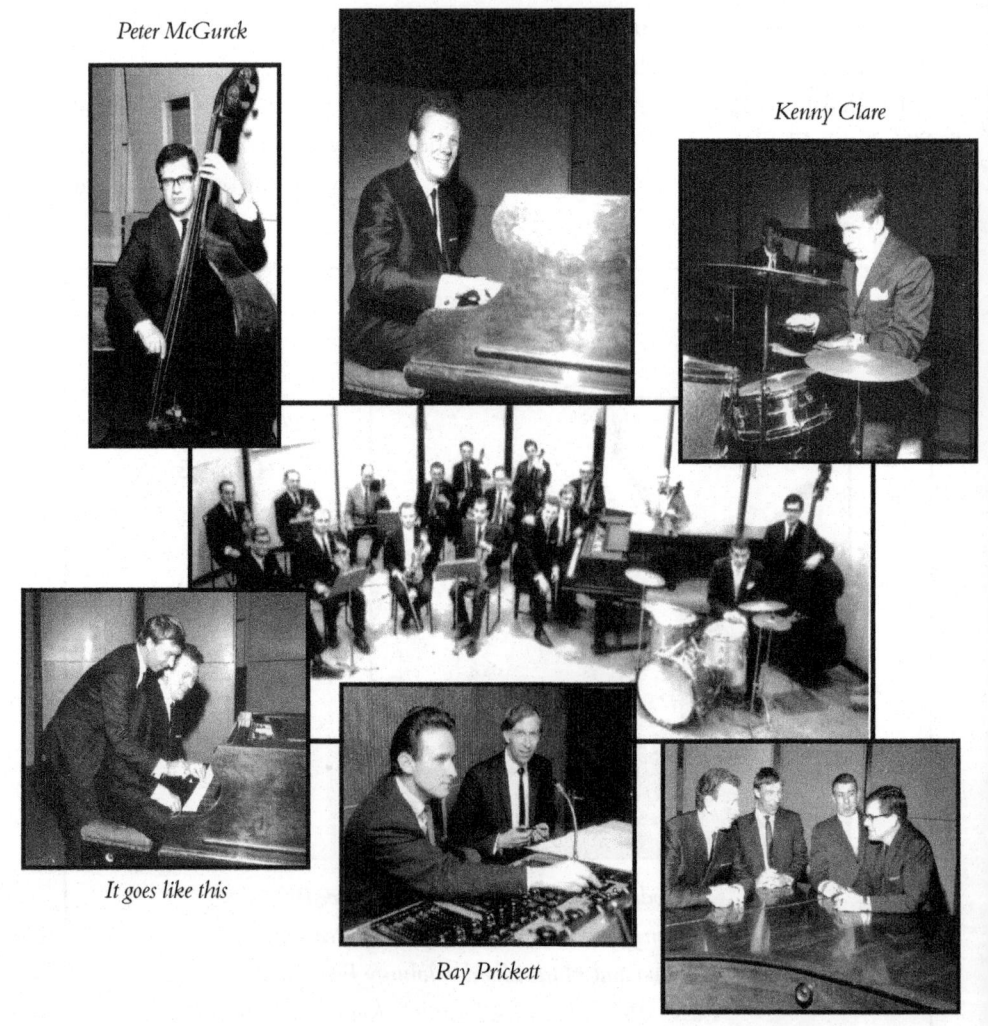

Kenny Clare

It goes like this

Ray Prickett

The A Team

The success of *"Cast Your Fate to the Wind"* was phenomenal. It made it to number 5 in our charts and was a chart record in every country of the world including America, where it made it into the top twenty in the Cash Box 100 chart. I was presented with the Melody Maker Award for the best instrumental record in Great Britain and the World. We even had offers of TV at the Olympia in Paris and doing a tour with Petula Clark.

I was presented with a Disc award for over a quarter of a million sales and a Pye Records Sales Award for the same thing. Both were presented to me by Louis Benjamin, the managing director of Pye Records. Total world wide sales were in excess of a million records!

The Awards Of Success

The Disc Award
Over 250,000 sales

The Pye Records Award
Over 250,000 sales

The Melody Maker Award
Best instrumental record in
Great Britain & The World

Putting Sounds Orchestral with a young boy's choir was an ambitious experiment but the piece of music I wanted to produce could well have proved to be an incompatible combination. The piece in mind was entitled *'Porcelain'* which melodically was very arresting being reminiscent of both Mozart and Beethoven.

The talented choir was borrowed from St Michaels Church Highgate and the very capable soloist was Michael Hutchinson. The recording session itself was naturally a little unusual with some time having to be spent beforehand by Johnny Pearson and myself with regards to rehearsal! After I had mixed the track I felt we had produced a piece of emotional musical magic. The media were sceptical with what they said in their reviews and were obviously not sure how to take it. In fact they labelled it 'Classical Pop' and it just might have made the charts with heavier air play.

In retrospect, it was probably too ambitious but it was still very worthwhile and I was pleased to have achieved it.

This arresting image portrays the true beauty and grace of Sounds Orchestral. Johnny Pearson and I have always strived for perfection but realistically there is no such thing even though we feel the music we have produced over the years has been very close. The true magic of Sounds Orchestral is that it will adapt to almost any mood you would like it to. I have even heard it said that Sounds Orchestral has been responsible for contributing to part of an increase in the Nation's birth rate!

'Cast Your Fate to the Wind' was the catalyst that brought orchestral music nearer to the understanding of the younger generation and because it is orchestral music it will remain timeless. Sounds Orchestral sounds as fresh and exciting today as it did when it was first conceived especially as a large percentage of the material recorded remains timeless in itself.

There have been no less than fifteen albums recorded and released by Sounds Orchestral over the years which includes compilations.

CHAPTER ELEVEN

Due to Sounds Orchestral's world wide success I found myself, with Benjie's blessing no less, going to New York to meet Marvin Schlacter and all the guys at Cameo Parkway Records, which was the American label that had released and promoted Sounds Orchestral. Marvin and his lovely wife Trudie were great hosts and made sure I was well looked after. I found New York incredibly exciting. By sheer chance I bumped into Benjie at the JFK airport on my way back to England. In conversation he discovered I had not been to Los Angeles or had the amazing experience of flying on a 747 jumbo jet which had only just gone into commercial service. He practically ordered me to stay in America as long as I liked, see Los Angeles and *a must* to fly the 747. I was overwhelmed with shock and even today I still can't believe that he had actually done that, especially taking into consideration the cost of it. Since then my feelings about Benjie began to change considerably. Did he have a heart after all? The aircraft and the flight were out of this world and so was Los Angeles!

Not too long after that trip I found myself on another jumbo but this time going to Johannesburg in South Africa, again due to the success of Sounds Orchestral. The Teal Record Company really went out of their way with the red carpet treatment. I even had a Cadillac at my disposal! I did an unplanned orchestral session with South African session musicians which turned out to be interestingly different! The boss invited me to his fabulous house which in pure white stone had a Spanish and Mexican look about it. Of course there was the swimming pool and there were the servants and God knows what else. He said he wanted me to meet Ruby. I thought Ruby was his wife but he took me into his bedroom and under his pillow was a hand gun. "Meet Ruby" he said. I was speechless.

Whilst all these things were happening with Sounds Orchestral my personal life also began to play a different tune. Karen Young, or Wendy, and I became much closer but although the relationship had its emotional moments she tended to treat me as her personal manager asking for my advice and approval of practically every modelling job she was offered and soon without realising it my own work was beginning to suffer. I made her aware of how I felt and suggested that perhaps she should change her Agency if she was not happy with what they were getting her. Finally she did this and things improved considerably, one of them being that she moved in with me at my apartment in Golders Green.

I didn't know how I could have been so naive not to have realised that Wendy was playing a very devious game, just as she did in the Welsh talent competition. She suggested that as we were now living together and sharing each others problems in such a together way why didn't we get married? It took me a while to get over the initial shock of that but then I thought having a wife looking like her would be the envy of many, and good for business. As for love, what's love got to do with it? This was show business!

The 14th November was the date that was set, but Wendy had a problem. She was a Roman Catholic and she was obsessed, and I mean obsessed, with wanting a white wedding, so she went to a hundred and one churches in the vicinity only to discover no one would condone a church wedding because I was divorced. She was beside herself with anger and disbelief, so out of desperation she turned to the Methodist Church. After a while she found that the vicar at the Methodist church in Neasden, which was practically on our doorstep, was agreeable to do the ceremony.

As weddings go it was superb. Wendy looked out of this world and had her pictures taken professionally by a hundred and one magazines. My boys, The Rockin' Berries with their first record riding high in the charts, supplied the music which went down a storm. All in all a memorable occasion.

It wasn't long before Wendy started on me about finance and that she felt that in accordance with our professional status we should now be living more up market such as in an olde worlde house in the country. Just to keep the peace we started looking, and ended up in Beaconsfield where she found a fantastic three bed roomed olde worlde house set in grounds of quarter of an acre. It was called 'Odd Acres'. There was a summer house, a stream with two wooden bridges, an old fashioned well and a very attractive court yard. The house itself had been built with hand selected coloured bricks. There was a sensational open fire place and the oak beams had apparently been rescued from actual ships of war. It was absolutely beautiful and she didn't have too hard a job in persuading me that this was *the* place. Even though realistically it was beyond our means it was also sadly not to be the happy home we had thought it would be.

Things began to go seriously wrong when Wendy started getting better and better modelling jobs and more and more money. I didn't see too much of her as she was always being wined and dined! She became very touchy and I dared not go anywhere near her, let alone speak to her on most nights for two and a half hours before she went to bed because she was meticulously doing her make up and preening herself with the "aren't I beautiful" look for the job in the morning! She developed a kind of aloof attitude which I found very difficult to live with.

There was the memorable occasion when she ordered a bra to be specially made for her by a French lingerie shop in Golders Green. Unfortunately I was with her on the day she went to pick it up. When she discovered it didn't fit properly she stormed out of the shop with bra in hand and me like a puppy following after. She got to the middle of Golders Green Road having stopped the traffic in both directions, turned to me screaming about the size of the bra and it not fitting properly and then threw it in my face saying I could take the fucking thing back.

One night I was in the Studio with Sounds Orchestral, and towards the end of the session Wendy walked in. Immediately all heads turned and there was silence. She knew she looked great in a tight dress with boobs and bum sticking out and she relished every minute of the moment. I could see the expressions on the guys faces as they quickly glanced at me as if to say "You lucky bastard having that to come home to."

Wendy spoke threateningly looking straight at me "If you are not ready in five minutes time I am taking the car and you'll have to walk."

I died a million times and virtually disappeared under the console. She took the car and I couldn't get home *again* because there were no trains to Beaconsfield at that time of night. This performance was becoming a bore and began to seriously affect my work and my state of health!

I walked out of the marital home one night never to see Wendy again. We got divorced and financially I lost everything. She got the house and I also got done for a monthly maintenance fee to allow her to keep the standard of living she was accustomed to: but although I cared I didn't care, because I was relieved to be out of her clutches and free again.

Where did I run to? Of course to good old Ma, where I poured my heart out and tried to sort my life out yet again. My father was really upset about the house. It was serious money and I had virtually given it to her on a plate by walking out of the marital home and leaving her with a small fortune. What my father understandably couldn't possibly realise was what it was like being married to someone who always put a stop to anything physical, in other words "you can look but you don't touch!" I was her husband for God's sake! I just couldn't stand it any longer. It was destroying me and my career so I had no alternative but to leave. She, on the other hand was far too clever to consider anything as drastic as that. I walked away feeling quite sick at the thought of her having got her hands on the property and how I had been well and truly taken for a ride.

Back with my parents again, and really nothing had changed. As usual anything important was always said or discussed over breakfast. My father, with a man-of-the-world type of smile said in a matter of fact tone of voice

"You will never learn will you? You might do yourself a big favour, and your mother and I, if in future you remembered the three fs – find 'em, fuck 'em and forget 'em . That way you might stay away from any more marital and financial disasters."

I had to smile to myself at those words of wisdom, because I now guessed how he got away with it when he went on one of his *cock* tours as my mother would say. There was no proof of course but I had at times noticed that twinkle in his eye!

My immediate concern was to find a one bedroomed apartment somewhere near Pye Records. I got lucky and within two weeks I made the move to the second floor at 4 Forset Court, which was an apartment block on the Edgware Road and only ten minutes walk from Marble Arch. This was to become my den of iniquity over the next few years. I actually felt secure and comfortable there and it was *my* home.

My apartment looked over the Edgware Road and I often used to mull over problems by sitting by the window and people watching. Edgware Road was certainly not short of some really interesting street activity. I was particularly lucky to have a public phone box right outside the front door of Forset Court and I could easily identify who was making a phone call. This became a very useful asset to my salacious activities devoted to making up for all the pleasures I had lost over the years due to my marital fiascos! Organising the coming and goings of the entourage of females I was fortunate to now have in my life was not too easy when there was no way you wanted them to come across each other. Therefore I made it a rule that they phone me first from the phone box outside the front door. Unbeknown to them I could then see who they were and panic accordingly!

Whilst wallowing in the glory of Sounds Orchestral, Terry Kennedy phoned me out of the blue and said he still managed Carter – Lewis and The Southerners (who used to be with me at Oriole). He said things with the group had changed, but would I still be interested?

I said I would certainly be interested to talk about it.

Terry pointed out that John Carter and Ken Lewis really appreciated all the hard work everyone at Oriole had put in behind the release of *"Sweet and Tender Romance"* and *"Your Mama's Out Of Town."* They both deserved to have made it.

But now they had decided to add a third member namely Perry Ford and to change the name of the group to The Ivy League. They were at the moment in great demand as a backing group and had already worked with such artists as P.J Proby, Paul Anka and Brenda Lee. As they were coming up with some very strong commercial material Terry had decided to take them into Southern Music's Studio and record two songs as a prospective single which he then played me. The intended 'A' side was *"Funny How Love Can Be"*

Inwardly I was very excited but decided not to show it. Terry said he would like me to work on the project with him. I said I would but I would have to be the Executive Producer having the final say regarding the material and what was ultimately released. I had no objection to him physically producing the product and being credited accordingly. Terry was quite happy with this and so a deal was mutually agreed with the first release being *"Funny How Love Can Be."*

I was proud to have them under my wing as their talent was undeniable. The working relationship between Terry and I was very easy going and quite compatible. We respected each other.

John, Ken & Perry

Once again the dreaded A&R meeting had arrived and I proudly presented the Ivy League and *"Funny How Love Can Be"*, my third record. I knew I had a good piece of product and this time there were smiles all around. Sounds Orchestral must have really given them a shock and had more effect than I imagined! Benjie was strangely affable, and I thought I had caught Tony Hatch looking a *little* concerned or was it jealous, since once again the record was voted to have strong chart potential and warranted the benefit of Johnny Wise's top promotional package.

WATCH OUT FOR THE IVY LEAGUE

At the risk of being trapped out on a limb, I predict that the Ivy League's "Funny how love can be" is heading for the higher reaches of the Pop 50.

This is only the group's second single under their own name but as one of the busiest backing groups in town they are on record with many top stars including P.J Proby, Billy Fury. Brenda Lee, Paul Anka and Pet Clark.

The trio – Perry Ford from Lincoln, John Carter and Ken Lewis from Birmingham – have been together for some six months. Prior to that says Perry, "We were just villains."

"We write most of our own material because, we know best how we feel. We all throw in ideas for the arrangements – this is why we joined together because we all think alike."

(NME January 1965)

"Funny How Love Can Be" by The Ivy League reached the number 8 position in the NME top thirty on February 4th 1965.

Further success was to follow.

On the 6th May 1965 *"That's why I'm Crying"* reached number 22 in the charts
On the 24th June 1965 *"Tossing and Turning"* reached number 3 in the charts.
On the 14th July 1966 *"Willow Tree"* reached number 50 in the charts.

Everyone involved had worked really hard to attain this and should be congratulated in achieving such a result. The talent of this group had been truly justified and I was proud to have contributed to its achievement.

The success of *"Funny How Love Can Be"* by the Ivy League gave me the hat trick of three hit singles in a row. I think Management was as shocked and thrilled as I was at the time, although they didn't really want to believe it. As such they had no alternative but to respect my achievement, which they did by making me feel I could do no wrong. *Funnily enough* I had no objections to this and they had no objections to anything I wanted to do or any new Artist I wanted to sign!

I felt good and I also felt at least for this moment I had achieved one up on Mr. Hatch!

The New Musical Express quoted: With Sounds Orchestral, Ivy League and Rockin' Berries in Top 30 John Schroeder making Piccadilly lights bright!

Tin Pan Alley

Tin Pan Alley, better known as Denmark Street lay in the centre of London's bustling Metropolis. It became the home of many illustrious Music Publishing houses for a long time. Taking a slow walk down that street opened your eyes and ears to an extraordinary world because every company you walked passed endeavoured to outdo the one next to it by playing something different and always louder. Every window was devoted to displaying sheet music of some kind usually their current hit songs. Anybody and everybody would be found visiting somebody in this street at some time or other. Music Publishers were a very important and integral part of the music industry and I personally valued and respected them very highly. My years with Norrie Paramor had done much for me in initiating a working relationship with many of them. Of course being a successful Record Producer with successful Artists made me particularly interesting to a Music Publisher. I would think at least fifty per cent of my appointments and time was taken seeing Music Publishers and listening to their latest material that they thought might produce a hit for the Artists I handled. I always respected a Music Publisher who came to see me with material knowing what Artists I actually produced. There was always that one who would bring a pile of songs and virtually throw them on my desk saying "here you are John, go through that lot!" Not appreciated!

The Music Publishing fraternity always seemed to have a particular air about it. I think it was in their mannerism and personality which was brought on by the nature of the industry they were in. They were always good for a laugh and had some wicked stories to tell. It was great having out of hour's relationships with some of them when we would go out drinking, clubbing and ultimately womanising, a subject that I was always willing to make the most of at this time of my life! I didn't like being alone too much especially at night!

Cyril Shane was a publisher I always had time for because he believed quite passionately in what he was doing. His expertise was acquiring foreign material that he believed had hit potential from countries such as France, Germany, Italy and many others. He would then commission a British songwriter to write a lyric and justifiably he would find himself throughout a year with a number of hit records.

I periodically went down to his office situated near Regents Park to have a listening session with him. Whenever this occurred there was always the important third member at the meeting and that was Pedro, his miniature poodle. Cyril religiously valued Pedro's opinion. Pedro would position himself on Cyril's lap and if he didn't like what was being played he would growl continuously until it had finished but if he liked what he was hearing he would pant heavily usually sticking his tongue out. After a while I also couldn't help myself respecting Pedro's opinion even though his comments at times were pretty demonstrative!

Before moving into the world of music publishing, Paul Rich used to be a Big Band singer. He joined Carlin Music and after many years devoted to the exploitation of songs, was promoted to the executive staff of the company.

Because he was a singer and a good one at that, Paul knew all about songs, their quality, their value and their potential. He was liked and loved by almost everyone in the music industry and he was particularly respected by record producers as someone who knew what they were talking about. He was very good at his job, often coming out with something totally unpredictable. One day he wanted me to hear the Italian hit record of a particularly beautiful love song. He gave me a copy of the English lyric and then as it was playing he was suddenly on his knees singing it with all the hand movements as well endeavouring to serenade me with the English words! I was speechless and I told him I didn't know he loved me that much! It was a good song and he did have a hit with it but unfortunately not with me, so he must have successfully serenaded someone else!

Most music publishers were very instrumental in helping with the promotion of a potential hit single; after all it was their copyright that was being exploited. They were usually well in with radio producers, D.Js and programme presenters so it was a concerted effort by many that ultimately contributed to a record becoming a hit record.

For a Record Producer, especially a successful one, the Christmas period was incredible when success usually *went to your head* because you would be invited to every type of party going. Not only that, you would be inundated with gifts especially from the Music Publishing fraternity, such as wine, champagne, chocolates and even food hampers containing a turkey. I had even received ornaments and jewellery!

I have to admit I was in my element at any of the Christmas parties because invitations for a bit of male relaxation from the opposite sex were so in abundance that it was just too difficult to refuse and always too difficult to choose!

Tony King

Tony King was a talented arranger who was beginning to have noticeable recognition for his success, particularly with Reggae and R&B Artists such as Bob Marley and Eddie Grant. It just so happened that he took an apartment two floors up in the same block as me, namely Forset Court off Edgware Road and so it wasn't long before we met. We both discovered we wrote songs and decided to get together to see if anything creatively worthwhile or productive came out of it.

We found we were very compatible in our ideas, helped by both of us having embraced almost every facet of the music industry at one time or another. Tony was also a very good musician and I was successful as a producer and songwriter and had access to quite a number of Artists, which put us in a strong position as far as our writing was concerned. We both had pianos in our apartments but Tony also had a 'porta studio', which he loved. He had a four track machine and all the accessories, so to an extent we could do our own demo which was a fantastic plus. We ensured we had regular writing sessions which were usually twice a week.

Up to the time Tony sadly became too ill to write, we had collaborated in no less than a hundred compositions many of which had been recorded by major Artists such as Nancy Sinatra, Amen Corner, Helen Shapiro, Status Quo and Geno Washington. This also included the infamous musical entitled *'Pull Both Ends'* which unhappily ran for only a short while in 1972 at the Piccadilly Theatre in the West End of London.

Sadly Tony had contracted Parkinson's disease, and to see him deteriorate in such a slow and painful way was extremely upsetting. He loved playing the piano so much that he used to play in an up market lounge bar twice a week but eventually seeing his fingers fumbling to reach the keys was truly painful. He was such a lovely guy, so placid and unruffled by any problem. Nothing was too much trouble for him. Sadly he died at 6.am on the morning of February 4th 2007. I miss him terribly and I always will.

Alan Tew

I think recorded music is taken for granted without realising how much individual talent is necessary to produce it. The end result is a team effort between musicians, the arranger/conductor, the Producer, the Artist and the sound engineer. Each one of these dedicated and talented people is as important as the other in achieving the end product although it is the producer who is ultimately responsible for its success or failure.

Keeping my eyes and ears open as to what was going on in the industry, I had heard the name of Alan Tew mentioned a number of times in connection with the arranging of certain product that was in the charts. I asked Sue to get on the case and track him down, which she did.

Apart from Alan's skills as both a brilliant musician and Arranger he was a very sincere and charming guy. Both he and I had considerable respect for each other and we became friends apart from the professional association. I started to give Alan quite a lot of my work since he was great in the studio and both musicians and Artists always had great respect for him. We were very compatible in our thinking musically, and he would always go out of his way to endeavour to get what I wanted. Our association developed to us writing together and ultimately having some quite considerable success.

Alan was blessed with a wicked sense of humour, and one day he told me the story of a rather serious car accident he was involved in which resulted in him losing vision in one eye and suffering numerous broken bones.

Apparently, a car hit him head on whilst trying to dangerously pass a lorry on a narrow country road. It was proven beyond any shadow of a doubt that it was totally the driver of this car who was at fault. Alan knew what he looked like and knew he had also been hurt and had ended up in a hospital too. One day Alan was in his hospital in a wheel chair casually going down the corridor to the cafeteria when he turned a corner and suddenly the guy who had hit him appeared at the other end of the corridor, also in a wheel chair. Alan stopped in his tracks with shock for a moment as he recognised who he was and then anger started to take over and he frantically wheeled himself towards the guy shouting at the top of his voice.

"Now it's my fucking turn. I'm going to get you, you bastard!"

Apparently a quick thinking nurse who had just about witnessed the whole scenario with all the shouting managed to stop another serious confrontation from happening which could have extended the hospital time for both participants quite drastically! Alan obviously couldn't believe his luck and unquestionably had hoped to seize this unexpected opportunity to seek some justifiable revenge!

Having *cast my fate to the wind* I had managed to sort my life out forcing myself to think more sensibly and logically. I had deliberately decided to cut my losses and bear the considerable cost of terminating wife number two's contract. Losing this element of stress in my life was incredible relief and having now found a new home in Forset Court I was beginning to enjoy life on my own but with the added high of having three records in the charts. It was just too good to be true. Even though I was enjoying every minute of basking in the glory of success I also knew there was a thin line between success and failure and I realised that to continue having chart records with every Artist I produced was by the law of averages just too unrealistic. Sadly I was right because the following Artists, whom I signed all in good faith, believed in implicitly and in the material I chose to record all failed to register. Peter Jay and the Jaywalkers *'Where Did Our Love Go?'* Without being biased I loved the record but it was a British rendition of a Motown classic something which I know Berry Gordy would have justifiably hated, Peter's Faces *'(Just like) Romeo and Juliet',* Antoinette *'There Goes (The Boy I Love'),* The Hellions *'Daydreaming Of You.'*

Even though these records and the follow-up singles failed to register with reasonably good air play the talent of these Artists contributed greatly in establishing the ultimate strength and direction of the Piccadilly label.

There are many factors that could cause the failure of a record to chart. It was usually impossible to pin point any one of them such as the strength of the song, the promotion, the advertising, the distribution and so on. It only needed one thing to be wrong and the record could be doomed.

Once again I was to live the nightmare of wondering where my next hit was going to come from. However, I was to have Clinton Ford, Helen Shapiro, David Garrick, Glo Macari, The Sorrows, Barbara Ruskin and Billie Davis all in the pipe line. Luckily the powers that be had no objection to the number of Artists I signed as they knew by my proven track record I was more than capable of producing the right product providing it received the right support.

The media had certainly got it right when they called it The Swinging Sixties or sometimes The Rock Music Explosion of the Sixties. I consider myself fortunate to have experienced it, worked through it professionally and lived through it pleasurably. In the whole of my career it was the most exciting time of my life, incredible music, incredible clothes, incredible women and incredible sex! This period also initiated the battle of the Cities who fought to out do each other in endeavouring to attract the greatest media attention. Liverpool certainly had a head start with the discovery of The Beatles, a musical phenomenon beyond anybody's imagination. But Birmingham and Manchester had plenty to offer. The Rockin' Berries hailed from Birmingham and the Sorrows hailed from Coventry.

One day a demo arrived on my desk and I was intrigued and impressed. I loved the image, all dressed in black which justified the musical direction of the band as leaning towards heavy rock. The majority of The Sorrow's repertoire was self penned but even though it was rock music it was impressively melodic and immediately identifiable.

They were a great band to work with in the studio because they took direction well and we had equal respect for each other but we needed that Hit. We had had two single releases, the first being *'I Don't Wanna Be Free'* which did nothing but the second entitled *'Baby'* deserved to make it but somehow didn't. However, it was received with strong interest and the potential of the group was particularly remarked upon.

One afternoon I was in Studio One doing some mixing when I heard some interesting songs coming from Studio Two. One of them especially caught my attention and I was thinking of The Sorrows. On investigating further, I discovered a guy called Mikki Dallon doing a demo session with some of his songs. We met in the pub later when I told him I was particularly interested in three of his songs for a group I had, called The Sorrows. I also told him one of those songs *'Take a heart'* could be strong enough as a single. Mikki was thrilled to pieces and arranged for the demos to be sent round to me immediately.

I must say as Mikki's demo of the song was very explicit, we didn't have to do too much re-arranging apart from putting The Sorrows' stamp on it. I got really excited having heard it back after Alan Florence and I had mixed it. It sounded a hit because it was so immediate and so different. The group were ecstatic and justifiably so when *'Take a heart'* reached number 21 on the 16th September 1965. This band were a bunch of some of the nicest and talented guys I have ever worked with and I really enjoyed producing their one and only album entitled *'Take A Heart'* which included the other two Dallon compositions namely *'She's Got the Action'* and *'Let Me In.'* The album surprised everyone by doing very much better than anyone expected.

Ironically Mikki Dallon formed Young Blood, his own record label some years later and he signed Don Fardon, the lead singer of The Sorrows. Guess what – on the 10th of October 1970 Don Fardon made number 3 in the charts with *'Indian Reservation.'* It was written by Mikki Dallon – of course.

For some reason I felt a little choked, perhaps for overlooking Don

Fardon's potential as a solo Artist but then the timing was not right so I should be pleased for both of them.

David Garrick was managed by Robert Wace who also managed the Kinks. Robert, who was highly respected in the industry was a very striking and eccentric character being over six foot tall, thin as a pencil, always carried a multi coloured umbrella and was hooked on pills because he was paranoid about headaches, stress, indigestion, stomach ache and God knows what else. On arriving for a planned lunch date at the pre booked table in a restaurant the first thing he did was to carefully place half a dozen bottles of pills in the centre of the table so he could stare at them throughout the meal as if his life depended on it which of course it did!

David Garrick was as bad but in a totally different way. He was a strikingly good looking guy, had a great head of hair, a wicked sense of humour especially with practical jokes, was blessed with an identifiable voice but nothing to shout about and unquestionably had the talent to bluff his way through practically anything. Strangely there was something very appealing about him. Robert Wace saw it and so did I. The problem we had was what to give him to record. Then I had the idea of *'Lady Jane,'* the Rolling Stones song. It was made for him, very camp, very infectious but thank God I got my next hit with it. It was released in May 1966 and made it to number 28 on the 9th of June. Now we needed something stronger as a follow up and Robert sent me over a record of an American song called *'Dear Mrs Applebee,'* written by Billy Meshel. It was in the American charts but there was no plan for its release here. I loved it since once again it was so David and we unanimously agreed that we should go for it. Alan Tew's excellent arrangement of the song was spot on and David excelled himself in the vocal department. However, Alan Florence, my engineer and I had a huge problem with the mix. We just couldn't get it right and Robert was complaining bitterly that there was something about the sound or the feel that didn't quite gel. It just didn't have the magic. We had to re-mix it four times before Alan and I managed to nail it. Robert was quite right of course and took an extra two pills on hearing the final mix! In September the record went to number 22 in the charts and was extremely successful abroad catapulting David into becoming a huge Artist commanding serious money. He always went down a storm in clubs, especially in Hamburg. He looked great and worked 'his bollocks off' on stage but he knew exactly how to milk his audience with a *cocktail* of high energy and sexual connotation. He was truly outrageous and he loved every minute of it. He also prided himself in being able to sing opera but I was unfortunate to have witnessed this. I could have sworn that I had heard the words 'Spaghetti Bolognese' and 'Fettuccini' more than once whilst he was on a high in this fantasy world.

I had the pleasure of meeting Billy Meshel who wrote *'Dear Mrs Applebee'* on two occasions, the first being when he came over to England to meet David and myself and the second, when I went to the States and he and Larry Weiss, another songwriter friend showed me the inside out of New York. There was nothing about anything those two guys didn't know so we had such a great laugh. We did the town in so many ways and I remember I was *very well* looked after!

Handling both the Kinks and David Garrick was more than a full time job for Robert Wace so most of the annoying managerial problems were put in the hands of Marilyn Davis, his personal assistant. Marilyn was very good at handling domestic fiascos created by both these Artists.

David was obsessed with orchestrating totally outrageous antics. As the story goes for some unknown reason he decided to go to the Earls Court Boat Show and impressed a certain boat builder that he was the personal secretary to Lord somebody or other who resided in the salubrious area of Knightsbridge. He said The Lord was interested in the 15 foot yacht that was on display and he would make it very worthwhile if it could be delivered to the Lord's house when the show had finished. He would arrange payment on delivery. Sure enough on the day after the close of the show and after two hours a very frustrated truck driver could find no such name and no such address! Needless to say the truck and the yacht which must have been at least 20 foot or longer grid locked the whole of Knightsbridge for practically all that day!

On another memorable occasion David had connived his way into staying with Liberace at his house in Los Angeles. Unfortunately due to some domestic difference or other David found himself out on the street with no means of getting home. He then had the nerve to phone Louis Benjamin, the Managing Director of Pye Records informing him of his predicament and asking him to arrange a ticket for his air fare home! How he did it I don't know *but he got the ticket!*

Billy, Me and David

I was always looking at cars. I could never stop looking at them and wanting them. Just like women, they enveloped me with their beauty, lines and performance. I was never happy with one for too long and I always wanted to change them for something better, sleeker and faster.

I knew nothing about a car called a **Marcos** until I had a very in depth conversation about it with John Maus of the Walker Bros. He owned one, praising it to high heaven and saying it was a fantastic big boy's toy. It boasted a top speed of 120 mph with a 1600 cc engine and because it had a fibre glass body its acceleration was dynamite. He thoroughly recommended that I go out for a test drive by calling or visiting the main distributor which was Hexagon of Highgate. All this sounded too exciting not to follow up. So one day I found myself behind the wheel of this incredible motor car with a driving position of being almost horizontal! It was truly an exhilarating experience to say the least and consequently I joined the one or two other well known show biz types such as Andy Fairweather-Low of Amen Corner who funnily enough had a hit with one of my songs *'High In The Sky'*, Carl Wilson of the Beach Boys and even Sam Wanamaker who had all obviously got bitten by the same bug!

Not only was I besotted with this motor car but also with one of the young ladies who had done much to sell it to me. Her name was Gloria and we were destined to enjoy many interesting 'rides' together! I was having so much fun with this car that I later brazenly traded it in for the 3 litre one which was stupidly amazing but it really went like a bat out of hell. Most of the time Gloria had her head turned towards the passenger window frantically making the sign of the cross which was a bit ironic when she was employed to help sell them.

Unfortunately I was to have a rather nasty experience with this car. I was driving up North on my own to see Geno Washington and the Ram Jam Band and accelerated hard round a 45 degree bend. The torque was so great that the car and the rear wheels decided to part company and go in different directions. It was a very harrowing experience but luckily it happened only a few miles from the Marcos factory. They sent out two engineers and fixed it in a couple of hours. Buy British – I was surprisingly impressed!

After a while the Marcos magic started to wear off a little particularly when certain other female friends of mine were too scared even to get in it. The final straw came when a very close female friend said "being horizontal was usually a pleasurable experience but being horizontal in that thing was quite something else!" I thought to myself "That thing was my pride and joy and saying that was not very nice at all" However, it did make me think, and I came to the sad conclusion that me and Marcos would have to part as I could not afford to lose any female TLC at this time of my life!

My world changed gear when I suddenly became hooked on saloon cars and in particular Mercedes, the first one being a Mercedes 280 SE. It was maroon and beautifully furnished. With this car I found I suddenly had more friends than usual and the abundance of room and manoevourability in it was very much approved of! Later on I even went one bigger and exchanged that for a Mercedes 300 SEL. This was really big and beautiful with a sumptuous interior furnished in wood with velvet upholstery. She was midnight blue, moved with such grace and she was so smooth and as silent as a ghost but – she was an alcoholic!

Even so I still came to the conclusion that my ultimate goal had to be the King of the Road, a Rolls Royce which I vowed I would have by the time I was forty!

More Love on 4 wheels!
From Marcos to Mercedes

CHAPTER TWELVE

As usual it had been a mad and hectic week but it was Friday at last. I enjoyed the ten minute walk from Forset Court to my office as it always seemed to clear my head. It was now 9.30am and Sue, my secretary was well trained not to do or discuss anything until she had presented me with my morning cup of black coffee. We then got down to business with the list of outstanding phone calls, the problems of the moment and the rundown of my appointments for the day.

Two meetings with two Music Publishers, one at ten and the other at eleven were first on the agenda so my mental faculties had to be well in tune. Not only did I have to listen to their songs but usually the latest update on their life stories as well. My full attention was essential. They could be holding the key to my next hit!

The afternoon would be totally taken up with a routining session with Barbara Ruskin and Alan Tew, my arranger on this occasion. It was Barbara's first recording session so it was very important to make her feel comfortable by making sure everything was absolutely right.

Sue then reminded me, as if I would forget, that I also had an evening session in Studio One with Sounds Orchestral, recording three tracks to complete the current album project.

This was a typical working day in my life which would also be interrupted with phone calls or Benjie screaming about something or other, and I probably wouldn't see my bed till one or two in the morning. It was tiring and hectic but I didn't really mind. This was my chosen life style and I relished every minute of it.

It didn't take me long to realise that Pye Records was a great company to work for, mainly due to its staff that always made you feel part of a team that really cared. Benjie was a bit of an ogre but I was to discover that even he and his management buddies were as wickedly normal as anyone else. I had by accident, caught them discussing in detail behind locked doors at the end of a working day, the attributes and availability of certain young ladies within the Company. "Would she be up for it? " I heard that question more than once.

I loved evening sessions, especially if I was working with Johnny Pearson and Sounds Orchestral. Out of all the Artists I produced they held a special place in my heart.

After any evening session I always looked forward to going across the road to the Double Time Café in the Cumberland as it stayed open till four in the morning. There were two specific reasons for this, one was to unwind after the session, and the other because there was a beautiful and attractive young lady called Anne-Marie working on her own behind the bar at that time of night or morning. Where there's a will there's a way, and after some dedicated perseverance we got on really well, but even though I'd come in there at all hours she never really believed me about the studio or what I actually did. So one night I decided the time was right to play my trump card. I invited her to come and witness one of my recording sessions then she could see for herself. I wondered why this offer always worked with very positive response! Pushing my luck I suggested that afterwards perhaps we could… Well, that *is* another story, fortunately with a very happy ending! After a while she took me by surprise by conjuring up a rather embarrassing pet name for me which to be honest I was quite proud of. She called me – her gentle genius!

Just before leaving to go to the studio one Friday evening, Sue asked me to deal with an outstanding call from Mike Rispoli from the Rik Gunnell Agency who wanted my confirmation of meeting him in Blackburn the next day, Saturday, to evaluate the amazing talent of Geno Washington and The Ram Jam Band. I called him to confirm it and he said he had arranged a special surprise menu of Rispoli hospitality just for me. I thought I wouldn't try to analyse that, but I soon came to realise that there was little Mike Rispoli did not know or could not achieve where entertaining someone who might be instrumental in concluding a lucrative business proposition was concerned. It made me feel important that he had gone to so much trouble.

I drove up to Blackburn on Saturday afternoon having nearly killed myself on the way in the Marcos. I was in a state when I finally arrived early that evening but Mike knew exactly how to take care of the situation. He and I soon became good friends especially as we found we had a mutual interest and interests!

"Geno! Geno! Geno!" They shouted! Screamed! Yelled! The place was packed. It sounded like a mini football match! I was totally blown away! A couple of minutes and The Ram Jam Band came on stage. Brilliant sixties type fashion, lots of colour, great spectacle. During their opening number *'Philly Dog'* the crowd were practically hysterical. "Geno! Geno! Geno! they yelled. Then the great man himself, born in Illinois appeared in some amazing 'gear'! Geno launched himself into a wealth of great soul classics *'Ride Your Pony' 'Uptight'*, *'Respect'* etc. The crowd's reaction was indescribable. You had to be there to experience it. This was the North and worth every minute of the drive up from London. I had never witnessed anything like it before and probably never will again.

Now I had to put my producer's hat firmly on my head! Geno had incredible charisma. He was a great showman but dare I say, with not too great a voice. However it didn't matter – he got away with it very well. They had a repertoire of fantastic soul songs and The Ram Jam Band, a strong act within themselves thanks to the talents of Peter Gage, provided a more than adequate backing. It was indeed a show within a show! But the greatest thing of all was that they had an incredible amount of bookings for a long time to come and a huge fan base. There would be no problem with a record deal but how was I going to capture all this and do justice to it on vinyl? It was vital to get a good recorded sound and at the same time not to lose one minute of the energy and hysteria of the whole show! I firmly believed their first release should be an album of what I had just witnessed and not go anywhere near a single at the present time.

On driving back to London I toyed with the idea of bringing a mobile recording unit to a gig but somehow I believed I could do better than that!

Perhaps I should record the band and Geno in the studio and then superimpose the audience? No good because there would be no spontaneity and Geno wouldn't get any audience feedback to help him. It would be a disaster!

By the time I got to London I had the answer. A brainwave hit me. I would convert Pye Record's Number One studio into a club, build a stage and invite an audience selected from his fan club. Soft drinks only of course! Re-create the show as I had just seen it. Get hold of top D.J Dave Cash to compere it. My biggest headache would be getting Louis Benjamin to agree! He would freak at the very thought of it, so I decided to put it to Les Cocks, his deputy as he would much more amenable to such a crazy idea. With some gentle persuasion he reluctantly agreed – providing there was proper control and security. On the actual night however, when he saw all those 'wild' kids arriving he was a complete basket case and beside himself with worry. I told him to go to bed and forget about it – which he did thank goodness! My adrenalin was pumping like mad and the whole event went off without a hitch. It was an incredible night! I have to thank Geno's management, and in particular Mike Rispoli, for controlling the event and to Alan Florence, my engineer for the technical side and for sharing a mammoth editing job to achieve such a great piece of finished product.

'Hand Clappin' Foot Stompin' Funky Butt …Live! was Pye's biggest selling album for three years running. There were others and I even took Geno into the studio and recorded *'Bring It To Me Baby'* written by myself and Tony king and *'My Little Chickadee'* written by Tony Macaulay backed by session musicians. He was an outstanding Artist and a joy to work with, but his forte beyond any shadow of a doubt was on stage. He owned it and he knew it. "Geno! Geno! Geno!" they screamed and that said it all. My favourite track? *'Michael'* which was recorded live and became our highest single chart entry.

It made it to number 39 on the 2nd February 1967.

Mr. James and the Vagabonds

Geno Washington, Mike Rispoli and I were having a serious discussion about working out the finer details to record a single using session musicians instead of The Ram Jam Band. Suddenly the door of my office was flung open and Benjie was standing there almost beside himself with frustrated anger.

"John what the bloody hell is going on with your Artists? I've got Jimmy James in the office next to me who has told me in no uncertain terms that he refuses to see you whilst you've got Geno Washington with you".

I answered apologetically, "Benjie, they don't like, or rather don't respect each other. I didn't know he was coming so can I tell you when I have finished with Geno which will be in a few minutes?"

Geno and Mike left rather confused about the whole scenario. I saw Benjie and said feeling rather uncomfortable

"It's O.K Geno has gone. Can you tell Jimmy James I can see him now".

I had to laugh about the whole fiasco. There was Louis Benjamin, the Managing Director of Pye records playing messenger boy between two of my Artists and what's more at my request. I knew I was in deep shit when Benjie next saw me. Surprisingly and shaking his head in disbelief he said with a hint of obvious sarcasm

"John – you are really something else! I was made to look a complete fool but luckily for you, it caught me on a good day and crazy that it was, the joke was on me. *Don't ever let it happen again*!" I breathed a huge sigh of relief.

The jealousy between Geno and Jimmy became quite a serious problem especially as they were both my Artists. Jimmy did not rate Geno at all because in his estimation Geno had categorically no voice. Geno did not rate Jimmy because he was totally useless and out of his depth as an entertainer.

Jimmy James was a fantastic artist to work with in the studio. To my mind he had a voice that was as great and as emotive as any of the big American Soul and R& B Artists. The album we made entitled "Open Up Your Soul" more than justified that. Our recording of Neil Diamond's"*Red Red Wine*" made the charts at number 36 on the 11th September 1968.

Helen's back

Helen Shapiro, my most successful association ever was uncommitted record wise at the time I moved to Pye. I felt it might be a worthwhile challenge to try to bring her back. In her favour was that remarkable voice which really was better than ever before because Helen was so much more experienced and mature. Against her were a number of years when nothing of real note had happened, certainly not record wise. I also considered that if the worst scenario did occur whereby the challenge failed then Helen, I and Pye Records would at least achieve some good, bad or indifferent media attention, which in itself would only be a plus. One thing was for sure – her past success was there forever and no one could take that away!

The Press Said:

Can Helen do it again?

*Helen's chance to
hit the high notes again*

*Finding success
the second time round?*

A fresh start for our one time pop princess

Due to the past, pressure was turned on me to come up with the song. It was difficult because I had to remember she was no longer in her teens but in collaboration with Tony King we came up with *'You'll Get Me Loving You'*. It was a simple song, very melodic with a romantic lyric painting a picture of 'one to one' love. I really thought it was a strong song and it did get excellent radio support. The reviews were mixed and annoyingly they seemed to take a delight in making most of the fact that Helen was out of favour at the present time.

> ## HELEN SHAPIRO: *You'll get Me Loving You (Pye)*
>
> *After more than six years with Columbia, Helen Shapiro has now switched to Pye – no doubt in the hope of achieving an improvement in her disc fortunes. And this record is a good showcase for her. It's an appealing rocka-ballad with a lilting rhythm and a faint continental quality which is accentuated by the mandolin effects. Very attractive tune, with strings and humming group. Makes thoroughly enjoyable listening. Many worse records than this have appeared in the chart but we can't ignore the fact that Helen seems to be out of favour.*

I battled on with further single releases, *'Today Has Been Cancelled'* being particularly noteworthy. Sadly, I eventually had to admit defeat and that a record come back for Helen and myself was not meant to be. Helen however, went on to being a very successful performing Artist especially when she formed a professional relationship with Humphrey Lyttelton and his Band. Perhaps more important than anything else is the fact that her voice has been heard all over the world!

Helen Shapiro will always be remembered with love and respect. At fourteen and a half years old she was quite phenomenal and arrived with such an unexpected impact that she will, for ever hold an honoured place in the pages of the History of British Pop Music. I feel justified in feeling proud, and dare I say pleased with myself since I did discover her and I did write all her biggest hits.

The John Schroeder Orchestra

The name Sounds Orchestral was born through a flash of inspiration and consequently eliminated the initial name of The John Schroeder Orchestra. My priority was now to find an orchestral direction for The John Schroeder Orchestra. This actually was a very pleasant task because I loved playing around with orchestral sounds. A large part of my track record was devoted to successfully producing Soul and R&B projects which in turn brought back fond memories of my association with Berry Gordy and Tamla/Motown. There were some really great songs around with performances by some amazing Artists. I thought it would be a zany and different idea to record them instrumentally using strings and brass but in addition using three girl backing singers to sing nothing else but the hooks or choruses of the songs. I asked Alan Tew, because he was passionate about soul music to work with me on the project. He produced some fabulous arrangements of songs like *'Where did our love go?', 'You can't hurry love,' You've lost that lovin' feelin', 'How sweet it is (to be loved by you)'* etc. The title I gave the album was "Working in the Soul Mine" and a distinctive sleeve depicting three black girls wearing miner's helmets helped it to sell beyond all expectations. It paved the way for further product by The John Schroeder Orchestra which pleased me immensely.

"Dolly Catcher" was my next piece of inspiration. The theme of this album was of course catching dollies, a pastime that I and many of us men thoroughly enjoyed doing. The chase was often better than the kill! The songs which were carefully chosen to fit the project were beautifully and cleverly arranged by John Cameron. *"Softly Softly Catchee Dolly" "But She Ran The Other Way" "I Was Made To Love Her"* etc and *"Explosive Corrosive Joseph"* which was written by John Cameron and featured in the film "Ocean's Twelve" were just some of the songs that enhanced this album.

My favourite John Schroeder album is quite definitely "Witchi Tai To"

The idea I had was to create a musical picture of the moods, atmosphere and feelings aroused by living in the world of today.

... Witchi Tai To ... Witchi Tai To ...

'What a spirit feeling ringing in my head
Makes me feel glad that I'm not dead'

There are some truly amazing musicians on this album, in fact the crème de la crème of British session musicians. David Byron, the lead singer of Uriah Heap actually pleaded with me to let him do the vocals and John Carter and Ken Lewis, ex Ivy League supplied the backing vocals. The arrangements were superbly handled by Lew Warburton and it was masterfully engineered by Alan Florence. Producing this album was magic for me and it became a very worthwhile and rewarding exercise. My sincere thanks to everyone who participated in it.

CHAPTER THIRTEEN

Ronnie Scott, who was a friend and the head honcho at Valley Music, called me during July of 1966. We met and he played me a demo of a group called The Spectres who had recorded *'I (Who Have Nothing)'*, the Shirley Bassey song. It took me completely by surprise because first of all it was an extremely odd choice of song for a group to do and secondly they had done such a different arrangement of it and yet had managed to pull it off in a strangely attractive sort of way.

Having evaluated this *demo* I felt there were things that could be bettered within the group but the overall sound and general picture appealed to me and came across as being really worth pursuing. Having seen them live, they had a 'je ne sais quoi' something that persuaded me to sign them to Piccadilly, much to the group's surprise and Ronnie Scott's delight.

Believe it or not, they had two managers, Pat Barlow and Joe Bunce and a fan club that was set up by Joe's daughter. Joe, who had something to do with waste paper, looked after the finance.

Funny how Bunce was just the right name for the job! Pat was a likeable rough diamond sort of a guy with a heart of gold. He was a plumber by trade and although his time was limited he managed to fix gigs and attend to other things mainly during his lunch break! What was so great about them both was their invincible belief in the group and it's potential. They both gave everything they had in totally dedicating themselves to 'whatever it takes to make *our* group happen'.

I have never signed an Artist that I didn't have implicit belief in that they had the potential to make it, meaning they were capable of having hit records. The first single was always a problem but at that stage there was little to lose and everything to gain.

After careful deliberation I decided *'I (Who Have Nothing)'* was different enough to create some reaction and even warranted some sort of media attention as a first release. This would then pave the way for something stronger.

The first time in the studio with any group was always a thrill as everything was a new challenge. The look of awe on their faces when they met Alan Florence, my engineer for the first time and saw all that fab equipment was a sight for sore eyes. But the biggest kick of all was seeing their expressions as they listened to the first playback through those two huge monitors! They were stunned and speechless. They could not believe what they were hearing. Fucking hell is that really me? Bloody hell is that really us? Us were The Spectres and they were: Francis Rossi – Lead Guitar, Rick Parfitt – Rhythm Guitar, Alan Lancaster – Bass Guitar, Roy Lynes – Keyboards and John Coghlan – Drums.

It would be hard not to forget the day that Pat Barlow came up to my office in his lunch break to discuss the next single since sadly 'I (Who Have Nothing) failed to make it. It was practically impossible to hide the look of surprise and amusement on our faces when he arrived in a dirty old boiler suit with a large spanner sticking out of his back pocket and well beaten up boots on his feet. As the manager of a rock band it all looked a bit incongruous but this man was a gem!

I asked Pat if the group had any original material that would be worth considering. Pat said Alan Lancaster, the bass player was always writing things and there was one song called 'Hurdy Gurdy Man' which was different and catchy. I liked what I heard and decided we should go for it as the next single. It was a good record and should have stood a chance but in spite of a great deal of effort it failed to impress. However, Johnny Wise, the Head of Promotion was just beginning to seriously take notice of this group's potential and that in itself was a big plus.

The dreaded third single was always a nightmare because I knew very well that Pye's policy, like E.M.I.'s, was to drop an Artist who had failed to really sell anything of significance or failed to have made the charts by their third single. Although everyone was aware of the gravity of the situation I dared not to allow it to dampen my implicit belief and enthusiasm that we could do it.

After listening to a hundred and one songs I eventually came across 'We Ain't Got Nothing Yet', which was an American hit for The Blue Magoos. With the right arrangement I believed it had the potential to give us that crucial hit. After all the song had already proved itself. Everyone supported the suggestion, so with plenty of praying we recorded it and it sounded great. We believed the final mix had 'Hit' written all over it!

It was released in February 1967 but amazingly even though the promotion and radio play was by far the best of the entire product released by The Spectres so far, it failed to make it again!

It was a dreadful blow. Disbelief and disappointment was written on everyone's face and I was cursing to myself

"What the fuck does it take to get a bloody hit with this band? I cannot afford to lose them. They're too bloody talented."

I could not understand what was wrong or where I was going wrong. Not only that, I could now see the recording contract being in serious jeopardy. Pat and the group were in another world waiting to hear their fate whilst I was also waiting for the dreaded call from Benjie.

Of course when I was least expecting it the phone rang. My heart raced and I really thought this was *bye bye* Spectres. The call however, was from Madeleine Hawkyard, the Contracts Manager. She said

"John, as you know The Spectres third single has failed and therefore the contract should be terminated but I know how strongly you feel about this Artist so I am not going to remind Benjie. You make another single and if Benjie says anything I will deal with it" Oh what a relief! I could have even kissed her! I was so grateful to Madeleine for that. We could all breathe again.

It was at this time that it was decided to change the name to Traffic to help make a fresh start. This backfired on us because unluckily it was also the name Spencer Davis had chosen for his group so we agreed on Traffic Jam. As for the next single I turned again to the group for original ideas. It was Rossi who came up with *'Almost but not quite there.'* Again it was a unanimous decision to go with it but this time more bad luck was to follow with it being banned by the BBC for its lyrical implication and so *yet again*…it fucking failed! Even Johnny Wise was a lot more than disappointed!

I was now at my wit's end because this time understandably, there would be virtually no chance of Benjie agreeing to yet another single, so I had to find some means of manipulative persuasion. My first move was to stay out of his way and make it impossible for him to contact me. If I saw or heard him coming anywhere near me I would hide in someone else's office. I had to have time to analyse the situation.

It occurred to me that there was an omen in three of the song titles namely *'I or We (Who Have Nothing)' 'We Ain't Got Nothing Yet'* and *'Almost But Not*

Quite There.' I interpreted that to mean the next single would make it, if God or Benjie ever gave me that chance. At present the group had no image or direction but as always I believed a Hit record would establish that.

It was pretty obvious to me that the material we had released so far was not strong enough and perhaps I had deluded myself in believing it was. Johnny Wise was so right when he said we were so near and yet so far but a miss is as good as a mile particularly in this business.

Once again I was looking for that elusive hit song but I still wasn't sure exactly what I was searching for. A music publisher brought my attention to a song called *'Gentleman Joe's Sidewalk Cafe'* written by Kenny Young, who had already had some success as a writer. Like the previous songs it was as good but even so I was convinced that ideally we needed a self penned song. It had to be immediately identifiable, be able to incorporate a catchy guitar riff, was melodically strong and had a rhythm feel that was unavoidably compulsive. Finally there must be no holes in the arrangement so that it held your attention from beginning to end.

I told myself that I was asking for too much but I still believed that where there was a will there was a way. I was after all once more fighting to save the record deal. I had to have the strongest case of all time, well prepared with the prayer of my life before going anywhere near Louis Benjamin. I needed to have *the song* ready to go into the studio immediately to avoid a mass execution. Besides I hadn't made a will and I didn't want a bloody funeral at this time of my career!

I had a heart to heart talk with the Band emphasising that it was really totally in their hands to find the inspiration to come up with something and quickly, that conformed to what I thought was necessary to save the contract.

I had now exhausted every other avenue. I appreciated it was a tall order. I told them my plan was to avoid Louis Benjamin tracking me down for however long it took. They were relieved to hear that but I also emphasised that my arse was on the line!

The situation was made worse for me by the fact that I had other Artists to think about and they were beginning to get fidgety because I seemed to be spending all my time with this group, which I was.

I did not hear a thing for three weeks and then Pat Barlow phoned me sounding very excited. He said Rossi had come up with a really strong guitar riff and an unusual idea. The Band were working on the song really hard and anxiously wanted me to hear it, with any suggestions that I might have.

We arranged to meet in the basement of one of their houses and I remember sitting on an orange box listening to the skeleton of the arrangement of *'Pictures of Matchstick Men'*. I told them I thought it was by far the strongest of anything we had done so far and that it should definitely be completed, with it being hopefully the next single in mind. The guitar riff was sensational and so was the title and lyric. I gave the boys my thoughts on the arrangement. They took it on board and when I heard the song again it was fabulous and I was really very excited, truthfully, for the first time. In addition to this, Pat suggested they changed the name again since Traffic Jam didn't really do it.

They had unanimously agreed on The Status Quo which was apparently derived from Quo Vadis. I agreed it sounded good but above all, it gave me another bargaining point to put to Louis Benjamin.

All I had to do now was to find a way to get round Benjie. I couldn't ask Madeleine again so my plan was to catch Benjie when he was at his most vulnerable which was when he was with Les Cocks every evening discussing the day's business and the night's pleasure. I chose the evening carefully and knocked on his office door. They were surprised but I was greeted amicably and asked to sit down. I thought to myself, in for a penny in for a pound. Looking at them both in turn I said quite emphatically

"I want you to agree to allow me to do one more single with The Spectres.

I have a fantastic song which they have written, rehearsed and ready to go.

There is a message in the titles of three of the previous songs which forecast that the next single will make it" Benjie responded quite firmly

"John, you have already breached the terms of the contract with the last single which I agreed and allowed you to make with Madeleine's blessing. That was the fourth single. Now you want a fifth. Let me tell you that even if we had a number one record with this group we would not recoup our losses on the previous four singles." I answered just as firmly

"I disagree, especially if by some freak chance it sold a million records with albums to follow. Not only that, but this time we want to change the name of the group to The Status Quo, so it would be as if they were a new Artist with their first record. And if we did drop them now, supposing they got a deal with another record company and recorded this song and it was a huge hit. What then? It would be rather embarrassing wouldn't it?"

Les Cocks had said nothing but had missed nothing either. He said to Benjie with a smile that I read as – "we should back off on this one Benjie."

"I know the company's policy well, but we must support our producers, especially with a case and belief in an Artist as strong as this one. John has more than proved himself with the product he has so far made for us"

I could see Benjie was relenting and with a sort of half threatening smile he said.

"O.K John I'll agree, but if this attempt fails there will be categorically no more" After I had thanked them both and shut the door behind me I thought to myself, "Les you're a gem."

Pictures of Matchstick Men

At last we had a song that I believed was right from every point of view. Rossi, thank God, had been blessed with some amazing inspiration. The group had taken on board everything I had said, in particular the fact that the song had to register in the first eight bars. The opening guitar riff was sensational.

The sessions went really well and Alan Florence and I had between us excelled ourselves in producing a fantastic mix. I must give Alan due credit as it was his idea to phase the lead guitar on the opening riff. The song registered as soon as the needle hit the deck. I was very sure we had a hit record on our hands and I felt inwardly proud and excited when it came round to me at the A&R meeting. I remained cool and calm showing little emotion during the playback of The Status Quo's first single. Benjie was really taken aback and looking at Les Cocks, and smiling begrudgingly, said "well now maybe at last we'll get some of our money back on this Artist". I declined to rise to Benjie's rather uncalled for remarks. Johnny Wise gave me A.1 support with promotion,and the single charted at number 7 on the 24th of January 1968.

Smiles at last!
Pictures of "Matchstick Men" charted practically all over the world, including America. The group even went there on a promotional tour. A well deserved Silver Disc Award.

The dreaded nightmare of a follow up was with us again. Should it be something similar or totally different? We went for a song that Rossi wrote called *'Black Veils of Melancholy'*. Wrong move, of course it failed because it was too similar to Matchstick. The gamble didn't pay off so it was in a way a major step backwards. It was Ronnie Scott who came to the rescue, bringing my attention to a song that he and Marty Wilde had written called *'Ice in the Sun'*. I liked it a lot and to my mind it had strong hit potential. I was proved right and on the 21st of August 1968 it went to number 8 in the charts.

Although we had now more than just tasted the charts and even the American Top 100 we still had not managed to establish any musical direction or image for the Band whatsoever and this was frustrating. Although no one made a real issue of it, the worry was there and I felt it.

I always looked forward to The Status Quo sessions. We had a lot of fun even though the sequence of events was sometimes unpredictable. I shall not forget walking into the studio control room one evening and was greeted with Rossi and Rick mooning over the console! What a horrible sight! However, I cannot recollect ever having had a disagreement of any kind. They always took their rehearsals seriously. They worked hard in the studio and they took direction well. I had to admire them for sustaining all they had been through. After a time they even got the courage to take the piss out of me and decided to nickname me 'Mumbles' because that apparently was what I did, although I was never aware of it and no one else had ever remarked on it! Perhaps I should take it as a compliment.

The biggest problem for Alan Florence and I was always Rossi's rather weak voice. Even though he was inwardly shitting himself every time it came to doing the vocals he never faltered once and always gave it his best. I really respected him for that. Because the voice was practically inaudible against the power of the backing we had to double track it every time on a mix. Without realising it we had created a really identifiable vocal sound which ultimately became the audio trade mark of The Status Quo. You just could not mistake it so it became a major plus in the band's future.

Strange though it may seem I was particularly impressed with Rick Parfitt's voice so much so that it inspired Tony King and I to write a song specifically for him. That song was *'Are You Growing Tired of My Love?'* Also as from this release the decision was made to drop the 'The' in the Artist name.

On the 28th of May Status Quo with Ricky Parfitt as the lead singer made the charts at number 46 and then re-entered the charts at number 50 on the 18th of June 1969. The song was ultimately also recorded by Jefferson and Nancy Sinatra.

A nice change of address

I had never noticed it was there because I had no reason to go to that side of Edgware Road except to the Lotus House, a very good Chinese restaurant which was right opposite Forset Court and which I and many others in the business frequented a great deal.

The Water Gardens and The Quadrangle, two very salubrious apartment blocks were situated next to each other behind The Lotus House and over looking Sussex Gardens. Being a lover of good taste, nice jewellery, nice cars and especially nice women, I was advised to check out The Quadrangle as there was an apartment that had suddenly become vacant. It was in fact Marilyn Davis, Robert Wace's P.A who had heard about it.

As soon as I saw it I was in love but the rent – that was not such a lovable proposition! However, as there were others waiting anxiously in the wings, my heart got the better of me and I found it impossible to avoid becoming the new proud resident of Number 12 The Quadrangle.

The majestic Quadrangle Towers faced my front entrance and I discovered none other than Barry Mason (See Tommy Bruce) residing there which was a very pleasant surprise.

I was a little concerned about having to tell Tony King as he might be upset and possibly a little jealous. Being Tony he was neither, and in fact he was very pleased for me and agreed it wouldn't in any way affect our writing since I would only be a five minute walk away from Forset Court.

Number 12 was a large two bedroomed apartment with a very long hallway leading to the rooms which comprised of a large and beautiful lounge with a balcony situated to the right off the hallway. The enormous master bedroom and second bedroom which was big enough for me to turn into an office were to the left. Since it was to be my home for some time to come I thought I might as well go all the way, so virtually with no expense spared I had the whole place fitted out with a thick pale orange *shag* pile carpet and some really expensive pale green Japanese grass wall paper. I also had fitted furniture in rosewood everywhere and two Country and Western type swing doors going into the lounge from the hall. I searched and found a lovely olde worlde king size bed and I persuaded a very reluctant David Garrick to part with a gorgeous sexy black and white pony skin rug for it. In fact it was three pony skins very cleverly stitched together. How could he refuse a personal request from his record producer! Even so I daren't think what David might have got up to with or even on it! Needless to say if luck prevailed I fully intended to carry on where he had left off!

I settled in there quite comfortably thank you, and what it did for my personal recreational activities is not printable! I really felt I had considerably moved up in the world.

CHAPTER FOURTEEN

Whilst I was physically doing all this moving and negotiating, my mind never for one minute wandered from the recording needs of every one of my family of Artists. They all had their own little boxes in my head and their careers were my responsibility and were of paramount importance to me. Sue was fantastic and was extremely capable of looking after the office, the appointments and prospective sessions etc keeping me informed throughout the day.

The stress of both the office and studio morning noon and night was beginning to tell. I felt so burnt out that any chance to get away from it, even for an hour or so was a godsend. My personal life seemed to have gone up a gear and I just could not resist the greater demands on my physical capabilities. I was also being inveigled into playing squash every day with someone or other in the music business which in turn often produced something musically lucrative other than just a good game of squash. All in all you could say I was burning the candle at both ends! I hadn't actually had a proper break or holiday as such for years.

I think Marilyn from Robert Wace's office had suspected my predicament and suggested it might do me the world of good to accompany her to deliver some Kinks records to a studio in Borehamwood. Sue practically made me go and I found the Devonshire cream tea in an olde worlde café in Borehamwood to be thoroughly enjoyable. I had forgotten what it was like to do and see something else other than the inside of a recording studio!

Marilyn told me a little about herself, in that her mother had died when she was very young and she had the task of looking after her father ever since, but as he was a bit of a gambler and loved the ladies, he used to give her money to keep her quiet, and as such told her to go and play with the traffic. I thought that was very sad but then she said she loved working for Robert Wace and having her time fully occupied taking care of the outrageous activities of the Kinks and David Garrick.

She seemed to be particularly fascinated by my song writing activities with Mike Hawker, Tony King and others and was surprised to learn that sometime ago more as a joke than anything else I had said I would love to write a musical. I had in fact already written some songs for it and even had a skeleton of a story line and a tentative title, namely 'Cinderella Smith.'

We got onto the subject of hobbies and I told her that music, cars, jewellery, clothes, aeroplanes and women were about my lot and of course The Quadrangle. She then suggested that as we were very near it we might as well have a quick look at Elstree Aerodrome before going back. This was a bad idea because once there and seeing and watching all those lovely little aircraft landing and taking off, my adrenalin started to flow and I was wishing how I would love to learn to fly. I just could not leave without finding out the cost and basic details. It was of course pretty expensive and time consuming but they reckoned on an average most pupils achieved a pilot's licence after ten lessons. I found it particularly interesting to notice that the car park had either very expensive motor cars in it or really tatty old bangers. There was nothing in between which would indicate that only those with money could really afford to fly but the remainder wanted to so badly that they sank every penny in to it and it was visibly crippling them financially!

Elstree and everything else about it was soon forgotten as we drove back to London and got ourselves mentally back into music mode again. I thanked Marilyn for the time out which was unexpected, thoroughly enjoyable and much needed.

Three Chord Genius

Francis Rossi, commenting on Quo's up and down track record, made a rather poignant remark, "direction wasn't as important as having a hit record – *any* hit record"

He was right to an extent because that was still the way the industry was geared. Without the continuity of Hit records there was no real future, although that was gradually changing. Image, longevity and musical direction were slowly becoming an important entity. It had become my goal to try to establish these things from the success of the material that was recorded. Status Quo had never blamed me in any way for the frustrating hit and miss situation we were experiencing. We had always unanimously agreed to record the material we did but the time had now come where they felt they had to deliberately instigate a positive image and musical direction. Understandably they were really as pissed off with the present situation as I was, and it was affecting their live gigs with them not knowing who or what they were trying to portray. They decided that jeans, tee shirts and Beatle boots were the way to go with a musical direction being much harder and much more exciting visually. They decided they really wanted to get into some serious rock 'n' roll. The hit records would hopefully come again in time but for now the live gigs were all that mattered. *'Pictures of Matchstick Men'* had already proved they were able to write a hit song and some of their self penned material was amazingly good.

They had obviously worked their butts off because the first time I saw them live, exploiting their new image to the full was a truly mind blowing experience. They were very much a different band to the one I had originally signed but a great deal of the self penned material we had produced on record was sensibly retained. The Spectres? Who were *they*?

A positive direction at last
©*Robert Ellis*

They wowed audiences wherever they played. They were loved because it was heads down and rocking all the way for nearly a couple of hours. The more gigs they did the better they became. They were so tight with such energy and telepathy on stage that I almost felt I had played a game of squash just watching them. Although sadly they had to suffer being ridiculed as a three-chord band there was no one in the world to touch them with what they did with three chords, and all that was just jealousy. Excitement was not the right word. It was far stronger than that!

We still needed the hit single, more so perhaps now than ever before to put the official public stamp of approval on the new image and direction.

Ronnie Scott was a genius in how he had managed to continually present me with really strong material that always seemed right for this band. There was no other publisher who knew an Artist so well. Mind you he did bring them to me in the first place but I bet he never envisaged anything like they were now. When he saw them, he couldn't believe it but he must have felt proud in having contributed to this success.

Ronnie played me a demo of a song called *'Down the Dustpipe.'* It was written by Carl Grossman, an Australian and we unanimously agreed that it was strong and had hit potential. We also agreed that it would be great to do live since it conformed to the new image.

It was strange having no more dramatics to deal with from Benjie and that I was able to go ahead and record *'Down the Dustpipe.'* without having to beg to do it. We had a lot of fun recording it because it was such an uplifting song and you really could not help dancing to it, the Quo way of course! It received a lot of airplay, but Tony Blackburn dismissed it on his Radio One show with the comment: 'well it's down the dustbin for this one.' I am really glad he was proved to be very wrong because on the 2nd May 1970 it made it to number 12 in the National Chart.

Three albums and many gruelling hours in the studio had been released so far but it was the fourth album entitled *'Dog of Two Head'* that I was really proud of. There was much more time and thought put into this album and Status Quo had matured considerably. The songs, being more in the direction that the band was now aiming for were so much stronger with all except one being self penned. Eventually the sales emerged as being surprisingly good with the album being classified as a cult album.

During this period I had the uneasy feeling that trouble was brewing. Colin Johnson had taken over management of the band and strongly believed that Pye Records were no longer the right record company for them to be with now that Status Quo had moved into heavy rock with a whole new image. According to him, Pye did not know how to promote this type of product. The band unfortunately supported this evaluation one hundred per cent which led them to deliberately breaking Pye's recording contract and signing a record deal with Vertigo. I couldn't believe they had done this, and rather cowardly behind everyone's back. Benjie, rightly, was not about to tolerate this and subsequently issued a writ with a court case pending. Finally the whole matter was settled out of court and Status Quo went on to have incredible success spanning more than twenty five years. Sadly for me I could not continue producing them because of my own contractual position with Pye Records. I had produced them for five years and I was considerably upset.

On reading Francis Rossi's and Rick Parfitt's autobiography of Status Quo I was angry and saddened to come across the following statement.

"John Schroeder, the producer at Pye, was a lovely guy, but he wasn't into hard rock. He was Medallion Man: the barnet was permed, he was beautifully pressed, he had high-heeled Beatle boots and a chain around his neck – everything was perfect. So he wasn't going to be right for us when we got into our jeans and T-shirts."

What a load of crap! What you look like doesn't dictate what you feel for God's sake! I was extremely hurt at this very personal remark.

I have successfully produced Classical music, Pop music, Orchestral music, Soul and R & B and there was no earthly reason at all why I could not have successfully produced hard rock especially having brought Status Quo this far over such a long period of time. We had as such, matured and grown up together.

I had given five years of my body and soul to this Band and very nearly lost my job at Pye Records more than once on their behalf. I have fought tooth and nail for their survival. Although proud of their achievement I feel justified in saying they might well not have made it without my patience and belief during those early years.

I hate the feeling of getting older and so I would much rather forget to remember January the 19th of any year including 1969.

Marilyn had made a point of not forgetting, and insisted on taking me out to dinner. She made it difficult to refuse. It was a good meal in a nice restaurant and over coffee she presented me with an envelope which she instructed me to open. I did this and to my surprise and joy she had presented me with a course of ten flying lessons at Elstree with The London School of Flying. I was lost for words and really didn't know how to thank her. She said it would not only give me a chance to get away from the office but also make a dream a reality.

Whilst driving and approaching Elstree for my first lesson I suddenly became choked up with a mixture of fear and excitement and at one point it even crossed my mind to turn around and cancel the whole thing.

I was apparently fortunate to have Captain Peter Conway as my instructor. He was very affable, in his forties and known to be very patient. From the start we got on really well, especially as he was fascinated by my show biz stories. My aircraft was a Piper Cherokee 140 registered 'Golf Alpha Tango Tango Hotel'. On walking round the aircraft Peter explained the outside checks that had to be carried out before every flight. Inside the cockpit it was a very different story with dials, numbers, switches, levers and the rest. Like everybody, I fell into the trap of trying to steer the aircraft on the runway thinking the joystick was a steering wheel as on a car and of course this did nothing because the joystick controlled the ailerons which controlled a left or right movement in the air and nose up or down in the air. The rudder which is operated by your feet controlled the direction of the aircraft on the ground and in the air. Your feet also operated the brakes.

Peter Conway was very thorough, but on the fifth lesson I had a bad day and he had me almost in tears with frustration. I really wanted to give up, thinking I would never understand all the bloody instruments or the bloody mathematics attached to map reading and such like. Peter had no sympathy and showed no mercy, subsequently giving me a relentless crash course on take off and landings, circuit procedures, emergency landings, engine failures on take off, map reading and compass headings etc. etc. We went through everything time and time again.

The dreaded tenth lesson had come and gone and I was now wondering when Peter was going to make me say my prayers by sending me up there on my own. By lesson twelve I had given up worrying about it but on the thirteenth lesson after we had landed Peter suddenly jumped out and said "Off you go. You're on your own. I want a perfect take off and a perfect landing. Good luck. You can do it."

Before I realised it, I was taxiing down the run way and in seconds was climbing to a thousand feet. Now I was really shitting myself wondering how the hell I was going to get the bloody aircraft down without fucking it up. Landing is much more difficult than taking off. Soon, with the runway in sight I had about a mile to go. I called the Tower "Golf Alpha Tango Tango Hotel – Finals" The tower replied "Roger. Golf Alpha Tango Tango Hotel. You are cleared to land." I had about three quarters of a mile to the runway and I had a massive amount of trees beckoning me to come down and have lunch with them! I cut the throttle to halfway and applied the first stage of flap then the second. Now I had about a half a mile to run and my height was five hundred feet. I applied the third stage of flap and holding the nose slightly high I skimmed across the trees swearing to myself as I did it. I closed the throttle completely and still holding the nose gently high and holding my breath and everything else as well, allowed the aircraft to sink and make a gentle bump as the wheels made contact with the runway. With the speed decreasing and letting go the pressure on the stick I applied the brakes and taxied slowly to the parking area. I was shaking and sweating profusely. Peter was waiting for me and coming over to the aircraft, congratulated me. He was genuinely pleased because with every new pass his credibility moved up and so did his salary. Now that I was safely back on terra firma it was an incredible relief but also an incredible high. I was shaking. I had actually been up there all on my own and got down. I had actually successfully completed my first solo flight and I had a certificate to prove it. I relived it God knows how many times! I received my official pilots licence not long after. I felt pretty pleased with myself as I was now permitted to fly anywhere providing it was VFR only (Visual Flight Rules) and with three additional passengers if they dared to risk it!

Surprisingly, I discovered the Music Industry was quite well represented at Elstree with Peter Sullivan, Wally Ridley's assistant at EMI, George Martin himself and Alan Florence my engineer at Pye all having flying lessons at the same time but somehow I had never seen any of them. Alan had never said a word. I wondered why.

My flying days unfortunately came to an abrupt end some years later when the cost of flying became completely unrealistic. When I first got my licence, hiring a plane was nine pounds an hour. Within six years this had risen to ninety pounds an hour!

Happily, by the time this came about I had notched up 500 hours of solo flying which included trips to Gatwick, Biggin Hill, Southend, Hatfield, Shoreham, Leavesden, Stapleford Tawney, Redhill, Lydd and even Le Touquet in France. Restricted to a height of 1500 feet The Channel was awesome but also frightening, eerie and rather lonely. Landing at Le Touquet was a relief but the reality of what I had done was amazing.

I have many memories both good and bad of my flying days but the following three are definitely at the top of the list.

I discovered having a Private Pilot's Licence gave me a particularly powerful 'dolly catching' string to my bow – and I made full use of it!

I needed no persuasion to take the lovely Gloria (remember my Marcos days) and her sister and a girl friend of her sister up for a short spin which to them was to be a first and undoubtedly a thrill of a lifetime. However, Gloria knew what it was all about because I had had the pleasure of her *flying high* with me on a couple of previous occasions.

It was a shitty day and it was touch and go whether we would be allowed to take off. But there was a moment when the fog lifted and five aircraft me being the last, were cleared but only providing we stayed within the circuit.

I was just turning on to finals having been up for fifteen minutes when the fog suddenly came down right to the ground with no warning whatsoever. I could not see the runway. I could not see anything at all. Shitting myself were not strong enough words to describe my fear and panic. I heard Peter's agitated voice in my head "Climb! Climb! Climb!" I reacted instantly but it was 3000 feet before I broke through the fog into bright sunshine! Peter's voice was there again "Put the aircraft into a steady 360 degree turn and maintain constant height. Use the radio". I called Elstree's Air Traffic Controller who said I was the only aircraft not to make it back (that was a very consoling thought. I don't think!) Had I any idea of my position and height? I said I had no idea but I must be somewhere in Elstree's control zone. My height was 3000 ft and I was holding a 360 degree turn. He came back and asked me what my fuel situation was. Sudden panic gripped me as I had forgotten all about fuel but once again the ever meticulous Peter had instilled into me to re-fuel the aircraft before every single flight and as a matter of habit I had done so without even realising it. Little or no fuel would almost certainly have been game over!

The Controller who, to make matters worse sounded even more stressed than I was said that as they had no radar facility he would call Stansted and see if they could pick me up on their radar. Sweat was pouring off me as I endeavoured to maintain the 360 degree turn and 3000 feet. I looked at Gloria. She was white as a sheet with hands and face soaking wet and eye liner running down her face. I turned to look at the girls in the back. One was knitting for fuck's sake! And both acknowledged how much they were enjoying it. Thank God they were apparently totally oblivious as to what was actually going on and it was lucky for me that they were at this moment. The radio had been silent for five minutes and it seemed like an eternity. I was becoming completely mesmerised by the fog which had the appearance of a thick undulating blanket with hundreds of hands and fingers trying to pull me into it. I desperately tried to fight it but finally I could resist no longer and I let go of everything.

I thoughtlessly pulled the throttle back which put the engine into idle losing all power. The right wing dipped sending the aircraft into a spin. I felt I was going to die and everything became so calm with just the sound of the wind. My eyes closed and I really did see sheep jumping over hedges in the meadow. Gloria was screaming at the top of her voice and the radio was going berserk both of which suddenly pulled me out of the momentary 'coma'. Being a right handed spin I slammed as hard as I could on the left rudder, pushed the throttle in and prayed. Eventually she righted herself and I climbed and climbed until we came into bright sunshine again with the expanse of beckoning fog marginally below us. We had lost 1000ft and I thanked God for my being at 3000ft because if it had been 2000 or 1000 we would almost certainly not have made it. It was Stansted Air Traffic Control who had been trying to get me to confirm the aircraft ID number, my height and present heading. They confirmed they had me on radar and gave me a new heading and requesting me to maintain a height of 1000ft. They said after fifteen minutes I should be able to see the runway as the fog luckily had dispersed over the airfield. I had to now deliberately lose 2000ft and at the same time maintain the given heading. This was a frightening experience having to fly blind in fog and being totally reliant on instruments. It required incredible concentration, especially as I did not have an instrument rating. At this moment the Air Traffic Controller was my best and only friend!

Suddenly the fog dispersed and the relief of seeing Stansted's main runway was indescribable. I confirmed I had the runway in sight and the Controller granted me a straight in approach having put all in coming traffic on hold until I was safely down. He talked me down to five hundred feet and I heard him warning another aircraft about to take off obviously on an alternative runway to look out for a Cherokee 140. Suddenly from nowhere this huge jet appeared and I swear to God I practically saw the colour of the pilot's eyes. Some of the passengers must have had the shock of their lives. Fucking shit I said to myself – that was a bit too close for comfort!

Although I had never sweated or shaken so much in my life whilst swearing my head off and gritting my teeth all at the same time, I somehow managed to land safely but quite definitely on a wing and a prayer. Gloria was a complete wreck and the two in the back although by this time somewhat unnerved, were saying how exciting it had all been! I don't think they realised how near they were from this world to the next. I was immediately ordered to report to the Air Traffic Controller and to apologise to him personally for fucking up Stansted's air traffic. Having reduced my self-esteem to half its normal size, the Controller finally allowed me to get away with it only because I had officially been given clearance for the take off. Someone at Elstree was in for a right old bollocking!

I was told to leave the aircraft at Stansted which left me with no other alternative than to get a taxi back to Elstree. I practically had another heart attack when I caught sight of the meter on our arrival. The girls, bless them, were happy to split the fare with me. When I finally walked into the flight office two and a half hours later I got a loud cheer and hand clap from all those that had previously got down safely and stayed behind to await my hopeful return. I was told in no uncertain terms how much anxiety, sufferance and worry I had put everybody through, especially the Air Traffic Controller. They indicated drinks all round would be the least I could do in gratitude for everyone's personal concern. Words totally failed me, made worse by the fact that as I had three females with me I could not answer back with language that probably would have banned me from flying forever!

The next day Captain Conway could not resist telling everyone that it was he who had saved the day. "*My* student nearly got killed and deserved a bloody medal for what he did but I had given him some sound Conway advice and without it he and his *female friends* would never have fucking made it – and that's a fact!" To quote him – he was fucking well right but did I detect a touch of jealousy?!

I wanted to conclude a music deal with a Management Company to sign a particular Artist that I felt exceptionally strongly about.

The business executive desperately wanted to feel what it was like to fly in a small aircraft since I had been excitedly talking to him about it in some detail.

We arranged the day and we were cleared for take off but at nine hundred feet the aircraft flatly refused to climb. I tried everything but she would not go up. There was no power coming from the engine. This was my biggest fear of all because engine failure on take off can so very easily be fatal. Panic seizes you and your natural instinct is to turn the aircraft towards the runway to get it down no matter what as quickly as possible. This is a fatal move because the aircraft will more than likely drop a wing and spin into the ground with no chance of recovery. Peter was with me again and although I didn't show it I felt I was about to have a fucking heart attack! Strangely my passenger seemed quite calm about the whole thing and showed no visible signs of concern. To make things worse fire engines and ambulances were lined up waiting for me. I landed safely and was embarrassed for my passenger as it was not a very good introduction to a first flight in a small aircraft. He looked a little off colour but with a smile he shook my hand and unexpectedly said "Well done". We subsequently concluded the music deal. I said I owed him one! We did fly again together and without any dramatics thank God!

Don, an Australian was a very good friend of mine. He held a powerful position being the Licensing Manager for a major record licensing company. He was ultra charming and had a lot of likeable natural charisma. Like me he loved female company and one day out of desperation he had the nerve to ask me for the loan of my flat for a couple of hours. I had to admire his cheek and why I agreed I don't really know. Not only that, this happened more than once and I even used to leave a bottle of wine in the fridge for *his and her* pleasure. Annoyingly there were the occasions when I had to wait before being able to get into my own flat because *he and she* had not completed *their* nocturnal gymnastics!

He had come flying with me on one or two previous occasions but he always had the annoying habit of sitting in one of the rear seats and falling asleep! I asked him many times why he did this, particularly as by doing so he was missing everything that was going on. He said it was the constant drone of the engine and the motion of the aircraft that made him do it but it did not in any way spoil his enjoyment of flying. I thought to myself with a touch of envy "More like the bloody nights he spent in my flat doing his own type of flying"

One day I decided to be decidedly wicked. I was up there enjoying myself at fifteen hundred feet and Don was fast asleep in the back as usual. The engine was giving out a monotonous drone which was quite loud as the revs were high. At about twelve hundred feet I viciously pulled back the throttle which immediately cut the engine and caused the plane to rapidly lose height.

Suddenly from the back seat "What the fuck! We're going down. We're going to bloody well crash! I'm too young to die. John for God's sake do something!" I didn't answer for some time to prolong the agony, keeping a close watch on our height. After a while I answered quite calmly

"Say your prayers Donny. I hope you've made a will!" He was beside himself with terror and I waited till we hit 500 feet then firmly closed the throttle. The engine responded immediately and we climbed back up to fifteen hundred feet again. I said with a hint of sarcasm

"We've been lucky I've managed to fix the problem. Now you can go back to sleep again" There was no answer. He looked like he had died and gone to heaven or was it hell?

He never really forgave me for that but we did go flying again and I ordered him to sit in the front seat and threatened that if he fell asleep again it might be too late and then there'd be no more nightly naughties in my flat!

That found the spot and that was definitely one up to me!

During the entirety of my career so far I can truthfully say I have never knowingly had anything derogatory said about me professionally or otherwise, in fact I have had many fantastic reviews and write ups. However, there was always the one! The article in question contained some disdainful comments by Paul Ryan, admittedly a good song writer who had written one or two hits such as *'Eloise'* for his brother Barry Ryan.

After the Rockin' Berries were no more I signed the lead singer Geoff Turton as a solo Artist and named him Jefferson which sounded a good name at the time. I personally loved Geoff's voice as it was immediately identifiable and he always managed to impart great feeling in whatever he was singing. *He's in town'* and *'Poor Man's son.'* proved that without any shadow of doubt.

Jefferson's first single entitled' *Baby Take Me in your Arms'* written by Tony Macaulay didn't for some unknown reason chart here but became a huge hit in America. The follow up entitled '*Colour of my love'* was written by Paul Ryan who happened to be flavour of the month for some reason or other! Everyone is entitled to their opinion. I gave him and Jefferson a hit record and I think the following remarks were unjust and personally insulting.

MY SONG WAS RUINED

THE FACT that Jefferson has a hit with 'Colour Of My Love' Isn't giving its composer Paul Ryan, as much joy as you'd imagine. He doesn't like the record even though it's given him his third hit in three months and established his name as a songwriter.

Paul Ryan says "Quite honestly, I think it's a load of rubbish. The production is terrible. Jefferson's a nice bloke, but it's very upsetting to hear what someone has done to your song. It's like someone framing a picture you're proud of in a tatty frame." (Disc & Music Echo May 24 1969)

On the other hand:

BILLY J. KRAMER – JEFFERSON

The Colour of My Love – Two versions of a very very good song by Paul Ryan and certainly one is destined to be a hit. I'd put my money (if I had any) on Jefferson. I feel they've been helped by an excellent production with the strings lifting at exactly the right moment and a very good lead singer who puts a lot of effort in all the right places. (NME)

Comment: *Having written many hit songs myself, quite frankly I would have been grateful for any recording of any of my songs, even more so by an Artist who had actually made the charts with it. As for the comment on production I have no words to say!*

Jefferson *'Colour of My Love' charted on April 9th 1969 at number 22.*

The Music Industry was certainly changing and quickly. The world of independence was making itself felt and was finding success in a number of different ways. I believe that Joe Meek (*Telstar*) was the innovator of independent production. He would license finished product which he had made and owned to various record companies and this happened as far back as the early sixties. The major record company would pay for the pressing, marketing, promotion and distribution of the product. When I was at Oriole Records he offered me an Artist called the Dowlands. They were two talented youngsters who had recorded The Beatles song *'All My Loving'* and of course the record was too good not to license the track from him.

Joe Meek – An acclaimed genius   *The Dowlands*

Joe Meek was an amazing talent himself, somewhat eccentric but never afraid to experiment with anything that made a sound – pots, pans, spoons and even a boiling kettle! He maintained, and rightly so, that independence was the only way to go even though it ultimately might spell financial disaster. At this stage of my career, much as I had thought about it, I was neither prepared to nor could I afford to take on such a heavy financial risk and so I stayed behind the secure walls of Pye Records. In retrospect I did have the track record so maybe I should have joined the likes of Mickie Most and Rak Records but I was truthfully too scared to do it.

Pye Records continued to support me and the product I made but a changing industry was making it harder and harder to get into those bloody charts. There were now as many as one hundred and fifty new singles released nationally every single week. Unless you managed to get on the BBC Radio One play list you were half dead before you started.

The biggest change of all was in the album market because Artists were at last being signed for their talent and expertise in a specific area of music.

Pye's policy had always been to make a quick turn over so Benjie, as astute as ever, formed two budget album labels namely Golden Guinea and Marble Arch. Both were to do extremely well. There was also another musical direction emerging which was labelled with names such as Underground, Progressive even Psychedelic and worse still Flower Power. As with all musical directions there were some very talented Artists that were to emerge from it. Keeping up with what was currently happening and not to be left out Benjie formed a label called **Dawn** to specifically accommodate these new trends.

CHAPTER FIFTEEN

My Artists

The Bystanders were an amazingly talented vocal harmony group. We were so close to having a hit record that it totally beats me how our recordings of songs like *'When Jezamine Goes'*, *'Royal Summer Sunshine Day'* and *'Pattern People'* were so near and yet so far from those infuriating charts. However, we did manage to achieve a minor hit with *'98.6'* a cover of an American song written by Andy Kim. After the failure of so many single records, like Status Quo a change of name, image and music direction was instituted. Jeans and long hair were of course the order of the day. The forthcoming material was totally self penned and much heavier musically speaking but the excellent lyrics always seemed to paint a picture. **Man**, as the group were now called, came up with an album concept that was different and clever but it needed to be clearly defined and imaginatively recorded. It was titled **'Revelation'**, the idea being the story of the birth and development of man through the caring of woman to his future in space.

Whilst recording this rather ambitious project we came to the subject of 'erotica' which to emulate properly, I needed the appropriate but genuine sounds. This track was to cause a huge furore throughout the industry culminating in it, and the entire album being banned by certain presenters such as Alan Freeman and Pete Murray who were acting on behalf of the BBC. However, the talented and ever perceptive John Peel loved the Band and the album and understood perfectly why this track had to be included. I can honestly say it was not there to create sensationalism as it was a necessary part of the story. Because it was taken out of context it created a great deal of publicity both good and bad. We had no objection to that!

There have been lots of rumours around as to how and where Erotica was recorded. One of them suggested it all took place in the solitude of a hotel bedroom but I can assure you that is not the truth.

Man and I had been working in Studio One all afternoon completing a further two tracks for the 'Revelation' album. By 7.00pm we had completed the backing track of Erotica and all we needed was the female voice making the appropriate noises which I insisted had to be genuine for the sake of mankind! The group were hopeless. They could not come up with any ideas, so we had a break to discuss the problem. After a while I said

"I will have a girl here by 11.00pm tonight" and they said unanimously

"There's no way you'll do that so we'll bet you an Indian meal and a drink for every one of us after the session tonight"

"And if I do?" I answered

"Then we'll buy you five meals and as much as you can drink"

After the break we rehearsed and recorded the backing track for the next song. The clock showed two minutes to eleven. There was complete silence in the studio. Eleven o'clock came and went. By eleven fifteen the group were feeling very happy with the thought of free food and drink and laughingly pointed a finger at me as if to say "We told you so."

I didn't show it but I did feel a little gutted since we had agreed a session fee and the young lady in question knew what I wanted. We had almost forgotten all about it when at exactly 11.20pm the door of the studio slowly opened and Anya gingerly and apologetically crept into the room looking very much the worse for wear. She told me she had been getting herself prepared!

The group were in the studio and when they saw her they were *absolutely* frozen in disbelief. I had moved up at least five hundred places in their estimation. But the really amazing thing about all this was that Anya knew Mickey Jones, the lead guitarist apparently *rather* well. This was to make things a lot easier.

Alan Florence and I fixed up some screens to create privacy (we would have preferred a public show!), gave them two comfortable chairs and a table. Alan set up a single mike for Anya and we gave them some appropriate liquid! I told them to relax and take their time. If there was a problem, to shout and I emphasised I wanted no sounds of any kind from Mickey. When I left them they looked like they were up for it and Mickey looked like the cat that had got the cream! We dimmed the studio lights and just waited. We ran the *Erotica* backing track and the sensuality of it obviously helped. We kept running the track and in a short while Anya impressed us all in more ways than one, and Mickey? We didn't hear a thing! How did he manage that! He wouldn't say but his face looked flushed and his eyes were unusually bright. However, there was no positive proof whatsoever that anything had happened but on listening to Anya's excellent performance it all sounded pretty genuine, if it wasn't she was a bloody good actress!

'*Sudden Life*' featured on the album, was released as a single, and received some excellent reviews with particular credit going to the production which I was *very* pleased about. But '*Erotica*' was released as a single in Sweden and made the top twenty there. At least the Swedes appreciated the artistry and creative genius that warranted this track being released as a single!

It took some time, but 'Revelation' did become a financial success which Benjie was surprised and thrilled about although he did deliberately say to Les Cocks at an A&R meeting with a smirk on his face and not daring to look at me

"I always thought recording studios were used for recording not shagging"

Les, smiling and quick off the mark answered "That's right Benjie. John *was* recording but recording shagging". Benjie had no answer!

There had to be a follow up album and there was, but this time each individual track depicted its own story, for example the first track entitled '*Prelude*' – '*The Storm*' distinctively paints a wonderful musical picture of a storm depicting gentleness that turns to anger and then returns to calm.

'2 ozs of plastic with a hole in the middle' became the title of the album primarily because no one could think of a better one and secondly because – well that was exactly what it was.

John Kongos

Due to Pye Records' distribution deal with Teal Records in South Africa I was asked during the Swinging London summer of 1966 if I would be interested in considering the talents of John Kongos who had already enjoyed some success in South Africa. I was impressed enough to produce and release a spate of singles on the Piccadilly label using no less then three different pseudonyms namely John T. Kongos, Floribunda Rose and Scrugg. The idea was to try to cash in on the ever changing musical moods of the current pop scene i.e. psychedelic pop, flower power (everyone was in love with everyone!) and progressive rock. Unfortunately, in spite of some great effort none of this came to fruition. Following this, John Kongos became a sort of John Lennon look-a-like and started writing songs with obscure and strangely deep meanings. He approached me with the idea for an album entitled 'Confusions of a Goldfish.' This appealed to me because the material contained influences of Dylan, Elton John and even David Bowie. This album actually became Dawn's inaugural album release.

John Kongos and I had a long professional partnership but it was annoyingly marred by success continually eluding us. I had great respect for his talent and was pleased to see that eighteen months after we had parted John Kongos had managed to achieve some of the success he justifiably deserved.

Quiet World – The Road

I have to admit in hindsight this album project was a mistake and maybe too ambitious. The initial concept created by three talented brothers was really too similar to Man's Revelation. The subject dealt with the feelings of an unborn child and the world it was going to have to endure.

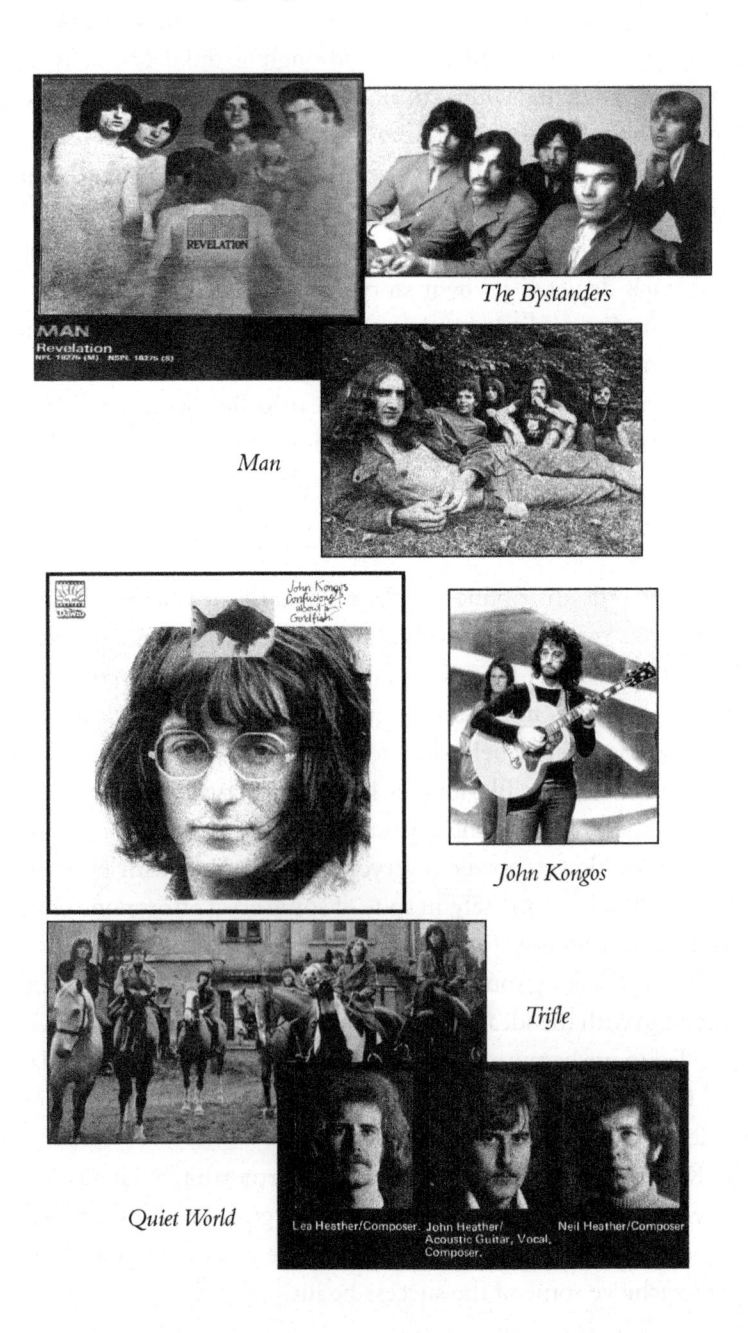

The Bystanders

Man

John Kongos

Trifle

Quiet World — Lea Heather/Composer. John Heather/Acoustic Guitar, Vocal, Composer. Neil Heather/Composer

I had made a promise to myself to have one by the time I was forty. I was driving through Streatham one day when my heart skipped a beat. Quite unexpectedly I spied a magnificent Rolls Royce Corniche parked on a garage forecourt with a FOR SALE notice attached to her. She was maroon with a beige vinyl roof and matching beige leather upholstery.

On closer examination she had sixty thousand miles to her credit. She had been very recently serviced and was showing just one or two tiny patches of rust. She had had one previous proud owner. Whilst test driving her I felt I was lost in another world, the world of opulence. She was so quiet, so smooth and so big. I loved her and I wanted her.

The Quadrangle was full of 'look at me' type of vehicles so my new Lady was not out of place. She immediately acquired a number of admirers and I was always greeted with a "Good morning sir" by the concierge in the Quadrangle Tower.

Over the next three or four years we had a lot of fun together. She was almost daily lovingly 'schroederised' and I thought she deserved a personalised number plate. I found **JS X12** (note the deliberate gap – name and flat number).

After a year I decided to be even more outrageous and treated her to a complete re-spray in an eye catching ivory white. Sometimes I found myself feeling quite embarrassed behind the wheel but mostly I enjoyed the sheer visible power of financial achievement. I loved taking her up North especially to a Geno Washington gig where Mike Rispoli had organised a permanent reserved parking space for her right outside the front door. She acquired a crowd of admirers, or were they groupies? She was obviously a turn on and being her manager I certainly had no objection!

I soon discovered that owning a Rolls was in itself a world of its own and without a doubt it gave me the feeling of *'having made it'* but it also incited both jealousy and surprising respect, especially on the road. People, wondering who I was would let me go first even when they had the right of way. Whilst this gave me a great 'buzz' there were those who went out of their way to deliberately antagonise by cutting me up. Normally I would rise to this but with a Rolls Royce you had to keep your cool, grit your teeth and bear it otherwise the last laugh would certainly be on you and you might have to get a bank loan to accommodate the cost of the damage. With every Rolls there was a list of recommended do's and don'ts but my Lady could match any room in a four star hotel and room service was always guaranteed to be excellent!

I was honoured that Alan Florence had asked me to be his best man at his wedding and the least I could do was to offer her Ladyship's services. Being my recording engineer, Alan had become a close friend both socially and professionally, and I owe a great deal to him. It was a wonderful and memorable occasion. Her Ladyship looked truly magnificent almost upstaging the bride!

Eventually the running costs such as servicing, parts and the cost of fuel to keep the Rolls on the road were becoming so high that I had to find some way to reduce these without having to part with her which at this moment I was reluctant to do. The solution I came up with was to look around for a good condition second hand Mini. In that way I could cut the cost by only using the Rolls if and when the occasion arose. I didn't have to look very far because there was a very smart Mini Clubman right on my doorstep owned by my illustrious friend Don. By sheer coincidence it was a white one with a beige vinyl roof. It was perfect and, after much haggling, Don and I came to an amicable agreement taking into consideration the *wee small* favours I had made available to him. Surely a real friend would have let me have her for nothing! Seeing the Rolls and Mini together they were very much mother and daughter.

Sadly all good things come to an end. It broke my heart having to say goodbye to that beautiful Corniche but she became just too demanding financially. As a memento I had her number plate transferred to the Mini.

We had had a great time together and thankfully she finally found a wonderful home in America. She was in fact one of the last hand built Rolls Royce's and I ended up with a £2000 profit and literally four years of free motoring. There's no way I could grumble at that.

It is impossible to count the incredible number of sessions which Alan Florence and I have worked together on since my having been employed by Pye Records. We have had our fair share of hits and misses and there have been some truly unforgettable moments in the studio.

British session musicians are amongst the finest in the world and many of them have ultimately become internationally famous – Jimmy Page and John Paul Jones (Led Zeppelin), Big Jim Sullivan (Tom Jones), Rick Wakeman (Yes), Alan Parker, Nicky Hopkins to name but a few.

The recording studio is a place of work and once in it there should be mutual respect by everybody for everybody to bring the session to a satisfactory conclusion.

I believe it was my first session at Pye Records with session musicians when on using the talk back I requested to hear some rhythm on its own. Alan and I were taken completely by surprise with what we heard back through the monitors – "Hurry up it's your move". On looking hard at the rhythm section I was amazed to see two of them playing chess! I immediately responded with obvious anger in my voice "You're wrong, it's my move and I want to hear some rhythm *now*".

I could not let this go and so I informed Charlie Katz of the incident since he had booked the musicians for this session. He was flabbergasted, and needless to say the two were severely reprimanded, jeopardising their careers with the possibility that they might not be booked for any sessions with anybody for a while. Charlie told me later that they were really sorry for what they had done and realised it was an incredibly unprofessional thing to do. Because they were so talented and virtually irreplaceable I did use them again even asking for them in preference to anyone else. On the first occasion I saw them after the incident in question they apologised personally to me. From then on I had ultra co-operation from them on all my forthcoming sessions. I put the incident out of my mind even though I shall never forget it!

I was in the process of recording an instrumental track with a fairly large Orchestra consisting of piano, bass guitar, drums. rhythm guitar, lead guitar, one trumpet, two tenor sax, one baritone sax, ten violins, two violas and one cello. As Alan and I were listening back to the third take with Lew Warburton, the arranger, there was a constant clicking noise every few seconds throughout the track. Strangely, about the middle of the track it would stop and then start again. I decided to let everybody have a break while we tried to find the problem. Alan virtually took the whole desk apart, checking and double checking everything thinking that it might be an electrical fault. He could find nothing and we just hoped that on the next take it would have disappeared. Everyone returned from their break and I asked for a run through from the top. There it was again, this infuriating spasmodic clicking noise. Alan and I then surmised that it must be coming from the studio since we had not recorded anything. I told Alan we'd run it again from the top but this time I'd go down to the studio. I listened and checked the rhythm section. I listened and checked the brass section. I listened and checked the string section and guess what? I discovered one of the viola players meticulously cutting the finger nails of his left hand with a pair of nail clippers! He had done the right hand before the break! When the sound stopped it was when he had to play. I told him quietly but in no uncertain terms that he had fucked up the possible master take before the break and caused us no end of problems and lost time in trying to locate the offending sound. The guy who must have been in his sixties started to shake and went white as a sheet.

After the session had finished a very upset Charlie Katz got hold of the poor guy again and pointed out to him that a recording studio was not a beauty parlour and that he was lucky to get paid for the session.

Hopefully he got the message. Maybe he was a new old boy on the block!

A very distraught Harry Benson told me that he could not find a drummer available on the day I wanted to do the Jan Burnette session. He had managed to book everybody else. Harry said he might be able to get hold of Phil Seaman but a little persuasion might be necessary and he would call me back at six o'clock. This was only an hour and a half before the session and I was beginning to panic. Without a drummer the whole session was in jeopardy. Harry phoned as promised and said he had managed to book Phil Seaman but there was one condition. Phil had to have his dog, a German Shepherd with him and refused to do any session without the dog being present. I could not believe what I was hearing. I said to Harry somewhat agitated "I suppose the dog expects a bloody session fee as well. What if he barks during the master take?" Harry had Phil's assurance that this had never happened and the dog had sat through numerous sessions without barking a word. Harry then made it quite clear – no dog no drummer. I had no alternative but to accept.

Like everybody else the dog, who I must say was beautifully groomed, arrived at the studio and made himself comfortable right next to Phil's snare drum. Rubbing salt into the wound, Alan Florence suggested putting a mike on him!

Having done two takes and made some minor changes we were now ready to do take three. Up till now, true to Phil's word, the dog had remained totally silent. As soon as the third take was counted in there was magic in the air – the tempo was great, the feel was great, the vocal was great, and the guitar solo was spot on. When the end came I almost shouted with excitement through the talk back "That's the one!" As soon as I had said that the German Shepherd let out two enormous barks. I virtually ran down to the studio and said to Phil Seaman in a very agitated tone of voice "Fucking hell I thought you said he would keep his bloody mouth shut" Phil answered quite casually.

"He was only agreeing with you that that take was the one. What he said was – YA…VOL, the German for total agreement.

I must be going crazy. Maybe the dog should have my job!

Much as I would love to, it is not possible to give individual credit to the enormous number of artists I was producing at this time. They all had undeniable talent and I took it personally when a record failed for whatever reason. Some of the Artists deserve a particular mention only because out of the band or group certain members were destined to become universally successful.

A Band of Angels should have achieved chart status but after three single releases it didn't happen and as per contract the Artist sadly had to be dropped. This band had a very talented lead singer who replaced **Paul Jones**, the lead singer of **Manfred Mann**. He also wrote some fabulous songs one of which entitled '*Handbags and Gladrags*' was recorded by **Chris Farlowe, Rod Stewart** and most recently by **The Stereophonics** which became hugely successful. I wish I had written it!

His name was **Mike D'Abo.**

Once again as per contract, three singles were released and didn't make it so I had to lose **The Loving Kind**. This talented three piece group were first brought to my attention by the late **Gordon Mills** who also managed **Tom Jones** and **Engelbert Humperdinck.** Although their own success failed **The Loving Kind** was to produce two major talents. **Pete Kircher** was to later join **Status Quo** and **Noel Reading**, the drummer was to join the great **Jimi Hendrix Experience.**

I signed and produced a group called **The Hellions** and yet again no joy. '*Daydreaming of you*' '*Tomorrow never comes*' and '*A little lovin*' sadly all failed. Later **Dave Mason** and **Jim Capaldi** joined **Traffic** and **Luther Grosvenor** joined **Mott the Hoople.** For me a personal loss and failure of three very talented people but thankfully they were to find justified success.

This Artist deserves a mention because in retrospect perhaps I should never have signed him. The song titled '*That's my life (my love and my home')* was written by the Artist. I commissioned **Frank Barber** to do the arranging and to this day I believe the song and the record were strong enough to have hit potential. The big problem, which at the time I wrongly assumed would be a plus was that the Artist's name was **Freddie Lennon** alias **Alf**, the late **John Lennon's** absent father! They didn't get on and were never likely to so there was no point in making further product. Personally as a record, I felt pretty strong about it even though the idea backfired on me!

Playing squash was very much a part of my life since it alleviated me of a lot of stress. I was in a League and playing a game every day often with someone in the Music Industry.

A memorable game with Lionel Conway, a music publisher was to leave me scarred for life. During this game he played an excellent shot which I returned but fell on the floor at the same time because my positioning and balance was totally wrong. He had no problem returning my shot and as I attempted to return his, having not got fully up from the previous shot I fell with all my body weight on to my left ankle. The pain was excruciating and my ankle swelled up very quickly to the size of a cricket ball. Lionel was in deep shock but managed to call an ambulance. The X ray showed a clean break on one side and a fracture on the other. The fracture proved to be the biggest problem so they inserted a three inch nail through the bones to hold them together. They set the clean break putting the leg in plaster. A week later blood was showing through the plaster. They found the bones had not been set properly (apparently a trainee doctor had done the job!) so they had to be broken again and re-set. I was lying helpless in bed in St Mary's Hospital Paddington. I was so mad with myself for putting my life on hold by doing such a bloody stupid thing. As for Lionel, I don't believe he went near a squash court again!

A short while after I had been released from hospital I got quite a shock when I discovered the head of the nail which had obviously been working its way through my foot was now about to break through the skin having been giving me constant pain whilst rubbing against my shoe. So it was back to hospital again. They removed the nail and my ankle looked like a piece of raw steak!

It was certainly a bad break in more than ways than one but I didn't realise I had so many friends. Whilst in hospital I had many surprise visitors and not only from the music industry. It was a chance in a million that two of the female kind who I painstakingly had ensured would never meet were standing there right in front of me. Fortunately the ward sister had the right stuff to treat the situation! Whether I would ever see them again was food for thought.

I had some amazing cards especially one from Pye Records that looked like the world had signed. I was touched that so many cared.

> *Get Well Soon*
> Hurry home Darling
>
> With I'll bring my clean laundry when I call - Get Well Soon!! Don't worry darlin', Peter
>
> Get well soon, John – I'm tired of all these frustrated birds around the office! Crafty Bridy

I also received a wonderful letter from Cyril Shane of Cyril Shane Music. I quote the following two paragraphs from it:

I have always thought that you were a bloody lousy squash player, but at least I thought that you might be able to stand on your own two feet.
  Seriously though, get well quickly as I need some bloody records and as you are the only idiot that records my lousy songs get well soon and get into the studio!
  Yours sincerely
  Uncle Cyril

Uncle Cyril never did anything without Pedro the poodle's approval. I can see him now reading the letter out loud to Pedro that he intended to send me. Pedro would be listening intently with ears pricked up after which he would be yelping with delight confirming his Master had said the right thing.

I had now been seven and a half years with Pye Records and I felt I was professionally in a rut. My enforced break had only made things worse. I needed a change and a shot of adrenalin. It felt like it was the end of an era and the time had come for me to find the beginning of another. I had to simply get out there on my own and take my chances like everybody else had done. On the plus side the industry had changed quite significantly, becoming much bigger, with more opportunities, mainly due to the successful emergence of many independent ventures. It was a sad day for me leaving Pye Records, more so than any other company. They were such a fun team of people with even Benjie and Les Cocks having their moments. I had made some good friends.
  I had to start somewhere and as I owned the name I began by negotiating

an independent deal with Pye Records whereby I could continue to produce Sounds Orchestral, perhaps my most treasured creation. Pye were very happy for me to give them a minimum of two albums a year. Both Johnny Pearson and I were more than pleased with this.

The industry began to realise that I had left Pye Records and was now on my own and as such, open for business.

I was approached by RCA to produce an album with Salena Jones. She was black, good looking and had a great voice which unfortunately was shamefully underrated. She was highly respected by other Artists and session musicians alike. It was an honour and an unforgettable experience to have worked with her.

I believe it was my past association with Robert Wace that was instrumental in my ultimately producing a group called Gnidrolog for RCA.

Their musical direction was as strange as their name and I was never really convinced about the envisaged album or its content. The overall title of the album was *'In Spite Of Harry's Toe-nail'*. One review started off by saying:

'This is musically deep, requiring careful and intensive listening'.

Unfortunately I have to agree with that, that is if you could be bothered to listen in the first place!

At the time, Paul Moriarty was a familiar face often seen in one TV drama or another. He was blessed with a wonderful speaking voice, which was perfect to portray the truly meaningful message and words of *'Desiderata'*. The record was released on Decca and titled *'Go Placidly.'*

If we took heed to what those words were really saying we would be contributing to making the world a better place today.

DESIDERATA

GO PLACIDLY AMID THE NOISE & HASTE, & REMEMBER WHAT PEACE THERE MAY BE IN SILENCE. AS FAR AS POSSIBLE WITHOUT surrender be on good terms with all persons. Speak your truth quietly & clearly: and listen to others, even the dull & ignorant: they too have their story, ♣ *Avoid loud & aggressive persons, they are vexations to the spirit. If you compare yourself with others, you may become vain & bitter: for always there will be greater & lesser persons than yourself. Enjoy your achievements as well as your plans.* ♣ *Keep interested in your own career, however humble: it is a real possession in the changing fortunes of time. Exercise caution in your business affairs: for the world is full of trickery. But let this not blind you to what virtue there is: many persons strive for high ideals: and everywhere life is full of heroism.* ♣ *Be yourself. Especially, do not feign affection. Neither be cynical about love; for in the face of all aridity & disenchantment it is perennial as the grass.* ♣ *Take kindly the counsel of the years, gracefully surrendering the things of youth. Nurture strength of spirit to shield you in sudden misfortune. But do not distress yourself with imaginings. Many fears are borne of fatigue & loneliness. Beyond a wholesome discipline, be gentle with yourself.* ♣ *You are a child of the universe, no less than the trees & the stars: you have a right to be here. And whether or not it is clear to you, no doubt the universe is un-folding as it should.* ♣ *Therefore be at peace with God, whatever you conceive Him to be, and whatever your labors & aspirations, in the noisy confusion of life keep peace with your soul.* ♣ *With all its sham, drudgery & broken dreams; it is still a beautiful world. Be careful. Strive to be happy.* ♣♣

FOUND IN OLD SAINT PAUL'S CHURCH.
BALTIMORE: DATED 1602

CHAPTER SIXTEEN

The magic, the beauty and emotion of orchestral music whether it be jazz orientated, classically orientated or otherwise will always remain with me as being something very special. I am proud of the fact that during my earlier career I had managed to bring orchestral music nearer to the understanding and appreciation of the younger generation significantly through the universal success of Sounds Orchestral and subsequently The John Schroeder Orchestra and The City of Westminster String Band. The beauty of orchestral music is that it is adaptable to whatever mood you have in mind. It speaks a universal language and your wish is its command.

The Beach Boys number one song *'Good Vibrations'* gave me the idea for an Orchestral Series called 'VIBRATIONS.' It was a modern word that had a good sound about it. It was also strong and meaningful but above all it could provide me with creating a million and one musical concepts i.e. Piano Vibrations, Dylan Vibrations, Latin Vibrations, Party Dance Vibrations, Love Vibrations and so on.

Polydor Records were very interested in the concept since they wanted to build their Easy Listening catalogue. However they made it very clear to me that to be financially viable it had to be produced as a low budget package which would deliver quality with economy. We did a deal whereby I agreed to produce ten albums during the following two years.

It was a tough assignment even though I used the crème de la crème of session musicians and the talents of a varied selection of top arrangers. As I had worked there for so many years I decided the sensible thing to do was to use Pye Studios with Alan Florence as my engineer. We found we were always having to fight the clock on every session and I am ashamed to admit that sometimes I had to forgo the quality to produce something adequately good that I myself was not one hundred per cent happy with. However, the series as a whole was a lasting success and proved once again that Orchestral Music is valued highly throughout the world by both young and old.

Rick Wakeman

Piano Vibrations is particularly worth a mention because it was the first album the very talented Rick Wakeman made as a solo artist. He was at the time a much sought after session musician and when I approached him he was thrilled and honoured to do it. The strong material on this album included *'Cast Your Fate To The Wind'* and *'Classical Gas'*. Of course a little later Rick Wakeman became a huge name himself both when and after he joined Yes.

It is interesting to note that Polydor Records Press Office described the Vibration Series as sophisticated pop, music for E types and young advertising men drinking at smart country pubs and music to be played on a nice stereo in a mews flat!... Don't look at me I didn't write it!

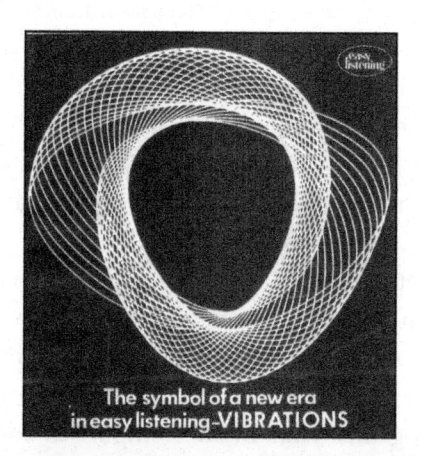

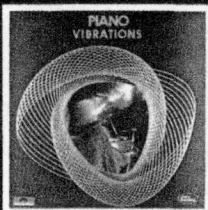

The Vibration Series
Pull Both Ends
'Let's write a musical.' I said it as a joke when Mike Hawker and I had written two number ones in succession for Helen Shapiro namely *'You Don't Know'* and *'Walking Back To Happiness.'*

Ten years later Tony King and I found ourselves working our butts off to complete writing the score to John Schroeder's 'Pull Both Ends' a new musical.

The whole saga was like a bolt of lightening that suddenly appeared from nowhere. Marilyn Davis had terminated her employment with Robert Wace to set up a theatrical production company called Present Productions with David Missen, her new business partner. Between them they wanted to bring my idea of a musical to reality and within a short period of time they had acquired the services of some heavy duty names.

Leslie Lawton was appointed the Director, Stuart Hopps and Nigel Lythgoe, later becoming the head of ITV would be handling the choreography. Alyn Ainsworth would be arranging the music and Malcolm Pride would be in charge of the set and wardrobe.

From a cast point of view Marilyn was in her element. She contacted Stewart Morris and did a deal with him for the services of The Young Generation, who were very big at the time. She commissioned the indefatigable Gerry Marsden and from recent auditions acquired Miles Greenwood as the two male leads. Christine Holmes who had a fantastic voice agreed to play the female lead with tremendous support coming from Judy Bowen.

Personally I thought Present Productions was taking one hell of a gamble simply because as such, there was no musical. We hadn't got a book and the songs were not complete, in fact many had not even been written. We didn't know who was going to sing what, when, with whom or where.

With the speed of so much happening all at the same time I had a problem knowing what day it was!

Marilyn got me together with Brian Comport to sort out the book. I gave Brian the basis of a very simple Cinderella type story which was centred around a Christmas cracker factory that was about to be taken over by an American Novelty Toy Company. Brian was a lovely guy but truthfully I was not that happy with the finished book. On getting together with Tony King we managed to sort out the songs and dance numbers and who should sing what and where. It took Tony and I three months to complete the score and it had no less than nineteen songs in it. The Show was now ready to go into rehearsal and then hopefully production.

Marilyn and David had managed to book The Palace Theatre Manchester for a two week preview to run from June 14th 1972. The big problem was getting the show into a London Theatre directly following the preview, that is if the preview was satisfactorily received, otherwise there would no way it would be going to London anyway.

Marilyn was young but highly respected by the theatre world especially for her tenacity to achieve success. She became very good friends with Donald

Albery, the Chairman and Managing Director of a number of London Theatres. With a bit of push and shove he was able to offer her the Piccadilly Theatre for an opening night on July 18th 1972. Even if Marilyn and David felt this was the wrong theatre they had no choice but to graciously accept the offer otherwise the show would never see The West End. This offer was also bound by the condition that it depended solely upon the success of the preview in Manchester whether it made it to London.

Annoyingly, Tony King and I were not allowed to go anywhere near the rehearsals because Management did not want emotional composers getting emotional and possibly causing uncalled for problems. I cleverly managed to find out where they were rehearsing but the nearest Tony and I got to it was looking through the tiny windows in the swing doors to the rehearsal room. All we could say to each other was "Amazing. I don't believe it. The songs and arrangements sound great."

The opening night in Manchester was an experience of a lifetime. I was in another world. "Was this really happening? Was this really the show that started as a casual joke without an inkling of reality about it all those years ago?"

As I waited for the curtain to rise, my heart was going into overdrive at the same time as I wanted to disappear under the seat in anticipated embarrassment. The opening number took the audience by complete surprise and thank God their enjoyment was sustained right to the final curtain. During the interval in the bar I was picking up people's comments and all I heard was how great it was to have a musical with such energy, colour, singable songs and wonderful dancing. All in all just a thoroughly enjoyable two hours of unpretentious pleasure and that was exactly how I had imagined it should be right from its initial conception. Marilyn and David were ecstatic, so were the cast and most of us waited up half the night in anticipation of the morning reviews. They were worth waiting for because they were excellent, way beyond anyone's imagination but the big question was –"Were we going to the West End?"

The phone rang and there was absolute silence, not a word or sound from anybody. Marilyn picked up the phone. It was the voice of Donald Albery. She put the phone down and let the anticipation deliberately linger for some more seconds and then she shouted "We're going to the West End everybody, opening night July 18th." The place went crazy. I was totally speechless and inundated with congratulations. If there was anything stronger than seventh heaven I was in it!

Of course after that success in Manchester everyone was saying there was no way it could fail in London. But London was a different ball game altogether and little did we know we were in for a big shock!

Seven nights were designated for previews before the opening night. Analysing the Manchester run Marilyn and David unanimously agreed that the show would benefit enormously if it had an electric turntable to turn the sets round more quickly and easily. It was installed at enormous expense and on one of the preview nights whoever was operating it should have read the instruction manual! Christine Holmes and Miles Greenwood were singing a very romantic duet which happened to be in a bedroom scene. Suddenly to my and everybody else's horror, almost as the song ended, a red telephone box appeared, being slowly lowered from the main gantry. The turntable had not moved, leaving Christine and Miles not understanding the audience's hysterics or why the orchestra had not started the introduction to the next number. The audience were now frantically pointing and as Christine and Miles looked up they were practically enclosed in the telephone box.

That should have stayed in. It was a killer of a moment!

The opening night in the West End of *my very own musical* was once again more than an impossible dream about to come true which again Marilyn had been instrumental in making happen. How many times had I imagined myself arriving at the theatre in a white Rolls Royce and standing at the back of the stalls with a big cigar in my mouth feeling the proudest guy in the world? In actual fact I did arrive in a white Rolls Royce but sat in the audience like everybody else. There was one big difference, I felt quite ill, beating myself up about so many things, especially the turntable scenario. The only event that kept me sane was the show's incredible and unforgettable success in Manchester which was an unbelievable experience. Could this be repeated in London?

The theatre was more than a full house with people even standing and I felt the cast's performance was in fact better than Manchester because everybody was on a high and so much more confident. There were Celebs there too. I wandered into the bar at the interval – listening. Generally the comments were good – young, energetic, vivacious, simply good fun with some great songs. I was pleased at that but at the same time there were a number of derogatory remarks mainly pointing to the fact that it was no more than a tarted up pantomime! That hurt. I was very upset on hearing that!

The second half looked just as good and received the stamp of approval with a standing ovation at the end! But we were all in for a big shock as we waited in the Green room as we had done in Manchester till two or three in the morning for the reviews. All the major papers had reviewed it and the comments, although hurtful were in some ways correct but also very scathing and very demeaning.

It put us all, especially me, on a dreadful downer, but Marilyn as brave as ever said – "What the papers think is one thing, what the public thinks is another. Let's keep calm and wait and see."

I don't think the cast were really bothered at all. The energy and input by everybody was just as emotionally strong. They were still dancing and singing their hearts out for quite a number of nights to come.

I took my mother and father to see the show and then did a tour of the West End so they could see John Schroeder's 'Pull Both Ends' advertised all over the place. I overheard my father of course displaying his usual 'I don't believe it' type of expression say proudly to my mother whilst they were looking at the huge hoarding that adorned the front of the Piccadilly Theatre.

"Well it's always been all or nothing with John. He failed his Accountancy exam and did nothing I wanted him to do and now the little bugger's got his name in lights all over the West End of London!" My mother replied rather emotionally "This'll teach you. You were always so wrong about John. He was born to be in the entertainment industry even though I would have never imagined this in a million years." At *last* the old boy had to bow down to what he was witnessing. For me it was a good battle to have won.

After a few weeks Marilyn told me the show was in trouble financially and out of desperation she had no alternative but to turn to her father hoping for some financial help. He agreed that after all everybody and the show had been through it must stay on for as long as possible as it might recover. Thankfully and surprisingly he committed no less than eleven thousand pounds to keep it going for some weeks longer. The writing was on the wall. The show was doomed and it was sadly forced to close after only four months. I saw the show two or three times and it was distressing to see the theatre only half filled and sometimes less than that. How different was Manchester!

Marilyn was pretty low, blaming herself for letting everybody down. I told her she had pulled off a miracle by getting the show into London at all and she should always think of those two fantastic weeks in Manchester.

When she and David were both in a sane frame of mind to discuss the show sensibly I told them *exactly* what I thought. The theatre was way too large but then I appreciated it was taking it or not getting into London at all. The Young Generation were also too large running up a huge and unnecessary expense. We could have done what they did and better with just ten of them. Tony and I were wrong in having nineteen songs in the show. It was far too many and ten would have been more than adequate. The sets were too lavish but the greatest weakness of all by far was the book and the story line. It was certainly my mistake in thinking the music would carry the show and all that was needed was a crutch for it to lean on, after all it was a musical!

E.M.I Records made a cast album at Abbey Road Studios, Studio One in fact which brought many happy memories back to me. It was engineered by the very talented Alan Parsons who was later to enjoy considerable success as The Alan Parsons Project.

I vowed I would never write another musical but all the dramatics, the numerous disagreements, the high and the lows of this show were worth every minute of the time, trouble and expense. I still today cannot believe that I wrote a musical which actually made it to the West End of London. Realistically speaking the chance of this happening was one in a million and luckily for me I was the one!

REVIEWS... REVIEWS... REVIEWS... REVIEWS

TAKING THE GOOD WITH THE BAD!
Manchester Evening News May 19th 1972
James Green (extract)

Re: Marilyn Davis, Producer "Pull Both Ends"

Quote: This is my first musical and the third show I have presented. The backing is coming from a Company of 'angels'. John Schroeder is being unduly modest because we believe there are twelve songs that could make the Hit Parade. The financial 'angels' agree with us. I jumped at the chance to produce this show.

Manchester Evening News June 15th 1972
by Beryl Jones

Marilyn Davis, *the young impresario who is producing a new £100.000 British musical 'Pull Both Ends' at the Palace Theatre Manchester.*

Picture by Tony Cordt.

From the first few bars of the overture there was that old black magic feeling about 'Pull Both Ends' at the Palace Theatre Manchester last night. This you felt was going to be something different – and it is, the liveliest most tuneful musical seen in Manchester for much too long.

The music and lyrics by john Schroeder and Anthony King are the greatest asset. The Young Generation have a swingin' smash of a number Cayo which will prove a show stopper.

Daily Mirror 15th June 1972
'Pull Both Ends' Palace Theatre Manchester

How nice to review a new British musical where songs don't sound all the same and where the choreography looks as if it had stepped out of an American show. It came over with a pace and swiftness that's unusual on first nights.

Daily Mail June 15th 1972
Patrick O'Neill 'Pull Both Ends' Palace Theatre Manchester

Cinderella put on her dancing shoes last night hopped into her blue jeans and jumped straight into potentially the liveliest new musical this year. Everything is centred around a Christmas cracker factory. The whole £100.000 production is set for the West End in July.

If you pardon a terrible pun – the show is a real cracker.

Daily Express June 15th 1972
Gerard Dempsey 'Pull Both Ends' Palace Theatre Manchester

The trouble with Xmas crackers is that the contents very rarely measure up to the wrapping. Something of the sort happens in this £100.000 new British musical – though in fairness the contents are a good deal more substantial than a motto, a paper hat or a novelty. Indeed the show has one very substantial novelty – it is certainly the first major musical in which the chorus is the star. The achievement last night was John Schroeder's music, a sequence of potential hit songs strung like beads on a line as thin as a filament.

TAKING THE BAD WITH THE GOOD!
London Financial Times July 19th 1972
Michael Coveney 'Pull Both Ends' Opening night
Piccadilly Theatre London

John Schroeder's not very new and not at all musical show is a cynically concocted piece of showbiz camp devoid of wit, heart, good performances, surprise and novelty aimed to trap a passing tourist trade which would applaud the Queen were she to step from the nearest ten foot silver papered cracker (she does indeed) and remember that in the halcyon days of their late middle age there was a pop singer who could smile without seeming facetious and who played with one of those shoddy groups who trailed in the wake of the Beatles as they emerged from the Cavern. The Young Generation for whom nothing from strikes to hairstyles is undeserving of a wet lyric and a vibrant gesture. What a sickening crew they are, to be sure.

TWENTY YEARS TOO LATE – THIS DUD CRACKER
Daily Express July 19th 1972
Theatre by Herbert Kretzmer 'Pull Both Ends' Piccadilly Theatre

It is hard to see what kind of audience the writers of this charmless new musical had in mind when they launched themselves into their labours.

Though the show is clearly intended to communicate the energy and zing of youth 'Pull Both Ends' tells a story so witless, dated and condescending I cannot imagine any young playgoer responding to it with anything but contempt.

'Pull Both Ends' despite its pretensions to modernity, is like a musical of the bad old fifties and arrives in the West End 20 years too late.

The Guardian July 19th 1972
'Pull Both Ends' Piccadilly Theatre London

The essence of the thing, if you must go, is the shining exuberance of fixedly smiling youth which falls a mile short of a 'Jackie' strip romance on a bad week. However one must report that a heavily middle aged and ulcerous looking audience shrieked with something akin to joy so maybe there's the appeal.

The Evening Standard July 19th 1972
'Pull Both Ends' Piccadilly Theatre London Review by Milton Shulman

To put the Young Generation into a dreadful musical called 'Pull Both Ends' at the Piccadilly is to face them with tasks for which they have little skill or talent.

Their singing for the most part pre-recorded on noisy tape, did little to distract us from the routine and repetitive choreography of Nigel Lythgoe.

The level of wit is well below the jokes in the crackers. The music and lyrics by John Schroeder and Anthony King can be commended only for nerve and persistence.

The Piccadilly Theatre London – Opening night July 18th 1972

CHAPTER SEVENTEEN
THE ROAD TO ALASKA

Having had a taste of independent production for a while, which always left me wondering where my next job was coming from if at all, I decided I needed something more positive in my life. The time had come to indulge in some serious gambling and at long last to set up my own Record Label. Putting my financial life on the line and with the help of an understanding and music loving Bank Manager, I carefully planned my method of madness.

The first step was the name. In a moment of pure genius I came up with, and decided to go with, the name **ALASKA** for three reasons. One – it was as such, an unknown and undiscovered territory. Two – it would be listed in the first twenty names in a telephone directory or similar, and Three – I just liked the sound of it.

Next was the design of the label itself and I had a picture of space, ice and loneliness in my head integrated predominantly by the colour blue. The final result, although possibly not immediately apparent, was subtle and hard to reproduce totally due to the atmosphere I had in mind.

After many attempts I was pleased with the final image which was enhanced by the carefully chosen typeset for the name. The label was immediately identifiable which was all that mattered.

Even though Alaska Records was still a dream away from reality I agreed to see a band that was rehearsing in the basement of a Soho Strip Club in the afternoon of October the 18th 1971.

After some trouble finding the place I was forced to stand inside the door for quite some time since it was impossible to move. The whole place, filled to the brim with black people was alive and jumping and even the floor boards were rhythmically complaining! I was totally mesmerised and taken aback by what I was hearing and witnessing. This was certainly *not* the band I had come to see. Although the musical excitement seemed to be emanating from one corner of the room it was hard to work out just *who was* in this band. It was the rhythms. They were so *damned* infectious. I had never heard anything like it before nor had I heard anything like the front line before. They were so *damned* out of tune! They called themselves Cymande, which apparently means Dove, the Bird of Peace. Their spokesman and presumed leader was Patrick Patterson, whom I had noticed played some *very* nice guitar. I made myself known and then explained what I did, why I was there and what had obviously happened. They introduced themselves individually, and excitedly said they had formed the band purely as a bit of fun for themselves, their friends and relations and anyone else who cared to come along. They all originated from the West Indies and although the lyrical content of some of the songs relayed some strong messages, they were eager to point out that the music they played was purely Cymande music. However, the names Rasta, Rastafarian and Nyah Rock appeared in many of the forthcoming interviews and write ups, as was Afro jazz.

I really wanted this band as I felt quite sure I could do something with them but I knew it would need a lot of work and particularly a lot of patience, especially with the front line. They clearly thought I was quite mad wanting to spend my money recording them *and* with no expense spared, *and* in a professional recording studio *and then* to release a record as well!

Cymande

SAM KELLY
drums

STEVE SCIPIO
bass

JOEY DEE
vocals

RAY KING
vocals

PATRICK PATTERSON
guitar

PABLO GONSALES
percussion

DEREK GIBBS
alto/soprano

MIKE ROSE
alto/flute/bongos

PETER SERREO
tenor

The recording contract was not easy to negotiate. Even though it was necessary that all nine members signed it I insisted that only one member should be responsible for the rest of the group, which included paying them individually and as such acting on each member's behalf. It was agreed by everybody that Patrick should officially remain the trusted spokesman and leader of the band, besides he and Steve Scipio were the only two members of the group who held a Bank Account. We mutually agreed a deal and contracts were subsequently signed and exchanged. With that out of the way we could now get down to some serious record business.

I suggested we took things slowly, got to know each other and went for three titles only to begin with. I selected these from their current repertoire which amazingly was all self penned. I felt they adequately demonstrated the versatility and potential of the Band. Now all I had to do was to record them which I was to discover was a major feat in itself, especially as I became very aware of numerous inter-group squabbles and jealousies which seemed to continually crop up.

It suddenly dawned on me that this session would be the first on behalf of Alaska Records. As I had decided it was Alaska's policy not to cut corners, especially as far as studio costs were concerned, I felt De Lane Lea Studios in Dean Street to be the right place for this project. This studio was a comfortable size and provided an excellent atmosphere. It also had all the up to date equipment.

By sheer coincidence Alan Florence, my lifelong engineering buddy had decided to go freelance just at this time. As he was available I immediately booked him for the Cymande sessions and I was very relieved to have him on board because I knew there were going to be plenty of problems and the first session proved exactly that.

That evening I arrived at the studio as arranged, and to my horror it was full of people, almost an exact repetition of what I had seen in the club in Soho.

As I tried to take it all in one guy stood out from the rest. He was black and must have been at least six feet tall, had a loud voice, wore a weird hat, snake skin boots and had a fur coat almost down to the ground. He was extremely intimidating, and as we faced each other I was beginning to seethe, especially when he remarked with considerable contempt "What you do to my brothers man? You take de money and dey get fuck all!" I thought that was pretty strong since I was paying for everything and taking a huge gamble. I got hold of Patrick Patterson and said to him very angrily "Who the fuck's that guy in the fur coat and who are all these people?! Unless you get them all out of the studio this minute there will be no fucking session." Patrick was taken aback at my unexpected tirade but then told me not to worry as he would take care of it. I told him that if it ever happened again there would be no record deal.

From that point on there were no problems except for musical ones. They had learnt a lesson and in exchange they were eventually rewarded by what they heard back through the studio monitors. They were so excited with disbelief. However my gut feeling told me that there was friction brewing, noticeably between Ray King and Joey Dee, the two lead singers. Unfortunately this was to finally bring about the departure of Ray King.

When Alan and I had finally mixed the tracks we both knew we had created something exciting and different. The varied rhythm patterns were amazingly infectious, bass and drums and percussion being so tight and Patrick's slightly jazzy guitar licks and solos being executed with so much emotional feeling. Even the always slightly out of tune front line added atmosphere and identity to the whole thing. Out of the three tracks *'The Message'* was definitely the strongest, commercially speaking but what was I going to do with them now? I couldn't release anything at this moment because Alaska had not been set up to accommodate this as yet. I did however, come to one definite conclusion. On the strength of those three tracks I decided we should seriously go for an album. Alan gave me that well known look which told me I was one hundred per cent right. When I told the Band that, the air suddenly became bluer than blue as all nine of them expressed words of totally uncontrolled excitement.

The magic that was Midem

Like the yearly Cannes Film Festival, Midem is the equivalent venue for The Music Industry world wide. It is also held in Cannes and usually takes place the last week of January. The opportunities it provides are incomparable since companies meet companies, people meet people, new deals are done and new product is heard, discussed and assessed. Anyone seriously in the music business cannot afford to ignore Midem.

Thank God I had the idea of going to Midem in the first place since I could meet and pre-warn other companies round the world all at the same time of my impending plans for Alaska Records.

I had a strong calling card because I had achieved an internationally known track record through my past successes with Sounds Orchestral, Jefferson, Status Quo etc. I already knew many of the European and even South African and American companies so I really had a trump card up my sleeve if I was careful to use it properly and create some strong product with some strong Artists in the coming year. Midem was also of course the ideal opportunity to take my three Cymande tracks with me to get an idea as to what the feedback and reaction might be.

The main Midem Festival Hall was packed with stands representing various Record Companies and Record Labels and it was not difficult to make appointments to see and talk to people you otherwise would never get near without making numerous trips around the world. Of course there was genuine interest but words had little effect because it was down to the product. As far as Cymande was concerned I had really positive response from Holland, France, Germany, and even Japan all of which I would follow up. They all agreed that an album was the way to go and to release a potentially strong single from it. I felt pleased that my initial thought as far as an album was concerned was the right move to make.

Midem's centre of social life was quite definitely the bar in the Martinez Hotel. Every evening it was packed but there was always a visible stand out collection of very good looking, sexually well dressed women inter mingling amongst the excited crowd of noisy music people. Someone whispered in my ear that if the guy operating the lift was made to smile with some financial incentive he could direct you quite discreetly to a 'what ever pleases sir' diversion, or was it perversion, into some of the other pleasures of life other than music!

Unashamedly, temptation mixed with fascination, and a bit of 'gotta have some of that' type of attitude made me totally unable to resist. After an hour I rejoined my friends at the bar with a huge 'worth every penny' smile on my face! I was informed *afterwards* that every year a carefully selected contingent of *talented* ladies was flown in from Paris to cater for the varying needs of all those lonely guys who loved and missed their wives so much but now had the golden opportunity to rise to the occasion and enjoy themselves just simply by being naughty boys!

Unexpectedly, near the end of the event I bumped into Marvin Schlacter. He and his charming wife Trudie had wined and dined me when I was in the States and riding high with the global success of Sounds Orchestral. He told me he now had his own record label called Janus which was run in conjunction with the Chess Records label which was owned and operated by Marshall Chess. I was to later discover that Chess/Janus was at this time recognised as a highly respected and successful label as far as the American market, and in particular black music, was concerned. I informed Marvin that I was in the process of forming Alaska Records and there would be product in a short while. He indicated very strongly that he would love to hear anything I had done or might be doing. I then said remembering how much he personally loved black music

"To tell you the truth Marvin I have not been able to stay away from the studio mainly because I believe I have found a multi talented and very different black Band. I have just cut three tracks with them and intend to start the album on my return" He then replied:

"Have you anything I can hear or take back with me?"

I gave Marvin a cassette of the three Cymande tracks, said my good byes and looked forward to hearing from him in due course.

Every year of the seven years of Alaska Records' life as part of the British Record Industry, nothing could ever prevent me from attending Midem. It was to become an important lifeline for two big reasons. One was money and two was to show my face and to reassure my international distributors that I had not gone out of business or something else as dreadful had happened. For my second year at Midem I decided to hire a stand since I had accrued some surprising publicity and had created some new and interesting product. All this helped to make the stand a showpiece that did attract considerable attention and indicated that Alaska Records was here to stay, for a while anyway. It was the one and only occasion I did this because the cost was too prohibitive but it had served its purpose and it had certainly helped in establishing the label.

One of my ingenious plans was to take to Midem each year the entire product range that I had made during the previous year. I then endeavoured to negotiate as many licensing deals as I could with advances which would then give me additional financial help in making the following year's product.

I shall never forget one particular year when on the last day I heard that there was a new Italian Company that were looking for product to service a huge range of juke boxes. Apparently they were paying cash so I frantically, with insane determination, searched for their stand. Believe it or not this was harder than it seemed but I found it eventually only to be told that there was no time left for any further appointments. How had I managed to miss out on something like this?

I was looking into the eyes of an awesome looking Italian Momma who obviously co-ordinated 'The Godfather's appointments'! I was not about to have this door shut in my face, so after five long minutes of some of my best chat up lines ever, and making the point that I had seven fantastic singles which he could not afford to miss out on hearing, she finally relented and I think even felt rather sorry for me. She disappeared for a minute and then with a 'you owe me one' type of expression (and I wondered what that meant!) informed me I had now been made the last appointment of the day.

Of course he had the blue pinstriped suit, dark hair and complexion and an unnerving abrupt attitude. He greeted me with a 'you hada better not be wasting my time' kind of smile which inwardly made me feel I was losing my nerve. He was understandably agitated because he had shut up shop and was preparing to go home. He said very hurriedly

"Come. Play play. Lette me hear. Play." After a small smattering of all seven singles he said "I lika de records. Good. Good sound. I take all."

That made-a ma day but as I walked through the 'Nothing to Declare' Customs area I was sweating like a pig not daring to look in a certain direction because a few thousand somethings were burning a big hole in my suitcase! However, I was smiling inwardly to myself – I'd be back again next year!

They got the message

Directly on my return, particularly as things seemed to be so positive I concentrated totally on getting the Cymande album into the studio even though I desperately wanted to progress things with Alaska.

I thought it a sensible decision to stick with De Lane Lea studios in Dean Street and called Alan Florence giving him the prospective recording dates. I allowed myself enough essential time to go into Cymande's repertoire a lot deeper as I knew I had to be very careful and meticulous as far as the selection of content for this album was concerned. I also had to go through the Band's arrangements of everything and alter them accordingly if necessary. I must say working with them in this respect was a beautiful experience. What they did was so bloody good and they were so thrilled and determined to get things together as I saw it. They were now listening, understanding and taking direction well. The changes were obvious and I was very happy. They were in fact learning fast how to be professional.

During the recording of this album, Alan one day mentioned to me that a young lady named Sandy who worked across the road at Warner Atlantic Records and was secretary to Phil Carson, the International Label Manager had heard the band and wanted to meet me. I was delighted to make my services available. Seven years later, Sandy and I were still enjoying ourselves making our own kind of music!

I had almost forgotten Marvin Schlacter and the cassette I had left with him at Midem. Practically on completion of the album, I received a telegram which said the following:

"Love the tracks and the Band. Want to release the Message as a single and the album at the same time. Any news on this? Let's talk a deal?" Marvin.

We talked a deal which was ultimately signed and agreed. Within four weeks a further telegram from Marvin followed:

"Message doing really well in both R&B and Pop charts. It looks like a big record. Album has also entered the charts."

I gave the band the news and they were speechless. Things started to move very fast with Marvin now suggesting an American tour with the band being *so hot* as support act to Al Green. He wanted me to meet Bob Schwaid who was Al Green's manager and for me to consider him also managing Cymande, certainly as far as America was concerned.

I spoke to Bob Schwaid on the phone voicing my agreement that I would be thrilled if he could put the package together. We agreed it was a great opportunity for both Artists and especially Cymande as they were presently enjoying a chart single and a chart album with both of them being cross over hits in the Soul/R&B and pop categories. Bob would let me have an itinerary in due course and we agreed to meet in New York before the tour was due to start. I told him we had been caught with our pants down since Cymande had never had a proper stage act in their life. I reassured him however, that they would have something awesome by the time they came over.

When I gave the band this news they were shitting themselves and at least two of them did not want to go to America as they were genuinely scared of flying and frightened of leaving home so they said! I reckon they were more scared of what Management at home would have to say on the subject! I emphasised that for a completely unknown and obscure British Band to have such success and such a huge opportunity land on their doorstep they simply had to get an act together, after all, what had we been working so hard for? This was the biggest thing in the world and I would help in any way I could. Patrick, being a Capricorn like me and uncannily being born on the same day as me, was very level headed and assured me they would have a stage act ready in time that I would be proud of and would even blow me away. I couldn't wait!

They had worked hard. The stage act was really good and I was proud, surprised and impressed. It looked right for the States and I thought Marvin Schlacter and Bob Schwaid would be more than pleased. With the runaway success of both the single and album, press and write ups etc started to come through thick and fast from all over the place.

Cymande: our loss is America's gain

CYMANDE: no luck in Britain, but a giant hit in the U.S

The very first black British band to hit the U.S Soul and Pop Charts well in advance of recognition at home…

News Sheet

One of the fastest selling hits ever released by Chess/Janus Records, "The Message" made its initial breakthrough on college radio stations. AM and FM stations then picked it up, enabling the record to enter one trade chart its first week at 85 with a bullet. The Cymande album is currently on the pop, soul and jazz charts.

Our special offer to you today is a free long distance phone call to London to speak to Cymande who will be making their first journey to America for a tour in April and May.

New York – Marvin Schlacter, President of Chess/Janus records, today announced an exclusive long term agreement with producer John Schroeder.

Cash Box — April 21, 1973

Cash Box

Cymande U.S. Tour Begins April 27

April 27	The Convention Center Louisville, Ky
28	Glassboro State University, Glassboro, New Jersey
29	Arlo Ballroom, Camden, New Jersey
April 30/ May 5th	Sugar Shack, Boston, Mass
May 6	Rutgers University, New Brunswick, New Jersey
11/17	Apollo Theater, Harlem, New York, New York
19	Independence Hall, Philadelphia, Pa
21	Constitution Hall, Washington, DC
25	Cincinatti Gardens, Cincinatti, Ohio
27	The Coliseum, Charlotte, N.C.
28	The Coliseum, Indiapolis, Ind
June 8	Chicago, Illinois
16	The Coliseum, Charlotte, N.C.
17	Memorial Auditorium, Greensville, S.C

CHAPTER EIGHTEEN

Well it was all systems go for Cymande's first American tour. It was decided the group should fly to America three days before to get themselves orientated, adjusted and acquainted with the new and very different way of life they were going to experience over the next few weeks. Meanwhile Bob and I had arranged to meet in New York beforehand.

Just less than one week before the group was due to leave I was annoyingly woken up with a phone call at four o'clock in the morning. Not being fully awake, at first I couldn't believe what I was hearing. Joey Dee was behind bars having been picked up by the police for being drunk, disorderly and having a dodgy passport. After the initial shock had sunk in and even after I explained the circumstances to the police in great detail they were not in any way about to release him, in fact on hearing the predicament, they were even more determined to hold on to him.

What a disaster! How could Cymande go to the States on their first tour with no lead singer because he was in bloody jail! I just daren't tell Bob Schwaid that. He'd probably have a heart attack!

I had to calm down and collect my thoughts. At the back of my mind I was sure I had heard of a company called Release set up by The Rolling Stones specifically to deal with Music Industry problems such as this. I found their number and within a few hours they were on the case. They pulled miracles and they actually got him released with a visa on the day of the band's departure. I was *so* grateful to Release. They were really pleased to have helped and better still with no expense whatsoever!

Harlem

The tour was going brilliantly with full houses everywhere every night. Bob and I were over the moon but on May the 10th Bob found a moment and whispered in my ear.

"Tomorrow we are playing The Apollo Theatre New York for a week. The famous Apollo, with an enviable track record of playing host to so many big names is in Harlem, a place where at the moment no white person would ever dare to tread, that is except me, because they would immediately be lynched. I am regarded as untouchable solely because I am Al Green's manager and he is regarded as a God. As long as you're with me there will never ever be a problem." I was grateful for that consoling thought.

As our limo wound its way through Harlem to the Apollo, Bob was right. The atmosphere felt very volatile and I felt pretty uneasy. It was really scary, with many weird looking dudes standing menacingly doing nothing, in front of their houses or on street corners.

For sure they had checked us out all right! The Apollo was such a nostalgic venue and Cymande had admirably done justice to it by commanding a full house every night of the week. Witnessing this will always remain in my memory as being one of my most treasured occasions ever.

Philadelphia

The Independence Hall was massive and yet not unlike a certain other place in London where I was also unable to move. Cymande came on stage and half way through the first number the whole place erupted with everyone standing on chairs, tables, bench seats in fact anything at all they could find to stand on. They also grabbed hold of anything that made a noise, knives, forks, spoons, plates, cups, glasses etc and as they became hypnotized by the Cymande rhythmic groove nothing in the world was going to stop them from letting it all hang out! It was a mind blowing experience and even Bob was shaken. Satisfyingly wild that it was, there was that undercurrent of discomfort and intimidation by being the only two whites in a room of about fifteen hundred people. Incredulously as I witnessed this unbelievable scene I thought to myself

"I had created this. Was this really the band I had come across by accident in that Soho strip club? This must all be a dream. This is not real."

Another example of unreality associated with Philadelphia was about to enter my life.

Bob was joined in Philadelphia by an extremely attractive young black lady called Laura. She was a shit hot PR person and Bob wanted to build stronger PR and promotion in the places and venues on the tour before we had actually got to them. He had not said a word to me about her coming and as the day wore on I became more and more besotted with Laura, so much so that I ended up spending the whole night on the hotel room to room phone desperately trying to persuade her to come down and sample some of my own special English PR. It didn't work, but before I put the phone down at about eight in the morning I jokingly told Laura I was going to New York at midday on the Greyhound Bus if she cared to join me.

As I sat on that bus feeling like death warmed up having arranged to catch up with Bob in Cincinnati I relived every moment of last night's fantastic gig including dare I say the rather frustrating marathon talk time with Laura. How could I ever forget Philadelphia?

The bus was just about to leave when suddenly out of nowhere this beautiful young lady plonked herself down right next to me. "Hi. My name's Laura!" She smiled teasingly and I detected an 'O.K you win. I give in' look about her. I felt good, very good!

We stayed at the Americana Hotel on Broadway for a few days and had a fantastic time, but one night we went out for a meal and didn't get back to the hotel till around midnight. With all the pleas in the world the concierge that night blatantly refused to let me go up to the room implying that Laura might well be a lady of the night and that was definitely against house rules.

Although I 'totally lost it' with the guy, Laura and I ended up spending the entire night walking the streets of New York. It was really scary particularly as she was black and I was white. I thought we were in real trouble a couple of times having caught the glimpse of a knife! That night we saw and mixed with the down and outs, the alkies, the druggies and witnessed the depravity that was New York. It was one hell of an experience. I think for Laura too.

At eight o'clock in the morning the foyer of the Americana Hotel was full and Laura and I sneaked up to the room and we did not appear for twenty four hours. Laura became a very close friend and I saw her practically every visit I made to the States. She was great at her job being very highly respected by all the major Record Companies and Management Agencies. She achieved a great deal in promoting and expanding Cymande's popularity and success in the States and in conjunction with Bob Schwaid she set up Cymande's second American tour. She was an amazing lady in more ways than one!

Chicago

Due to Cymande having had two successful tours under their belt and their popularity still remaining high, Marvin Schlacter asked me if I would like to record the Band in Chicago at the famous Chess Recording Studios that had played host to the likes of The Rolling Stones, Chuck Berry, Fats Domino and lists and lists of other famous acts. How could I refuse that? It was really an unbelievable honour. The Band was thrilled with this idea but I emphasised that we would need a considerable amount of new material. Once again Patrick assured me they would come up with it and they did. This resulted in the recording and release of two further albums namely 'Second Time Around' and 'Promised Heights'.

There was a memorable moment in the studio during one of the sessions.

I can't remember the title but the backing track was complete and we needed to put the lead vocal on (Joey Dee) with three of the other guys handling the backing vocals. The engineer set up two mikes, one for the lead and one for the back up. They were set up so all four guys would be facing each other.

I was just about to ask for some lead vocal when I suddenly heard a torrent of heated words emanating from the studio floor. The main bone of contention seemed to be centred on body odours and especially feet. They were refusing to stand next to each other!

I couldn't believe this and voiced my anger accordingly.

"Oh for *fucks sake* we'll do the lead vocal first but I flatly refuse to put each one of you on separately. You're supposed to be professionals!"

That apart, the finished product we produced was something else – shit hot, very different and beautifully infectious. It was in fact Cymande music at its best and Marvin, on hearing the finished product excitedly had singles and albums already lined up for future release. Due to lack of time some of the mixing had to be done in England. Just for the hell of it Alan Florence and I decided to use and experience the huge De Lane Lea Studio complex in Wembley. This was the biggest recording complex in the country costing well over a million to build but in retrospect I don't think it made any difference to our finished product since the magic was already in the grooves and tracks we had created.

Alaska Records Ltd was incorporated in April 1972 and I made its place of business 12 The Quadrangle as I had already established an office there. I invested in an attractive looking desk, hopefully for an attractive looking secretary, who would be sitting attractively facing the front door to help and advise the hundreds of people who would be clamouring for my services!

There was no point at all in setting up a record label without a distribution and pressing deal. I needed someone reliable and trustworthy and so I started at the top and approached E.M.I Records, after all I had worked there for four and a half years. They appeared to be very supportive of my plans for Alaska Records and I was relieved and pleased that we came to a deal.

Strangely I had not seen Marilyn for some time since the musical, but as if by magic she reappeared just at this time. She suggested that it might be a nice gesture to throw a lunch time buffet for the guys from E.M.I Records since they were going to be so important to the future of Alaska Records.

I thought it was a great idea so the truly lovely Veronica, or rather Ronnie Jones, my newly appointed gorgeously attractive secretary whom I had filched from the lovable Alan Freeman (not Fluff), sent out the invites to all concerned. Ronnie and Marilyn then got the drinks and buffet organised for the day in question. When it had all been set up it really looked 'the biz'.

It was planned for 1 o'clock. By two o'clock one person, a secretary had arrived. By three o'clock she had enjoyed some of the wonderful food but eventually felt quite ill due to the embarrassment caused by not one of her colleagues showing up. By four o'clock I had had enough. That was the end for me and practically the end *of* me. There was never one word of apology forthcoming from E.M.I. Feeling gutted was not strong enough for the way I felt. I consoled myself by accepting the fact that this was all part of the madness I had brought upon myself with wanting to do this mad project in the first place and I had only myself to blame. Undeterred, this only made me more determined and madder to carry on to the bitter end or whenever.

Ronnie, my fearless secretary was an absolute godsend. Ron Poms, as I nicknamed her was outwardly so gentle and warm and yet her ability to organise was amazing. She had the affectionate habit of calling me 'Boss Boss'. To tell you the truth I loved it. She found her time was *constantly* cut out making umpteen cups of coffee because she was *constantly* making appointments for me to see Music Publishers, Managers, Agents and everybody who was anybody in the Record Industry. She also set up dates for me to audition new Bands and Artists at all sorts of strange times and venues.

Ron O'Shea had been recommended to me by two or three reliable sources as the sort of guy who wouldn't take no for an answer and was blessed with a more than average amount of gift of the gab. We arranged to meet in a coffee bar in Tottenham Court Road.

"You need me as much as I need you" he said quite emphatically. For one long minute there was silence but then the mutual respect between us began to kick in and we felt as a team we could bring Alaska Records the success that was so positively envisaged. We did a deal, with Ron temporarily carrying the title of both The General and The Promotion Manager of Alaska Records. A short while later I employed **Alan Heather** as Head of Promotion and also **Ian Stephenson** as a record 'plugger.'

Somehow I have always been fortunate with Radio as well as the Media. I have contributed to numerous radio programmes across the country and I am proud to have had many excellent write-ups not only on myself personally but as an Artist, as a songwriter, as a Producer and as a Label Manager. I have had some incredible support for many of my musical adventures over the years, Sounds Orchestral being one good example.

Alaska needed every ounce of Media help it could get and that is why I independently employed the services of **Roger St. Pierre,** not only a talent in this field but he was also familiar with my track record. Likewise I employed the services of **Dick Barnatt,** brilliant at picture taking, to handle advertising and photography. Last but not least I retained the services of **The Margaret Brace Copyright Bureau** with regard to compiling Royalty Statements, Music Publishing Agreements and Artist Contracts.

As with any Artist, a record label should have or must have a positive musical direction. I knew I wanted to make quality product. I knew to compete and be seriously accepted I needed to have Hit Records. I also knew I wanted to create longevity with my Artists and this surprisingly came very quickly with no warning at all, in the form of Cymande. I was also open minded to considering prospective talent in all musical directions because my own make-up dictated it.

After a great deal of time, deliberation and frustration I had at last got what I considered to be the right team behind Alaska Records. My number one priority was now to build the Artist roster and get the right product into the market place.

I knew for Alaska Records to be successful I needed to draw upon every ounce of recording experience I had acquired over the previous years of my professional career. There was such a wealth of it but uncannily, once again it was Norrie Paramor who was whispering in my ear. "Remember you have to implicitly believe in the Artists that you sign and the material you intend to record with them. You have to know exactly what it is you are after and what you want to hear as the finished product and you also have to be sure to get the result in the allocated time period because time is the essence of money. Above all go with *your* gut feeling and do what *you* believe in. There is no substitute for that."

When it's your own label the mixture of financial stress and creative drive can be a lethal combination and often brings about the temptation of cutting corners such as using an inadequately equipped studio to save cost which then becomes a possible threat to the success of the finished product. With every project I had in mind I endeavoured to avoid this trap. It wasn't easy!

Since practically all Alaska's released product was my decision, the burden of success or failure was squarely on my shoulders. However this was also shared by the skill, talent and dedication of the highly supportive team around me who always had to bear in mind and live with the fact that we were a small label struggling to make our voice heard in a highly competitive industry. We intended to give it our best shot!

The Office, Alaska Records Ltd,
12 The Quadrangle, Cambridge Sq, London. W1

The Heart of Alaska

John Schroeder
Label Manager – Producer

Ronnie (Ron Poms) Jones
Secretary

Ron O'Shea
General Manager

Ian Stephenson
Promotion

Alan Heather
Head of Promotion

Mustang is GO!

Cool Dudes!

Not So Cool Dudes!

It was all Ron's idea. He loved American cars and desperately wanted one. Knowing how weak-minded I was about cars, he managed to persuade me that it would be a good idea to invest in an old pale blue Ford Mustang that had caught his eye. "It would provide us with something different to bring attention to the label," he was quick to emphasise with a persuasive smile. He knew I couldn't resist the temptation and suddenly there she was! We had an Alaska logo imprinted on each side of her and I have to admit I just loved it.

When our baby ran, and that was not too often, she did create considerable attention and we all felt and believed we looked like 'super cool dudes' but when she broke down, and that was rather too often she also created considerable attention and making us feel and look like ' super dumb dudes'! This was more than embarrassing to say the least.

One rather nasty uncalled for and hurtful remark I overheard was "Their fucking Mustang's broken down again just like the sound of their records!"

Must have been jealousy – what else?!

CHAPTER NINETEEN

We were at last officially open for business, and once Alaska's whereabouts through word of mouth and the media became known we were inundated with prospective Artists and recording propositions. My first signings and first releases started to make their presence known. Surprisingly, initial reaction and response was far greater than any of us expected.

> Friday December 21st 1974 – The Entertainment News
>
> Record Companies
>
> *In this day the giants hardly give the small labels a chance, yet 1973 found many companies holding their own. ALASKA is rapidly becoming a brand name and CYMANDE their most widely marketable product. They can only get bigger so watch out!*

Ron, Alan and Ian were all firing promotion bullets in the right places and many were hitting their target but it was distribution that gave us our number one headache. It was a proven fact that when a kid walked into a record store with the money to buy a single record and that record was not there he would definitely spend his money on something else. We lost a lot of sales through product not being available for two to three days when the demand was there. I strongly believe at least three potential hit singles were lost in this way. Distributors were far more interested in meeting sales demand with major Artists and Record Companies before getting round to a small independent label like ours. I was in fact forced to change Alaska's pressing and distribution deal three times in four years!

There was no question it was tough out there, especially as competition was so fierce, but as I have mentioned before our greatest success and income came from abroad where our product was far better received and far better evaluated. It was so nice to do business with people who really appreciated the effort, the product and the belief of what we at Alaska Records were trying to achieve. This resulted in us having chart success in France, Germany, Holland and even Japan. We also provided the initial recording opportunity to many Artists that later became established names such as The Dooley Family, or The Dooleys as they became known.

The Artistic Power of Alaska

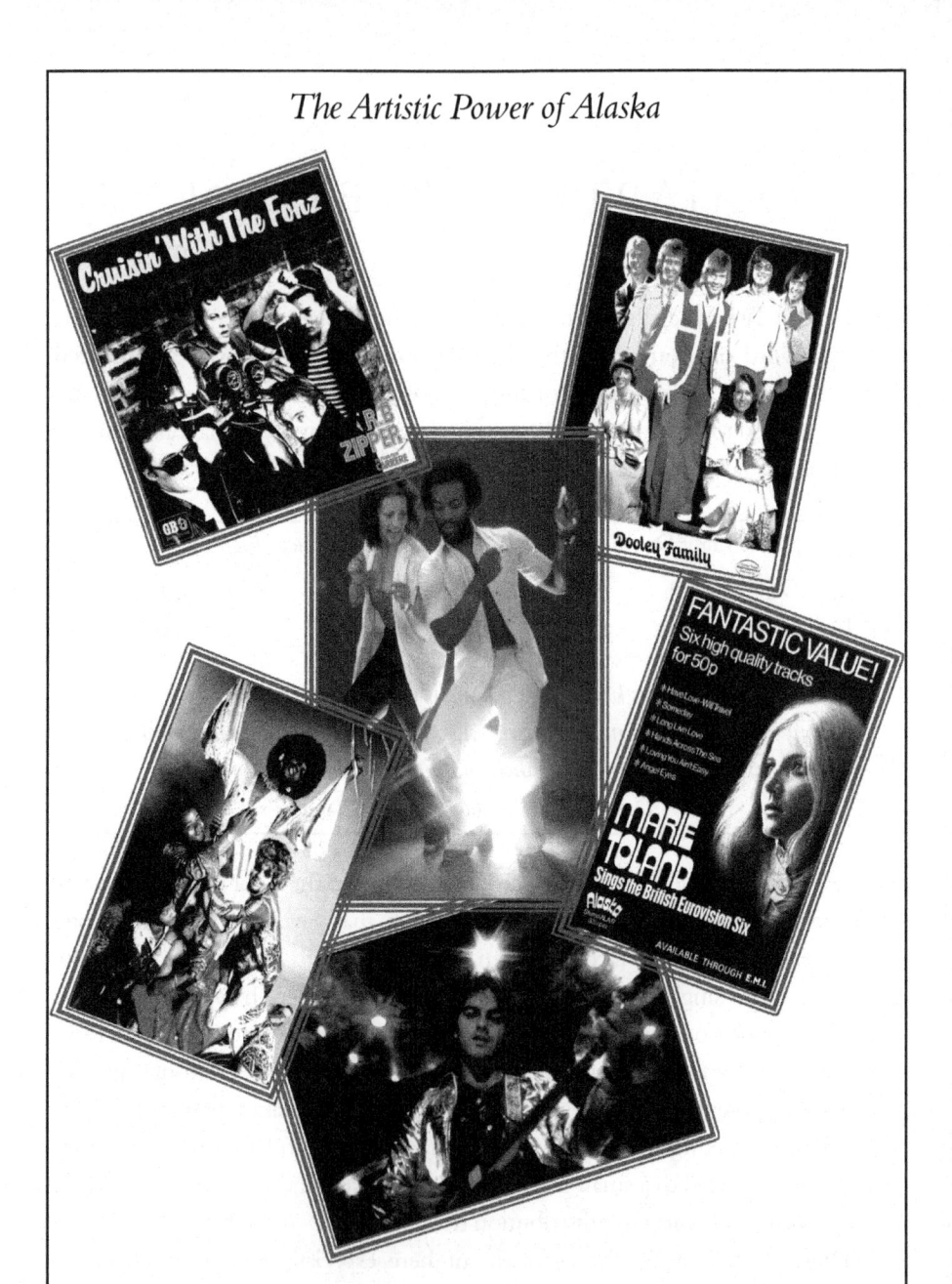

R B ZIPPER *(Trevor Horn (far left) the well known producer, was in this group)*
THE DOOLEY FAMILY *(Later had numerous chart hits as The Dooleys)*
LOVE DIMENSION *(Recorded much played disco version of Smile)*
ERASMUS CHORUM *(Britain's first gay rock band)*
MARIE TOLAND *(Six Eurovision song entries including 'Hands Across The Sea', 'Loving You Ain't Easy' 'Angel Eyes' etc)*
JULIAN LITTMAN *(So talented so underrated Soul Rock artist)*

To bring attention to a small label it had to be consistently active, doing things, sometimes crazy things all the time, that were strong and interesting enough to arouse the attention of The Media. One of these projects gave us our first Chart Record.

One day a songwriter named Nick Ryan played me a demo of a song called *'Naughty Naughty Naughty.'* The idea was based on the catch phrase of the Punch and Judy character. It was extremely infectious and insane enough to be a Hit. Nick also brought my attention to Joy Sarney, the young lady who had made the demo. I had to agree that she was vocally well suited to it. I liked the whole idea and the only problem I could foresee was to find an authentic Punch voice. By chance I had to go Clacton one weekend, and lo and behold I came across exactly what I was looking for in the form of Tony Green who was performing in his usual residential spot on the pier. Needless to say he was surrounded by kids who were still enthralled by the rather violent antics of Punch and Judy. Tony, bless him was only too pleased to do what I wanted. We had a fun day in the studio recording this rather unusual scenario. For his sins, Tony also ended up having to do the song on Top of the Pops. The record ultimately sold 250,000, made it into the top Twenty and did Alaska a power of good, making its reality much more universal even though it did little to further Alaska's envisaged musical direction.

The success of this record was a great morale booster for all of us, especially our Artists, since they now felt an element of pride in sharing this success and being part of what was now a successful label with a track record!

Marvin Schlacter, head of Janus Records, has for many years been a close friend of mine both professionally and personally. Our association goes back to the days of Sounds Orchestral when he was responsible for orchestrating the breakthrough success of *'Cast Your Fate To The Wind'* in the States.

Now with Cymande's first album being the fastest selling album in the New York market that Janus had ever released, and the single *'The Message'* becoming a solid Top Twenty hit in both the Pop and R and B categories, Marvin had set the stage for the first Alaska single releases in America.

Billboard April 14th 1973

John Schroeder made his future with CYMANDE.
He assures it with two singles about the past.

"Happy Birthday Sweet Sixteen"
by **Gulliver**

"Wash My Mem'ries"
by **Chance**

John Schroeder is associated with music that people remember. Like his Cymande album, now an international hit. That same kind of excitement is being guaranteed by a new group called Chance. Which is NOT how you'll discover this exciting single.

We're proud to have John Schroeder part of the Chess/Janus family

Black Bear and Harbor

Following four years of miraculously 'still hangin' in there' I felt the time was right for Alaska to have a sister. Black Bear was formed specifically as a show case to exploit my love of Black and Soul music, pointing the finger of attention to the undeniable talent of such Artists as Joanne Williams, Steve Haynes, Mel Nixon, James Jamieson etc.

Harbor Records on the other hand was formed specifically as a showcase to the acquisition of both American and European product.

Music Week October 13th 1979

HARBOR RECORDS is John Schroeder's new label, which he believes will play a part in his own personal "fight against the lethargy and general depression in the music industry"

Schroeder has therefore decided to be led by his own track record, looking to America to sign Artists directly to this UK label and he has been there twice to establish a further dialogue between himself and US artist/managers.

Steve Haynes and Richard Stepp (Canadian artist signed at Midem) are the label's first releases. Other signings are American rock band Zingo and UK Band Hooker

The Artistry Of Harbor And Black Bear

Richard Stepp, Joey Dee, Steve Haynes, Mel Nixon, Joanne Williams

How I got so heavily into Seventies Rock 'n' Roll I'll never really know, but there was a big revival going on at the time. Both Bill Haley and Chuck Berry came over and did some mind blowing gigs. I got presented with a really impressive and commendable self made album by a Band called The Flying Saucers. I went to see them live and they were good, very good. In fact they were so good that they were asked to actually back Chuck Berry, and they were also the support band with Bill Haley and the Comets. Most of their material was original and self penned by the very talented Sandy Ford, the Band's lead singer. We had considerable success abroad, especially with a sensational track entitled *'Keep on Comin'*. We got good reaction here but didn't quite manage to pull it off.

The Cruisers were another Seventies Rock 'n' Roll Band that were originally very much into 'doo wap.' I loved this band. They were so tight and their vocals were excellent. I consider we produced a great version of the classic *'Get a Job'* which really deserved to have made the charts. They also had the honour of appearing on the same bill as Chuck Berry.

On reflection I think I must have been the only person and the only record label apart from Charly at the time crazy enough to support a rock 'n' roll revival. I just loved the music, and the talent of the Artists I became involved with was unquestionable.

Crazy Cavan and the Rhythm Rockers also didn't escape my attention but at the request of their management I produced them independently for Charly Records. They were a band with personality plus and totally magnetic on stage. To get away from the aura of a studio (Olympic Sound Studios to be exact) we built a large stage in the middle of the studio to help them feel *on top of things* but this time I couldn't get away with inviting an audience. (Thoughts of Geno Washington!)

Olympic Sound Studios situated in Barnes had an outstanding reputation with a track record of name Artists a mile long. But it was also thought to be haunted! The front reception area was connected to the studios by a very long corridor and the ghost, believed to be friendly dragged a chain down this corridor at night every so often. I swear to God I was mixing the Cavan album at three in the morning and during one of the tracks there was this intermittent clinking noise. The engineer thought it was a technical fault in the console and so shut everything down. There was a deathly silence and then this scary metallic clinking noise sounding exactly like a chain being dragged started then stopped and then started again, moving from left to right. This went on for two minutes which seemed like an hour. To say we were shitting ourselves would be putting it mildly!

Ironically, the album which was entitled *'Our Own Way Of Rockin'* had a front sleeve with a picture of a hand with a bicycle *chain* wrapped round it. For me a chilling reminder!

Rock 'n' Roll Showcase

Phil Carlson at Warner/Atlantic Records asked me if I would be interested in producing an album with Ronnie Barker entitled *Ronnie Barker's Unbroken British Record* for K-Tel Records but also allowing me to release two tracks from it on the Alaska label. I chose Pismonunciation and The Vicar of St. Cain and Abel. I didn't have to think twice about this offer because to produce such a talented Artist with such an enviable track record was a really huge honour. I felt proud to have been asked.

Ronnie Barker was one of if not the easiest Artist I have ever worked with. His material was always well prepared and it would be very rare indeed for the necessity of a second take. He was very amenable to direction and would consider any professional suggestions. He was a prime example of a perfectionist. No room was big enough to hold his talent. Out of the studio he was very quiet and charming but behind those eyes there was always that glint of mischievousness. I greatly respected and admired him and am so grateful to have had the opportunity of working with such a genius.

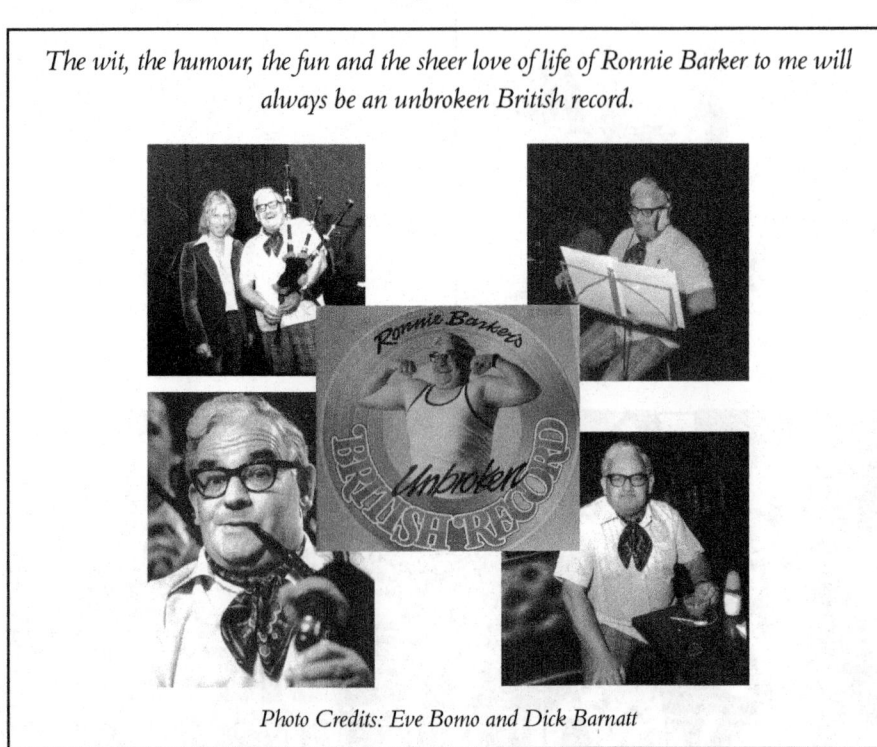

The wit, the humour, the fun and the sheer love of life of Ronnie Barker to me will always be an unbroken British record.

Photo Credits: Eve Bomo and Dick Barnatt

CHAPTER TWENTY

HTS

Running a record company, however small, and especially your own, is unquestionably one helluva headache, especially financially.

One of the biggest expenses was the continuous use of the services of a professionally high standard tape copying studio. We needed tapes copied all the time particularly copies of masters requested by various companies round the world. Eventually I came to the conclusion that it would be cheaper to create a comprehensive studio and tape copying service ourselves which could also include editing and equalisation. It would not only be able to cater for our own requirements but other record labels as well. On the face of it, it seemed a solid financial proposition, and there was a demand for it. I virtually knew everybody that was anybody, so I figured there would be no shortage of business.

Finding the right premises was a headache since they needed to be easily accessible and situated in the heart of the music industry which meant Central London. Eventually I got lucky and found a suite of offices on the third floor of 73 Newman Street, which was just off Soho and not far from Tottenham Court Road which was really an ideal location.

Some time before this idea came to me, I met Bill Crompton, a songwriter who had emigrated to Vancouver Canada but periodically came over to London. He happened to be a professional carpenter, and for no particular reason I told him in the course of conversation of my intended new venture. He saw the premises and consequently offered to adapt them to my requirements in return for a piece of the business. We ended up with a small reception area, the studio itself which was fairly large, an impressive console, speakers and tape machines, in fact all the necessary hi tech equipment for copying and reduction, my office which was a nice size and a further studio where we installed multi racking to house numerous video machines of virtually every conceivable format. Video, particularly promotional video, was becoming a major industry so we were now also equipped to provide a very high standard video duplication service. There was one other office which I decided to rent out. This was taken by Ged Doherty who today holds the very enviable position of Chairman of Sony BMG . At the time he was managing Paul Young and the Q Tips. The whole place was very functional and pretty impressive, becoming quite a den of activity.

The Company was named **Harbor Tape Services,** since it was envisaged as a subsidiary to Harbor Records, and of course I had to inject a considerable amount of hard earned capital into it.

Bill Crompton obviously did not charge the Company for his input nor did he contribute any speculative capital into the business but he did end up having a very nice percentage of the Company.

The Reception

The Studio

The Office

I was lucky to find Graham Watts, a trustworthy and talented young recording engineer who was equally at home working with both audio and video. He operated the two studios very efficiently whilst the lovely Karen Jackson whom I employed as *the* secretary looked after the admin and studio bookings. Surprisingly, advertising was not necessary since word of our existence got around so quickly. It wasn't long before we had work coming in from RCA, CBS and EMI. Our rates were very competitive but our greatest asset was being able to turn the jobs around almost immediately since none of us had any objection to working half way through the night to do it.

The little white Mini Clubman I bought a while ago from my illustrious friend Don, primarily to reduce the running costs of that unforgettably beautiful white Rolls, was to serve me well for some years to come. With her wooden dashboard, wooden console and alloy wheels she also stood out from the crowd especially as I had retained and transferred the personalised number of **JS X12**. Eye catching that she was, I had already got caught out on one or two memorable occasions being seen somewhere and with someone I shouldn't have been! For some dangerous excitement I considered a bit of 'in your face' ego was well worth it!

I dreaded it but I knew at some stage it was inevitable that there would be no more trips to Alaska, the Alaska I had developed and financed over the last few years.

Without my really realising it, my professional life was changing. Since the studio was doing so well I was spending far more time at Newman Street than with the running, upkeep and progress of Alaska Records, Harbor Records and Black Bear. Alaska was now in its eighth year of madness and becoming an ever increasing financial burden, mainly due to industry changes and the increase in pressing, distribution and studio charges. It had had a good run for its money with Cymande's success, Joy Sarney's success and the label's consistent achievement and recognition abroad over the years making it all very worthwhile.

When it was finally put to sleep there was really no great financial gain or loss, only those many unforgettable moments, some sad some glad. I have often asked myself what had been the point of it all anyway. It was of course the challenge of coming up with the skill to make it successful and for me not knowing unless I gave it my best shot. The worst scenario was the Artists themselves. I was upset to see some truly great talent go to waste as it was to witness the failure through impossible odds of some unquestionably chart orientated product.

To be honest I would never attempt such a venture again, the financial gamble especially being far too great unless of course there was outside investment. I am not sorry for one moment to have done it but in retrospect the weakness lay in myself. I was trying to wear too many hats at the same time when I should have stuck to the one I knew best which was record production. There were basically too many company-type every day problems to be able to concentrate solely on one thing at a time although I am adamant that the actual making of the product did not suffer. If only I had my brother's business acumen things might have been different!

On the plus side, it had been an exciting but scary roller coaster ride producing my own company's product. However, once again I had the opportunity of working with so many talented people both technically and artistically all over the world which was the reality of an impossible dream. The Alaska team was dedicated and conscientious having achieved against all odds some unbelievable results but with the industry changing daily like it was, we all knew the writing was on the wall. Music at this time and what it stood for was never so far down the list of importance. Accountants, Managers and Lawyers were now the stars of the show.

After the trauma of the burial I transferred all Alaska's assets into the ownership of John Schroeder Enterprises Limited which to this day controls anything relating to Alaska Records and its associates. I ran my life from Newman Street which became a really busy place with audio and video work coming in from so many sources, even off the street.

It soon became evident that the additional facility of a fully comprehensive video duplication service was to put our studio one step ahead of the other guy.

Initially instigated by Bill Crompton's shady contacts whilst in London, we sort of unavoidably found ourselves caught up with the duplication of blue videos. Bill thought it was a bit of good business acumen but I thought we should, for obvious reasons distance ourselves from the product we were professionally involved with as it was not our concern to ask what where and why. But in this case word got around so fast and since the video studio was so conveniently comfortably furnished, suddenly from out of nowhere and not being able to stop it (as if I truthfully wanted to) we had an exclusive 'music biz' video club on our hands which met once a week to view the latest piece of pornographic art. At one point I thought we were going to need a 'bouncer'! (Just joking) For some strange reason there was a distinct increase in our overall business!

Young Graham was a gem but I had to keep him on his toes.

Video fascinated me, especially from the production point of view. It was a different adventure but it was becoming clear that the music industry was demanding that every new record released needed to have a promotional video with it. To do this was initially extremely expensive and really only name Artists were at this stage able to benefit. This was a plus for us from a duplication point of view because down the road we were driving in an unknown and unfamiliar direction but one which was looking invitingly optimistic and financially lucrative.

Esme

Having played squash most of my life, and prided myself in keeping physically fit by even going to the gym, I suddenly began to realise that through the medium of radio, television and video more and more emphasis was being put on to health, food and fitness in relation to our daily lives. Due to the out of nowhere success in America of a keep fit video made by none other than Jane Fonda, it wasn't long before women in particular over here, were about to get hooked on to what I believed proved to be a forthcoming craze. The craze of looking good feeling better.

It was purely by accident that one day at my squash club I had the pleasure of meeting Esme Newton – Dunne who was *Cosmopolitan's* much respected and envied fitness teacher. I was fascinated by her vast experience of the subject and the fact that she had written two books, appeared on TV and taught keep-fit regularly. On hearing this *and looking at her* I reckoned that I could create a keep-fit video with Esme but with a more personal approach. I imagined the viewer participating in a specialised programme of simple exercises with her in the comfort of their own home and at times that were convenient to them. They could for instance do ten minutes with Esme before going to work each morning. I also had in mind to show ways of lessening stress with everyday things, for example the right way to pick up a heavy bag of some kind such as a shopping bag. When you think about it there are so many things we do each day that are stress related and there are so many ways we can learn to reduce this stress – listening to and watching this video hopefully being one of them.

I had no experience of video production at all except that I knew what I wanted to create. I was lucky to come across Michael, a video cameraman who had already acquired an enviable track record. He loved the concept of this video and for sure without his input I could never have produced it.

I believed it had to be like a book and have a beginning, a middle and an end. I remember filming the anxiety of trying to hail a cab in the rush hour for the opening sequence. I remember going to someone's house, probably Esme's, and filming everyday stress related things in the home. I remember we virtually converted a squash court into a studio to film the series of exercises that Esme had spent so much precious time in working out. Then there was the music and the editing which was a work of art but a living nightmare. Looking back, it was creatively exciting but frightening for me being in unknown waters without complete control. I was pleased with the finished product but had I created a saleable commodity?

Walter Voyda at Precision Video believed I had, agreeing with me that the interest in keep fit was about to become very much bigger, huge in fact. He really wanted to release **Looking Good Feeling Better**.

Precision did a remarkably a good job with the advertising and promotion of it but unfortunately it proved to be just a little too much ahead of its time, like a few other things I had done throughout my career.

Esme – looking good

Recently someone who must have known me, Esme and the video intimately went out of their way to send me this as an inspiring reminder of an historic occasion!

I don't play squash for nothing ya know!

CHAPTER TWENTY-ONE

Things were going good, too good really. HTS was prospering and there was plenty of work but for some reason I felt very uneasy. It wasn't long before I was proved right.

Although there was a great deal of work coming in from the major Record Companies they inclined to become, dare I say, lackadaisical in their paying of invoices within a reasonable period of time and in fact beyond the period initially laid down in the terms of agreement. I was forced to make them aware of my concern even to the extent of offering them a discount for payment within twenty one days of completion of the work. They replied that whilst they sympathised, the present time scale of payment was now the company's policy as far as their accounting was concerned and no special conditions could be applied even with the offer of a discount. It is strange that they all had said the same thing at the same time.

I was gutted as I felt blackmailed by the fact that they knew I could not afford to lose their business and they knew seventy five per cent of it came from them. The offer of a discount meant nothing. The real crunch and almost the final straw came when Ampex decided to join in the fun.

Ampex unquestionably manufactured the best virgin tape which we totally relied upon, as without it there could be no business. They were now *politely* suggesting that they could no longer supply their product without payment within seven days of receipt. This was crippling, especially as major Record Companies insisted on us using Ampex tape for their copying needs. Our business was being seriously threatened as we now found ourselves with a serious financial problem on our hands.

I was having hardly any sleep through the intensive worry of all this when the phone rang at two o'clock one morning. It was the police who said I should go down to the studio immediately as it had been broken into. They would not tell me anything further. As I drove down there I can't describe how I felt. I have never felt so unwell. When I arrived, there were police all over the place and I was greeted by walking straight into the shock of seeing all our video and audio machines stacked up downstairs inside the front door presumably ready to be transported out of the building! The front door to our suite was smashed to pieces. It was alarmed but the wires had been cut. The two studios were virtually bits of broken wood but neither my office nor the reception area had been touched.

I cried in despair but the Senior Officer in charge was either endeavouring to be vaguely sympathetic or plainly sarcastic. He said in a matter of fact tone of voice

"Consider yourself lucky Mr. Schroeder. You've still got all your machinery. At least we stopped that going out the door. You'll need to get hold of a lock company now and get the front door secured and re-alarmed. There's an insurance guy here and he'll get that sorted for you. I reckon they knew what they wanted and they knew all that stuff was in here. They don't like failure you know and they could easily come back again, usually it's within two weeks."

I was shaking with the shock of it all. To get the door fixed, the studios repaired and the equipment put back and up and running was going to take at least a week especially as Bill Crompton was not in the country. With desperation in my voice I said

"Couldn't you put a guard, just one guy even on the premises for a couple of weeks? Just being there he would act as a deterrent"

"Oh no sir we couldn't do that. We couldn't spare one man. We're far too busy dealing with serious crime like murder and violence!" he said quite unemotionally.

Where was he when I needed him most? Bill could have fixed that damage in no time but it took Graham and I with the help of a hired carpenter and an understanding insurance company a good number of sleepless nights before everything was back in place and running again. Our clients were surprisingly concerned and did show some understanding and sympathy but basically we were still left with the same financial problems.

Two weeks had gone by since the burglary and we started to relax but it was inevitable that we found ourselves running out of stock of virgin tape. It was time to see the Bank Manager to put him in the picture regarding our cash flow problem in the hope that he would help us out of our immediate predicament. Persuading him to come down to visit the studio when we first opened was a smart move and thankfully I consequently had no problem with securing a bank loan. We were back in business putting the last three mad weeks behind us.

"No! No! No!" I screamed to myself down the phone "not again please God not again not after all we've been through."

Would you believe the bastards had done it again but this time the equipment had really gone and the clever little sods had taken it out through the roof of the building. Unlike the previous occasion, this time there was hardly any damage done to anything at all. The alarm had been professionally cut off again and great care had been taken in unplugging all the machinery and carefully extracting it from its location. There was no damage done to the front door of the suite and no damage done to the recording console, speakers or the video and audio racks. The biggest insult of all was that in my office I had some drink and on my desk were four empty glasses with an empty bottle of Champagne standing next to them. The bastards had drunk to my health having practically given me a heart attack!

The police were not much help but believed the job was well organised and planned by someone who knew the premises, knew the equipment and knew just how much time they needed to complete the operation. Together we went through the books, through every one likely I could think of in my mind, our clients, people off the street and even our staff.

The last straw
There was nothing anyone could say. Karen, Graham and I stared helplessly in disbelief at the bare rooms that had once again been a hive of activity the day before. It was a sickening sight not only because it was the second time in three weeks but we had worked so fucking hard to recover from the first fiasco. The money had been sorted out, the place re-built, the equipment re-installed and orders were coming in but now we were faced with the embarrassment of having to tell our clients to go elsewhere since we had no equipment to service the orders. Both the Police and the Insurance Company were in no hurry to sort it out; after all it wasn't a *serious crime was it!*

Graham and Karen, bless them understood perfectly when I told them in all honesty that I had no inclination whatsoever to put Humpty Dumpty back together again. I had had enough and the thought of it happening again would always be there. I felt it was like having had a bad accident in your car, the car being repaired but never feeling quite the same again. There were also too many loose ends and too many unanswered questions. I had to admire the nerve, but drinking *my* health with *my* glasses, *my* champagne and in *my* office was the last straw. I was not amused!

I had the awful feeling that my career had been brought to an abrupt, quick and final end. This was not what I had envisaged at all. Perhaps HTS and all that it stood for was just not meant to be. My love in life was making music and making people feel happy and romantic with the music I made. I found myself in the frame of mind of just wanting to run away from everything and everybody so I made a big decision and went to live in Canada.

During my time there I produced several Canadian artists both in Vancouver and Toronto. It was necessary to also produce them in French since Canada is a French speaking country. Luckily I could speak French myself which was a great help!. I remember being very impressed with Little Mountain Studios in Vancouver. I was also honoured to be invited as a judge on a national television talent show entitled "The Fame Game".

It was only through my parent's ill health that I subsequently returned to England in 1990, ten years later.

I came back to find Status Quo with their album Rockin' All Over The World almost at the top of the album charts. I began to realise nostalgia, especially in relation to the Sixties and Seventies period was becoming big business with re-issues and compilations being avidly put together. The original sounds thanks to modern day technology were being enhanced and given a totally new lease of life. The music I had made was being heard, played and appreciated all over again. I was thrilled to pieces.

One thing led to another and out of the blue I was asked by John Judd, Helen Shapiro's husband, if I would do the honour of becoming the President of the Helen Shapiro Fan Club since Humphrey Lyttelton was retiring. I didn't know there was still one in existence. I was honoured to accept and I could not believe how big and internationally minded it was. It had its own monthly Newsletter and suddenly I found myself signing autographs again! What a shot of adrenalin it was. I felt a million dollars and even though it was a blast from the past, I was made to feel and felt I was literally once again *Walking back to Happiness!*

Whatever my inner most feelings might be I still get a kick every time I see, hear or read about Status Quo and the adventures of Rick and Rossi. I smile to myself knowing that there has never been a band that has survived and been acclaimed as long as the Quo. The traumas I endured and the years that I stuck with them at Pye Records will always be very much a satisfying but hurtful achievement even though I was not invited to Morecambe for their twenty fifth anniversary. The greatest personal accomplishment was the recording and subsequent success of *'Pictures of Matchstick Men', 'Down the Dustpipe'* and the *'Dog of Two Head'* album.

Also high on my memory list was the record I made with Rick Parfitt who sung the lead on a song that I and Tony King had especially written for him. It was the sound of his voice and the emotion he was able to portray that had inspired it.

'Are you growing tired of my love?' achieved a phenomenal review in Disc on its first week of release. Today one of my biggest wishes in the world is that song making it into the charts recorded by one of today's Artists possibly a boys Band such as Boyzone or Take That. It wasn't so much that I had written it but that it was and still is a very strong song both lyrically and melodically, and without being biased has hit written all over it.

> ## Quo's best ever
>
> STATUS QUO: *Are You Growing Tired Of My Love? (Pye)*
>
> *If I had heard this disc without first seeing the label I would never have suspected it was Status Quo. It's a complete change of style for this group, and is totally removed from the distinctive sound it created in "Matchstick Men"*
>
> *All the same, it's an excellent record – in my opinion, the best that Quo has ever made. Opens quietly, with the air of moodiness heightened by clanking piano and deep throated cellos. Then it breaks into the melodic chorus – a beautiful melody that's still in my ears. The stringy backing is imaginative, the boy's harmonies are colourful and the beat is solid enough for dancing – particularly when it intensifies in the latter stages. Very good indeed – with, I thought, a hint of the Bee Gee's about it*

The discovery and recording of Cymande in 1972 will always remain a high point in my career. At last the world, or some of it, had woken up to this fantastic Band proclaiming its infectious talent and amazing writing ability.

A top twenty single, a chart album and two American tours, one supporting Al Green in 1973 was an extraordinary achievement suddenly coming out of nowhere. It makes me feel proud because it condones my implicit belief in an Artist, financing the project when I could ill afford it and against all odds achieving universal success even though it has taken thirty years to do it! This Band and their music was way before its time and I believe there have been no less than thirty two Artists who have sampled their material amongst them The Fugees and MC Solar. I feel elated every time a request for the use of something connected with Cymande is put before me. Today their music is not only being used on Television but has even found its way on to the big screen.

Sanctuary Records upheld their belief in this Artist with material being consistently released and licensed all over the world. My personal thanks goes to Lorraine Jones, Sanctuary's licensing manager for her relentless help and undivided attention in this respect. Currently a CD containing all the Cymande material digitally re-mastered is receiving and will go on receiving solid attention especially on radio. They and I have recently been featured on Soul Britannia, a TV programme dedicated to the strength and popularity of Black Soul Music in this country.

"Has there been anything in your career that has meant more to you than anything else?"

How many times have I been asked that question and how easy actually it has been to answer it? Without a doubt it was the discovery and subsequent recording of *'Cast Your Fate To The Wind,'* but more than that was the fact it provided the means of bringing Orchestral Music nearer to the understanding of the younger generation. That was the challenge and ultimately the achievement. I also pride myself that Sounds Orchestral was a very clever name.

Once again I was recently overcome with the feeling of the return of the excitement of, dare I say my memorable past when Sam Szczepanski, a highly talented and charming young lady who carried the title of Special Projects Manager at Sanctuary Records came up with the idea of a CD compilation containing forty four instrumental tracks all digitally re-mastered and all carefully selected from the vast repertoires of Sounds Orchestral, The John Schroeder Orchestra and The City of Westminster String Band.

SOUL COAXING – the many moods of JOHN SCHROEDER does do justice in showcasing *my way* of how I feel about some of the best songs ever written, some of the best recordings I have ever produced and featuring some of the best and most talented musicians this country has ever had to offer.

The reaction to this CD took me completely by surprise. It has received some excellent reviews with certain tracks being singled out and played consistently on local radio stations across the country. Thanks Sam!

The release of this CD also triggered considerable interest in the request for my participation in various interviews based on my many years in the Music Industry. One particular radio station was so impressed with the amount of material that it put the interview out in three parts. I shall never forget the Presenter's final words at the close of the third part.

"John we're running out of time but as heard by the records we have played it is very noticeable how much belief, feeling and emotion you put into the music you make. I must confess that my wife absolutely insisted that *'Cast Your Fate to the Wind'* be played at our wedding otherwise there might well not have been one! Is there any way you can express or describe your feelings about the music you have given us and what it has meant to you over the years?

There was a momentarily pause whilst that question sank in.

I looked him straight in the eye and then repeated it quite passionately and quite emphatically.

"All that I have done successfully or unsuccessfully I can truthfully say has been done… **all for the love of music**."

FRINGE BENEFIT
Soul coaxing – the many moods of John Schroeder

★★★★☆

As well as penning hits for Helen Shapiro, John Schroeder was the man who introduced Tamla Motown to the UK. His talents extend to composer, arranger and producer, contributing to Sounds Orchestral's Million seller Cast your Fate to the Wind. Throughout the 1960s and 1970s he released a string of underrated albums featuring trademark, multi-layered, swirling, pop/jazz like interpretations of original and cover material such as Love is Blue, Wichita Lineman or Parisian megastar Michel Polnareff's

Glorious Soul Coaxing. The surprisingly funky side of Schroeder's slant on cheesy listening, evident on tracks such as Spinning Wheel, Get out Of My Life Woman and Papa's Got A Brand New Bag, appeals to both loungecore and Northern Soul DJs, while his work with Brit-funk protégés Cymande has influenced the likes of MC Solaar and the Fugees. Schroeder's presence continues with his Explosive Corrosive Joseph on the Ocean's Twelve soundtrack.

Keith Barker-Main. Music Week. April 2005

POSTSCRIPT

Out of a delegation of businessmen who went to Russia in the early sixties only two were instrumental in consummating a business deal with the Russian's, one of them being my father seen here shaking hands with President Kruschev.

The mystery of the letter written to me by Sir Joseph Lockwood, the Chairman of EMI Records in 1957 was disclosed to me by my mother when she was desperately ill. Apparently my father was doing business with E.M.I. at the time and mentioned to Sir Joseph Lockwood that I wanted to make the Music Industry my career more than anything else in the world even though he was vehemently against it. He also told him, and I gather quite proudly, that after waiting six months I had actually been accepted for a job in the Sales Office of E.M.I Records.

With the way my father was feeling about me and my career at the time, he didn't have to say anything to Sir Joseph Lockwood so it probably took him some courage to do it, or did he do it out of love or did he just do it out of guilt?

I shall never know but he did it!

ARTISTS PROUCED OR CO-PRODUCED THROUGHOUT MY CAREER

1957 – 1962

Artists produced with Norrie Paramor as Assistant to Norrie Paramor – Columbia Records

Michael Holiday	Billie Anthony
Tony Brent	Helen Shapiro
The Mudlarks	Tommy Bruce
The Avons	Frank Ifield
Pearl Carr and Teddy Johnson	The Norrie Paramor Orchestra
Cliff Richard	The Big Ben Banjo Band
The Shadows	Dickie Pride
Eddie Calvert	Jimmy Crawford
Brendan O'Dowda	Dave Sampson
Reginald Dixon	Ricky Valance
Ido Martin	

1962 – 1964

Artists produced as Label Manager for Oriole Records

Maureen Evans	Johnny Pearson
Brett Ansell	Jan Burnett
Tony Sheveton	Ray Pilgrim
The Dowlands	Mark Dwayne
Jackie Trent	Tony Raymond
The Spotniks	Brian Weske
Jacques Jordane	Rey Anton
Jackie Lee and The Raindrops	Alan Klein
Sue and Sunny	Deek Rivers
Intimate Strangers	Col James
The Gary Edwards Combo	Christine Quaite
Frank and The Barbarians	Sol Raye
Susan Singer	Paul Hanford
Carter – Lewis and The Southerners	Faron's Flamingos
Clinton Ford	The Jeff Rowena Five

This is Mersey Beat Artists:-
Rory Storm and The Hurricanes
Sonny Webb and The Cascades
Ian and The Zodiacs
The Del Renas
Earl Preston and The TT's
The Nomads
Faron's Flamingos
The Merseybeats
Derek Wilkie & The Pressmen
Mark Peters & The Silhouettes

1964 – 1972

Artists produced as Label Manager for Dawn – Pye – Piccadilly Records

The Rockin' Berries	Ebony Keyes
Peter's Faces	Peter Jay and The Jaywalkers
The New Formula	Sounds Orchestral
The Ray King Soul Band	The John Schroeder Orchestra
Stella Starr	The City of Westminster String Band
The Knack	Status Quo
Jackie Challenor	Band of Angels
Paddington Bear	The Lovin' Kind
The Factotums	Geno Washington and The Ram Jam Band
Jimmy James	Jimmy James and The Vagabonds
The Ivy League	Kes Wyndham
Antoinette	Glo Macari
Shirley Abicair	David Garrick
The Sorrows	The Hellions
Helen Shapiro	Jan Panter
Barbara Ruskin	Dodie West
Keith Powell	Billie Davis
The Bystanders	Man
Christine Quaite	Shakey Vic
John Kongos	Clinton Ford
Jefferson	The Timebox
The Wackers	Mal Ryder and The Spirits
Quiet World	Ted Rogers
The Dedicated Mens Jugband	Felders Orioles
The Montanas	The Carnaby
The Village Idiots	Nita Rossi
Sounds Around	Guy Darrell
Floribunda Rose	Mark Peters
Freddy Lennon	Peter Nelson
The Worrying Kynde	John Christian Gaydon
The Spectres	Trifle
Barley Bree	Keith and Billie
Margo and The Marvettes	Platform Six
The Undertakers	

1972 – 1980

Artists produced as Label Manager for Harbor – Black Bear – Alaska Records

Cymande	Sloane
Jan Burnette	Chris Kelly
Mike Rose and The Colours	Harmony Blend
Hooker	Velvet Love
Alan Lee Shaw	Steve Haynes
Marie Toland	James Jamieson
Joy Sarney	Bookham and Riskett
The Stops	Joanne Williams
Scarlet Jade	Love Dimension
Photograph	Julian Littman
Carol Crosbie	The Flying Saucers
Danny McCree	Sandy Ford
Bullet	The Cruisers
Chance	R.B. Zipper
Gulliver	The Dooley Family
Astra Nova Orchestra	Brian Keith
Jupiter 4	Paul Moriarty
Zingo	Teaser
Erasmus Chorum	Mel Nixon
The John Schroeder Orchestra	

Artists Produced independently

Salena Jones	The Vibration Series
A.S.P	Gnidrolog
Ronnie Barker	Steel Mill
Crazy Cavan and The Rhythm Rockers	

A PERSONAL MESSAGE OF THANKS

Little or no credit ever seems to have been given to the amazing talents of Arrangers, Recording Engineers and especially session musicians I have worked with over the years. It is impossible to name them all but without their dedication the music I have produced would never have come to fruition.

Thank you is not enough!

Studio Engineers: Malcolm Addey (E.M.I) Peter Bown (E.M.I) Stuart Eltham (E.M.I) Geoff Frost (Oriole) John Wood (Oriole) Alan Florence (Pye) Ray Prickett (Pye) Terry Evenett (Pye)

Cutting engineers: Malcolm Davies (Pye) Howard Barrow (Pye) Michael Greene (E.M.I)

Arrangers: Martin Slavin, Norrie Paramor, Frank Barber, Lew Warburton, Ken Woodman, George Chisholm, Johnny Harris, Johnny Pearson, John Cameron, Alan Tew, Nick Rowley, Tony King, Alyn Ainsworth, Colin Frechter, Zack Lawrence.

Piano/keyboards: Nicky Hopkins, Rick Wakeman, Ronnie Price, Johnny Pearson, Alan Hawkeshaw, Mike Moran, Harry Stoneham, Gerry Butler, Jim Lawless.

String Bass: Frank Clarke, Peter McGurck, Lennie Bush, Tony Reeves.

Drums: Kenny Clare, Ronnie Verrol, Bobby Orr, Alf Bigden, Clem Cattini, Simon Phillips, Barry Morgan, Phil Seaman.

Percussion: Tony Carr, Dennis Lopez, Barry Morgan, Jim Lawless, Frank Holder.

Electric Lead Guitar: Jimmy Page (Led Zeppelin) Ernie Shear, Chris Spedding, Alan Parker, Mike Morgan, Frank Ricotti.

Rhythm Guitar: Judd Proctor, Eric Ford, Vic Flick.

Bass Guitar: John Paul Jones (Led Zeppelin) Big Jim Sullivan, Brian Odgers, Herbie Flowers, Les Hurdle

Brass/Woodwind: Stan Roderick, George Chisholm, Don Lusher, Albert Hall, Ray Davies, Rex Morris, John Scott, Derek Goldsmith, Bobby Hockey, Red Price, Jimmy Skidmore, Tubby Hayes, Ronnie Scott.

Harmonica: Harry Petch.

Strings: Charlie Katz, Reg Leopold and everyone else that I have had the good fortune to work with in this department.

Backing Vocals: The Mike Sammes Singers, The Vernon Girls, Maggie Stredder, John Carter, Tony Burrows Ken Lewis, Reg Dwight (Elton John).

Session Fixers: Charlie Katz, Harry Benson, Barbara Mandell.

I shall never forget any of you!

PERSONAL ACKNOWLEDGEMENTS

By the time you read this, hopefully you will have read an enjoyed my story. It would be nice to think that it had also jogged your memory into re-kindling some happy and unforgettable moments and times. It was, after all, a period that will never be repeated. 'Sex Drugs and Rock 'n' Roll' as the Press labelled it was a reasonably accurate description.

In retrospect, it wasn't that easy to write and although it has taken me three years it took on the aspect of being a true labour of love. One of the greatest things for me was that it resurrected contacts with those I had not spoken to or seen for years. Sadly I was also to discover that some of my best Music Industry friends had passed on to that better place.

My personal thanks go out to everyone I have known or even spoken to in my professional capacity. However, I would also particularly like to thank Ann-Marie Gordon, Kate Calloway at EMI Records, Simon Lindsay at Sanctuary Universal, Oswin Brenner at Polydor, Ged Doherty and Nick Kadrnke at Sony/BMG, Adam White and Daryl Eastlea at Universal, Ronnie Bell, Cherry Fletcher, Trevor Simpson, Steve Knowles, Tony Barrow, Paul Nixon, Bob McClure, Roger Dopson, Sam Szczepanski and Lorraine Jones and many others of course who have all in one way or another assisted me along the way and even kept me from becoming too despondent over the pressure and worry of it at all times.

PHOTO/ALBUM SLEEVE ETC. ACKNOWLEDGEMENTS:

EMI Records Ltd, Polydor Ltd, Sanctuary Records Group Ltd, Oriole Records/ Sony/BMG, Motown Records Archives, Alaska Records Ltd, Harbor Records Ltd, John Schroeder Enterprises Ltd, Mrs Mavis Hurley, Richi Howell, Carousel Artist Management, Tony Cordt, Robert Ellis, Sam Kelly, Steve Scipio, Dick Barnatt, Eve Bomo, Flair Photography.